# The Lazarus Effect

# The Lazarus Effect

*A Novel*

Ben Witherington III
and Ann Witherington

PICKWICK *Publications* · Eugene, Oregon

THE LAZARUS EFFECT
A Novel

Pickwick Publications
A Division of Wipf and Stock Publishers
199 W. 8th Ave., Suite 3
Eugene, OR 97401

www.wipfandstock.com

ISBN 13: 978-1-55635-964-4

*Cataloging-in-Publication data:*

Witherington, Ben, 1951–

   The Lazarus effect : a novel / Ben Witherington III and Ann Witherington.

   vi + 264 p. ; 23 cm.

   ISBN 13: 978-1-55635-964-4

   1. Archaeology—Fiction. 2. Lazarus, of Bethany, Saint—Fiction. I. Witherington, Ann II. Title.

PS3605 W55 2008

Manufactured in the U.S.A.

To the memory of James Arthur West, Ben's grandfather
"Assuredly blessed are those who die in the Lord."

And for our old friends Ed and Bev Robb

Finally, to our various friends who may recognize some
of these characters a bit
Imitation is the sincerest form of admiration.

# 1

# Art for Art's Sake

A RTHUR JAMES WEST HAD spent the summers of the last quarter century knee-deep in ancient sands—from Israel to Turkey, Jordan to Greece. As a young doctoral candidate at Johns Hopkins, drafting his dissertation on "The Relevance of Artifacts for the Study of New Testament History," he had been inspired to attend that institution because of the work of W. F. Albright, one of the progenitors of American archaeology.

Unfortunately, Albright died in 1971, but his writings and work served as a living legacy pushing West to explore the interface between NT studies and archaeology. His thesis raised a few eyebrows by exhibiting an expansive grasp of early Jewish and Ancient Near Eastern as well as Greco-Roman history. Through the aid of a family friend, Professor John Bright of Princeton, Art was offered a place on a dig in the early 1980s.

It was on that dig while sifting sand in the nether layers of a tel that he looked up and saw, much to his surprise, one of his archaeological heroes—Yagael Yadin, the father of modern Israeli archaeology. It was only a brief encounter, for Yadin was just visiting the site during a break in his final year of serving in political posts prior to retirement. Apparently West had been born just a little too late to work with the real legendary figures in the field.

Nevertheless, this auspicious career beginning led first to a postgraduate stint at St. Andrews in Scotland and ultimately to faculty positions at two prestigious schools of divinity—Vanderbilt and Duke. He managed to sidestep the first roadblock of academia, "publish or perish," by having his dissertation accepted by the Cambridge monograph series, and by authoring a humorous "digging on a dime" journal piece which came to the attention of the Discovery Channel. And now, after more than twenty years in the field and in the classroom, West could add "television host" to his vita. *Biblical History*, much to the delight of his producers, had developed a loyal following that crossed demographic lines. With the grace of a seasoned scholar, Art moved effortlessly between the hallowed halls of the ivory tower and the paneled walls of family rooms across America. Older audiences appreciated his scholarship, while younger viewers saw what his students saw—a man who could tell really cool stories and make sorting potsherds sound fun.

With years came experience, rock-solid credentials, and a sterling reputation. Art was ready to venture out on his own. In 2004, he secured permission from the IAA (Israeli Antiquities Authority) to begin digging in the small village of Bethany, situated just a few miles outside Jerusalem.

What the years had not brought was a wife or family. That first professional dig had sealed his bachelorhood, whether or not he knew it at the time. He once likened archaeology to a pick-up game of sandlot baseball—the one 8-year-old boys dream about—the one in which you just happen to be hangin' out with Carl Yastrzemski, and Ted Williams drops by wanting to "hit a few." He'd been seduced that summer of '81—by the heady must of newly unsealed tombs, by the intellectual magnetism of the mentors that would become friends, and by the thrill of the laborious but delicate search for artifacts. As with most jokes, there was some truth in the adage that an archaeologist's life is constantly in ruins. Art, with little premeditation, chose the ruins, and thus filled his life with centuries-old dust rather than decades-old regrets.

He also pursued his work with the vigor of anyone answering a call from God, for that's what archaeology was to him. Summers were spent traipsing through the Judean and Galilean regions in search of the breakthrough find that would revolutionize the study and understanding of the Bible. West was not only a researcher, but also a devout evangelical Christian.

Just this morning, he selected Psalm 112 for his morning devotion: "Even in darkness light dawns for the upright . . . Good will come to him . . . who conducts his affairs with justice." But a clutter of prayer requests had jumbled his mind. For the first time in his career he arrived at a dig site without funding. The third quarter NASDAQ dive had left the usual coffers empty. Nothing short of a preeminent find would secure a major grant.

Right now, all that shined down upon him was the 89 degree, 7:30 a.m. sun. When scouting locations for this year's dig, he first set up an extensive series of conversations with Mustafa el Din, the property steward of the nearby Church of Mary and Martha, home to the oldest known graveyard in Bethany. He had spent the previous week surveying the south end of the Kidron valley, honeycombed with graves and tombs stretching from the Mount of Olives to this tiny burg. Yesterday he settled on the site. Today, before the temperature climbed to its usual 95 degree high, he hoped to complete a preliminary inspection and choose a tel. Approaching the site, his eyes fell upon a small mound. Giving it an optimistic once-over, he offered up one last thought, "Maybe, just maybe, God, you'll shine the light of Providence on me today."

Unlike the Orthodox Jews of the region, Art had no real qualms about poking around old graveyards. Instead, removing a spade from the large duffel bag he carried, West eyed the variety of limestone rocks and slabs that surrounded the mound. With a deep breath, he selected a spot and, using all of his 6'2" 195 pound frame, began the hard labor that defined the beginning of any dig. He worked methodically, alternating between his collapsible pickax and spade, until he encountered a stone much larger than usual. With sweat pouring from his brow, he finally managed to budge the boulder just enough for it to slip to the bottom of the sandy tel. Dropping the spade and mopping his head, Art estimated that he could probably squeeze himself into the opening— head first.

Switching on his flashlight, he first peered into the hole and discovered a surprisingly large chamber. Too symmetrical to be a normal hole in the ground, the room appeared to be surrounded by carved walls. Shadows cast by the flashlight hinted of niches here and there. West noted that this was no place for a claustrophobe. Throwing caution to the wind, he thrust his head, then his shoulders, into the dark, dank space.

Slithering on his belly, he thought back to his youthful days as a Boy Scout. While spelunking in the North Carolina Appalachian caves, he'd nearly gotten trapped in a narrow crevice. Hoping for a less harrowing experience this go-around, West pushed and shoved a little quicker. Finally in, he tried to unfold himself to his full height, only to bang his head on the limestone ceiling.

"Art, Art, Art," he muttered, as he rubbed the rising welt where he once had hair, "You're a man of modern times— not a five-foot ancient!" As he informed his often surprised students, most people of the first few centuries, even the men, grew no taller than 5'4" or so, a fact demonstrated long ago by ancient skeletons discovered and measured by the Israeli archaeologists of this region.

He turned his attention to the back wall. Sure enough, there *was* a niche, a niche with some sort of stone object lodged within. Crawling towards it on his knees, he immediately recognized the object as an ossuary, a bone box used for ancient reburial.

As periodically explained in episodes of *Biblical History*, the practice of osslegium, or the disassembling and storing of a skeleton in an ossuary, probably began about twenty years before the turn of the common era and continued in the Jerusalem area until the fall of the city in AD 70. Scholars debated the origins of the practice, but West was sure that the rise of the Pharisaic movement in early Judaism had played a hand. As in all cultures, burial practices reflected the societal conceptions of the afterlife. Drawing on the famous "dry bones" story in Ezekiel 37, Pharisaic Jews believed that God would one day raise the righteous from their graves and so it made sense that they would rebury the bones intact.

He grasped the end of the stone box and pulled. From its size he determined it to be a one person adult ossuary. Because only a minority of ancient Jewish ossuaries bear inscriptions, he was a little surprised to see the encrusted Aramaic letters.

*Eliezer, son of Simon*

Though a common name, readers of the English translations of the Bible were familiar with the famous Lazarus of Bethany, whose Hebrew name was actually Eliezer. Trying unsuccessfully to check his excitement, he reminded himself that an inscription alone does not an identification make.

A quick scan of the wall with his flashlight revealed two other small, but empty niches. However, just above the compartment that contained the Eliezer ossuary, the light fell upon a protruding rock, approximately three feet in width. Centuries had taken a harsher toll on the rock than on the ossuary. Pulling out a small brush from his backpack he whisked away the top layers of dust. Then, holding the flashlight in his mouth, he poured some water from his canteen onto the limestone facing. As the letters came to light, his heart beat accelerated. He saw the words . . .

*Twice dead . . .*

And was that next word "under"?

*Twice dead under . . . Pilatus.*

As if the limestone facing knew an encore was expected, the inscription continued:

*Twice born of Yeshua, in sure hope of resurrection.*

His breath caught. In his mind, the verses of John flashed by at marathon pace, finally coming to rest on chapter 11.

*. . . Jesus called out in a loud voice, "Lazarus, come out!"*

*The dead man came out, his hands and feet wrapped with strips of linen,*

*and a cloth around his face. Jesus said to them,*

*"Take off his grave clothes and let him go."*

Fumbling with the zip of his pack, he quickly pulled out his digital camera and began shooting pictures of the ossuary and the inscription. But as he moved to shoot the full wall, he heard the ominous scraping of stone against stone. And then, but for the beam of his penlight, all went dark.

# 2

# An Overturned Stone

Sixty-four and nearing the twilight of his career, Dr. Patrick Stone bore the bitter scars of a life that failed to meet expectations. With a doctorate from the University of Chicago in Ancient Near East Studies and a second from Tübingen in Germany, no one could dispute his skills as a scholar. His personality and resulting personal life were another thing altogether.

Few knew of the failed romance early in his graduate days. He'd fallen as deeply and hopelessly in love as possible for a narcissist with the daughter of his master's thesis advisor. The match, in Stone's view, couldn't have been more perfect. Her intellect nearly matched (without, of course, eclipsing) his own; her 5'1" trim figure perfectly accentuated his own 5'5" Napoleonic stature; and she understood intimately the life of an archaeology academic. And therein, as they say, lay the rub.

It never occurred to Stone that she wouldn't want a life any different from the one from which she came. She enjoyed his company, to be sure, and she had stayed with him throughout his doctoral work. But when it became clear that he intended to pursue a fourth degree, in Germany no less, without so much as a conversation about it with her, she left.

On rare occasions, usually helped along by one glass too many of Glenfiddich, he still remembered the unkind predictions she made—based on her father's shortcomings. "My father—he never made department chair in all his years at Chicago!" And, "My father—he abandoned his family year after year, months at a time, for archaeological crumbs!" She had no intentions of recreating that life for herself, or for the children he would never commit to fathering. All this she delivered in lieu of the "yes" he expected when he proposed to her with a replica of an ancient marriage band made especially for her during his last trip to Jerusalem.

Since then, he'd sworn off women—completely. He might well have become a monk, except that monasteries were neither conducive to accumulating personal accolades, nor known for the tolerance of envy. While his work continued to draw praise, few wanted to seek him out, or even claim him as a colleague. As others in his field gained acclaim, rather than celebrate their discoveries, he fumed about being passed over.

For years Yale had been his academic home, but recently Stone began spending more of his time in Israel researching the material culture and social networks of Second Temple Jerusalem. His Yale colleagues were only too glad when Stone was granted a research position that allowed him to spend more time abroad. No one knew quite what he expected to achieve, but rumor had it that he sought nothing less than a first century A.D. document that would cast doubt on traditional Christian claims.

Raised in the South, Stone still had a mama's boy devotion to his sole surviving parent, who lived in a Kingsport, Tennessee nursing home. He dutifully sent the monthly support for her care. Holidays were spent in Tennessee; vacations were spent in Tennessee. Summers were divided between research trips—and Tennessee. Some semblance of peace was found visiting with her and walking the woods behind the boyhood home he still maintained.

Stone's undergraduate years at a conservative Protestant college (in Tennessee, of course) led him to entertain the notion of Christian ministry. He quickly realized, however, since he was already one of the biggest intellectual fish in his small pond, that life held the potential for something much more lucrative than ministry. So he transferred to the University of Chicago and stopped attending church altogether. Though it has often been said that there is no believer so zealous as one converted later in life, it may also be said that no unbeliever is so zealous as one dissuaded from faith as an adult. Patrick Prentiss Stone was most certainly the latter.

Over his black, unsweetened morning coffee, Stone ruminated on Art West's return to the region. He knew his self-appointed rival had arrived several weeks previous to his own, permits in hand, to excavate in Bethany. Wanting to stay abreast of any interesting developments, he'd given his research assistant, Ray Simpson, the unglamorous (not to mention, unscrupulous) task of following the new darling of popular archaeology. "How that guy got a TV show, I'll never know," he grumbled. Every time West touted a new discovery Stone seethed with envy. Not once had the twit mentioned him or any of his books on the show.

He gave a start as his cell phone began chiming the first movement of Beethoven's Fifth Symphony at full volume. Blinking his beady gray eyes, he reached for it, finding a very excited Raymond Simpson on the other end of the line.

"West just disappeared into a tel! It's got to be a tomb!" the graduate student reported. Stone jerked to attention. "Say that again, Simpson?"

"West just climbed into the hole he's been digging all morning. He's been down there for at least fifteen minutes!"

"Well, well, well. Must have found more than sand if he's still in there. Stay put. I'm on my way. And don't let him out of your sight!" He rang off and hurriedly grabbed his keys from the Egyptian bowl on the hall table.

"Let's see if we can't find an old cemetery ghost to scare Mr. Biblical History away long enough for me to get a good look in that pit." Stone's mind danced with possibilities as his white Volvo sped towards Bethany.

# 3

# Lost and Found

"THAT BOY SCOUTING MEMORY must have been a premonition,"
thought Art. "Never go *swimming* without a buddy . . . ha! . . .
never go digging without one either!" He'd lost track of time, mostly
because he'd spent more than the first few minutes repeating the inscription over and over again.

> Twice dead under Pilatus
> Twice born of Yeshua, in sure hope of resurrection

Soon, however, fear replaced fascination. Perfect for storing bones inside stone boxes, the conditions were anything but accommodating for
living, breathing six-foot men. He tried to focus his thoughts, taking a
mental inventory of his pack. Besides the waning flashlight, dwindling
canteen, and digital camera, he had a handful of brushes, a small notebook, pencil, and a bar of Halvah, a Middle-Eastern answer to a candy
bar. What else?

He had tossed the collapsible spade aside before diving into the
mound, so prying the stone loose was out of the question. "Think man,
think!" His cell phone! Normally he hated the things—he used his
sparingly, sharing the number with only a select few and keeping the
ringer turned to silent. Silently offering a prayer that he had enough
battery power, he punched in the numbers to the caretaker's office.
Gratefully he listened to one ring after another until he began to worry
that Mustafa had, for some reason, left the property. "*Salam Alaykum,*"

came the faint Arabic greeting in the familiar soft-spoken accent of Mustafa.

"Mustafa! Mustafa! Dr. West here! I'm trapped in a tomb on the back side of the mound you showed me yesterday. Please, *please*, hurry!"

"On the way," came the reply, as the man of few words hung up the phone and dashed out of his office.

"Oh the irony!" thought West. "I finally find something interesting and almost get buried with it." He tried to slow his heart rate as he made a futile attempt to staunch the torrents of sweat pouring down his neck and back. No more than five minutes passed before he heard the ping of a shovel tapping from above. Using his canteen, he tapped back. Within minutes, Mustafa had used the discarded pickax to pry the stone loose.

"Thank God! I don't know what I would have done if you hadn't been there! *Shokrun*! I'm forever grateful, friend." Handing the caretaker his digital camera, West clamored out into the blinding, stifling day. Looking at his watch, he discovered it was already after ten o'clock.

"Mustafa, someone intentionally moved that stone to seal me in there. Did you see anyone? I've got so much to share with you, but first I've got to get over to the IAA and I can't do that without cleaning up a bit first, so I've got to run by my flat! And we've got to cover that hole. Can you do that for me? I'll make a call to have the area secured. I promise to fill you in just as soon as I can. Again, I can't thank you enough for saving my life!" When West finally ran out of breath, Mustafa, brown eyes smiling, acknowledged the task with a nod and slight bow.

Propelling the bright blue Mini Metro towards his apartment, Art's thoughts bounced like pinballs. "Who would seal me in a tomb, for Heaven's sake? Did someone follow me? A prankster? Why didn't I see them? Hear them?" Only briefly did his thoughts turn to Mustafa. A man of honor, the Palestinian Christian had shown him nothing but friendship over the past several months. And had he been culpable, he certainly wouldn't have answered the call for help.

Just after passing the Pool of Siloam and the old City of David ruins, Art turned onto a quiet side street, and whipped into the fourth driveway on the left. Barely taking time to remove the keys from the ignition, he headed straight for the bathroom. He didn't even bother with the hot tap—cold water rinses soap and grime just as well, he reasoned, and he desperately needed a respite from the heat.

Clean, cooled, and quenched, West set the empty water bottle on the weathered table that served as his desk. He needed to start making phone calls, but in what order? IAA or press first? He should probably start with the IAA's director, Dr. Samuel Cohen, and see if he couldn't come right over with the pictures. For years Art had cheerfully turned over any findings or artifacts to the IAA, most of which found homes in various museums in and around Jerusalem. And this practice had not only fostered an easy and amicable relationship with the Antiquities Authority, it had also given rise to a most enjoyable friendship between Art and Sammy. Yes, he'd start with Sammy, and later, he'd give his friend Israel Steinmetz a ring at *Ha'Aretz*, one of the two leading daily newspapers in Jerusalem.

Cohen answered his phone on the third ring with a hearty English "Hello."

"*Shalom alechem*" began Art, in Hebrew.

"*Alechem Shalom*," replied Cohen. "Art? Is that you?"

"It is indeed! You'll never believe what happened this morning! What I found. What I think I found. I've got pictures. Pictures you've got to see to believe . . . that is until you can get to the tomb. The tomb. You've got to have it secured, cordoned off, be sure no one gets in, be sure no one gets trapped like me . . ."

"Art. Art. Slow down. As usual you speak too quickly for these ears. You've found something. You've got pictures and you want to show them to me. Certainly. How's noon? I'm tied up in a meeting until then. Now what's this about being trapped in a tomb?"

"I'll get to that when I see you. In the meantime, you've got to get someone over to the Church of Mary and Martha in Bethany to secure the site! There's a caretaker there, Mustafa, but he's got other duties. Oh, and could you contact Grace Levine's office and see if she can join us? I want a second opinion on this Aramaic inscription . . . " West trailed off to catch his breath again.

"An Aramaic inscription. Secure a tomb at the Church of Mary and Martha in Bethany." Art could hear the furious scratch of Sammy's pen against paper. "And a call to Grace Levine. Done. Anything else? A plate of fresh hummus and some peeled grapes perhaps?" Sammy joked with his friend.

At the mention of hummus, Art suddenly remembered he hadn't eaten since five this morning. "Yeah, that would be great! I'll see you at noon."

~

As he made himself a quick sandwich he thought about the look he'd soon see on Grace's face when she read the inscription. Picturing her round face framed by a riotous mass of still-black curls, brown-green eyes dancing behind funky red spectacles, his stomach lurched. While he'd been looking at his watch graveside, he should have been sipping lattes with this lively department chair from Jerusalem's Hebrew University. He knew she would forgive him when she saw the pictures, but she should have been the first call, he thought ruefully. "I'll apologize in person," he thought. Grabbing his camera and a small notepad, he started towards the door to the garage when his home phone rang.

"Greetings, my friend." The deep voice of his old friend Kahlil El Said boomed from the receiver. "I have news of the James ossuary. Let us meet at our usual spot behind the Shrine of the Book this evening. Say nine? We will talk. You are free?"

Art smiled just hearing the voice of the Muslim antiquities dealer. They had met during that first dig back in the Eighties and had shared a lifetime since. Art had become a frequent guest of Kahlil and his wife, Sheema, and had been present at the marriage of their only child, Hannah. When Sheema's cancer had gained the upper hand, he'd taken the first available flight. Like Jews, Muslim's bury their dead within twenty-four hours, and Art had promised her he would look after Kahlil in the early days following her burial. It was then that they inaugurated their tradition of meeting in the quietude of the park to discuss everything and nothing, away from the bustle of Kahlil's shop and of Art's various projects.

"For you? Of course I'm free. Nine o'clock it is. I look forward to seeing you old friend."

"Bless you, my friend. Until tonight then. *Salam.*"

Art knew Kahlil would be thrilled to hear of his find—and horrified to learn of his early interment. He might have to skip that part. Though ten years had passed since Sheema's death, Kahlil avoided almost all conversation of her, of sickness and of death in general. Best not to mention his near miss, at least not tonight. Camera and notepad in tow, he stuffed himself into the Mini and headed for IAA office.

# 4

# Grace under Pressure

EVEN THOUGH IT WAS only mid-morning, most shoppers on Ben Yehuda Street were looking for shade. Grace Levine had found hers under the awning of her favorite coffee shop, Solomon's Porch, where she sat sipping, not coffee, but a more refreshing blend of orange and papaya juices. As she worked her way through the morning papers, *Ha'Aretz* and *The Jerusalem Post*, she gave a short prayer of thanks that neither led with a headline of overnight terrorist activity. Mercifully, for the past several weeks, all had been quiet on the Middle-Eastern front.

The same could not be said for the usually quiet stretch of stores, cafes, and restaurants along Ben Yehuda. Her thoughts of Art West and his uncharacteristic lateness were interrupted by the growing throng of onlookers looking for the source of commotion at the end of the block.

"Non-kosher, close it down! Non-kosher, close it down!" A shouting individual had swelled to a small chanting group of men.

Grace rolled her eyes as she slipped her feet back into the sandals she'd kicked off beneath the table. The McDonald's protestors were at it again. Surely this band of Haredi had better things to do with their time than spend it scaring off American tourists. The last time she looked, the Haredi didn't control the whole city—just thought that they should.

Raised to know her mind before she spoke it, Grace had grown up in Brookline, Massachusetts, to observant Jewish parents with a keen sense of intellect and social conscience. She almost never passed up a chance to debate, especially when she felt strongly about the topic.

Dropping her cavernous tote behind the outdoor coffee counter, she smiled wryly at her friend Sarah Goldberg, proprietor of Solomon's Porch. "Keep an eye on my table for me, yeah? I'll be back in just a sec." Sarah urged, "Go get 'em tiger!"

Grace had quickly scaled the ancient academic walls of both Brandeis and Yale, finishing her doctorate in only four years. The predominately male environments had emboldened her, cementing her commitment to academic excellence. Her dissertation on the Herodian period in Judea and its multi-lingual culture, published not as an obscure academic guide, but as a trade title, had even enjoyed mention in more than a few popular magazine columns. By the time she celebrated her thirty-fifth birthday, she'd bought a flat in Jerusalem and established herself as one of the preeminent authorities on Aramaic translations. But now, as she confidently approached the growing fracas, it was her bulldog tenacity, not her academic prowess, that fueled her stride.

Pushing herself into the midst of the melee, she at first drew curious stares from the jumble of tourists, vendors, and street musicians who had gathered. By the time she reached the center of the commotion, she found herself the target of a dozen or so pairs of eyes, undisguised with disdain and outrage. Undaunted, but without actually making physical contact, she brought herself nose to nose with the self-appointed Master of Ceremonies, Rabbi Menachem ben Schlomo.

"How dare you use your position to incite riot! Surely you realize your actions affect the entire commerce of this block, Jewish and non-Jewish alike? Is there not enough *tzuris* in the world without you adding to it?"

Stunned by her audacity, the rabbi's *minyan*, dressed in the traditional black suits and hats of the ultra-orthodox, held their collective breath. Unused to impudence, especially from a woman, the rabbi, tight-lipped and seething, addressed the crowd.

"Who is this woman?"

Refusing to be belittled or ignored, she answered for herself. "I am Dr. Grace Levine, professor and Chairwoman of the Department of Biblical Languages at Hebrew University, and I respectfully ask that you and your students return to your *yeshiva* and find a way, other than this disgraceful demonstration, to honor ha-Shem." Not normally a stickler for so-called political correctness, she'd purposely emphasized her position as chair*woman* for added sting.

Hoping to sting back, the rabbi, again not addressing her directly, quoted Proverbs to his disciples, "To what shall I compare a nagging woman, it is like a continual dripping of water."

Glaring, she threw back her shoulders and made a great show of planting her feet. "I can assure you, rabbi, that *this* nagging woman will not leave this spot until you and your students take your business elsewhere."

Sensing a change in the temperament of the crowd, the rabbi gave an almost imperceptible nod to his followers, and, grimacing, he led them away. Near the back of the line of disciples, a young lanky student paused before her.

"You, a Jewish woman, should be ashamed of yourself. You should know your place better. No one speaks to Rabbi Menachem like that—especially in the presence of *Goyim!*"

Apparently satisfied with his rebuke, he hurried to catch up with his brethren. A few tourists smiled gratefully at Grace before heading into McDonalds to satisfy their American appetites. Returning to the café, she smiled in response to Sarah's raised eyebrow.

"Mission accomplished. Thanks for watching my stuff."

Retrieving her tote, she returned to her table. As she reached into her bag for a tube of chapstick, she noticed the light on her cell phone blinking. Assuming it was Art with an explanation, she was surprised to hear Sammy Cohen's tenor on her voicemail. "Grace, we need your expertise over at the IAA. Can you join us at noon? Give a call and I'll fill you in." Intrigued, but still worried about her American friend, she dialed Sammy's office to confirm.

# 5

# An Israelite with Guile

IN THE WAKE OF a Hamas attack on his home in Gaza, Sedek Hadar joined the ranks of a radical orthodox movement in his native Israel. His parents, siblings, and a grandmother had all been reduced to casualty statistics of the massacre. His wife of only a few months also sustained serious and life-threatening injuries, and rather than celebrating his first year of marriage with the blessed birth of a son, he instead spent it sitting *shiva*, mourning yet two more losses: his beloved Miriam and their unborn child.

Since then, out of work and out of sorts, he'd found solace within the confines of the Sons of Zion, zealous followers of Menachem ben Schlomo. Rabbi Schlomo did not believe that the secular Israeli government represented true or biblical Israel. He considered the Zionist movement a hopelessly compromised mess. Brokering land for peace was folly. True Jews, he espoused, knew that there'd be no peace in the region until Messiah came. Until that time, they, the true Jews, would stand as sentinels of the land, protecting the holy territory and the biblical prerogatives of their ancestors at any cost, including violence and death.

An orphaned, disillusioned Sedek had found first comfort and then purpose in the person and teachings of Rabbi Schlomo. At the rabbi's urging, he began keeping an eye on the plethora of archaeological sites in the region. Observing escalated to policing, then stalking. Distrust grew to anger against anyone he perceived to be desecrating

Israel and her heritage. On a few occasions he anonymously contacted the IAA with reports of theft. He dutifully reported back to the Sons of Zion who, in turn, gave Sedek all the moral support and encouragement he needed for his spying operations. He was only instructed to be discreet, to operate with a certain amount of savvy and guile.

His hatred of Palestinians had long ago spilled over to encompass any non-Jew—any non-orthodox Israeli Jew, really. Grace Levine was a case in point. What self-respecting Jewish woman would think she could speak to any man, let alone a rabbi, with such brazenness? And tousling those wild curls about for all to see! He realized that not all Jewish women covered their hair these days, reserving it only for the eyes of their husbands, but, he assured himself, no man of any merit would deign to call her wife. Before he could lose himself in memories of his Miriam's own black ringlets, he turned his thoughts to his ever-growing roster of suspicious characters.

Ever since the James ossuary debacle, involving some prominent Jewish antiquities collectors as well as dealers, collectors, and foreign archaeologists had headed his list. This week, Dr. Art West and Dr. Patrick Stone topped his hit parade—apparently with just cause. Just before joining the Sons of Zion on Ben Yehuda Street, he'd tailed Stone to a mound in Bethany. It was high time he returned to the site to see what havoc the little man had wrought.

# 6

## Facing the Artifacts

### *Easy Come, Easy Go*

Fʀᴏᴍ ᴛʜᴇ ʟᴏᴏᴋs ᴏғ things, Sammy Cohen's office could have been easily mistaken for that of an American CPA, mid-tax season. Filtered by the parchment-colored roller shades, the midday sun added a soft luminescence to the troupes of dust mites dancing in the air. The low hum of the window unit air-conditioner did little to disperse the heat, but a fan was out of the question—years of files and reports stood in precarious piles throughout the room, many topped with replicas of ancient scrolls and original artifacts. To an untrained eye, the office could have qualified for national disaster relief. To Sammy, it represented more than twenty years of dedication to the preservation of Israeli history. He knew the contents of each stack, so what did it matter how it looked?

In anticipation of the noon meeting, he methodically reassigned positions to the files inhabiting the chairs around the chipped Formica conference table. Balancing the last file on a new pyramid, he looked up to see the doorway filled by his friend Art West. Setting his camera, notebook, and file down on the first flat surface he could find, the American came forward to pull the Israeli official into a bear hug. Before they could even begin their litany of pleasantries, a voice piped up from behind. "And where's my hug? Don't I rate anymore?" Art turned to embrace Grace in a more gentle squeeze just as she threw a playful right fist into his arm. "What happened this morning? We said ten o'clock at Sarah's right?"

"We did. We did. And if I hadn't been sealed in a tomb I'd have been there!"

"Arthur West. I've heard a lot of wonderful stories come out of that mouth of yours, but really, you expect me to fall for that version of the 'dog ate my homework?'"

"Grace, really, I—," Art's explanation was interrupted by Sammy.

"Grace, my dear, wonderful to see you too!" diffused the Director, motioning to the conference table and chairs. "Art's had quite a morning; let the man tell his tale!"

Art dashingly reached the table in time to ease out a chair for Grace. She could hold her own with the most chauvinist of men, but he also knew she secretly loved chivalry. She flashed him a grin. "It'll take a lot more than 'coats over puddles' to get back in my good graces."

Art grinned back. "Would a little Turkish Delight pave the way at all, ma'am?"

"*Ahem*, children. Do I need to sit between you?" Sammy interrupted again. "Art, let's have it."

Removing the photos from the file, Art's heart began to race. He carefully laid all ten on the table for his friends to see. "I took these this morning, on the property of the Church of Mary and Martha." He gestured toward the first few. "Here you see the inside of the chamber. And here, notice the niche. Now," he gestured toward a third image, "note the ossuary *in* the niche and the inscription above." Fighting to keep from sounding like a toddler on Christmas, he pushed three more pictures towards Grace, "How would you, *Dr.* Levine, translate the Aramaic?"

Unfolding her red reading glasses onto the bridge of her nose, she examined each of the three close-ups before translating aloud, "*Twice dead under Pilate, twice reborn in Jesus in sure hope of resurrection*" she confirmed.

"That's how I read it, before the lights went out!" agreed Art. "Now, look closely at the letters etched on the end of the ossuary."

Grace shared the three photos with Sammy. "Eliezer son of Simon," she declared. "This is a pretty ordinary ossuary inscription, Art, nothing particularly of note . . . unless . . . " The light began to dawn. "Unless you think this refers to *the* Lazarus!"

Art could only respond with raised eyebrows and a somewhat goofy grin. He wanted to see her go the rest of the distance.

"And if it is *the* Lazarus, that would make this ossuary, this tomb, a tangible, certifiable, outside-the-Scriptures reference to the idea of resurrection!" she finished triumphantly.

"Almost. A slight correction, if I may, your esteemed professorship. This would actually be our earliest attestation not of the idea of resurrection, but of the *actuality* of it. But we can save the textual nuances for later!" he teased. "First we'll need to do the usual testing—date the inscription, determine that the lettering is of the same hand as that on the box, carbon date the whole lot, but knowing what we do about the practice of using ossuaries in this region, this has got to predate AD 70, wouldn't you agree?"

Sammy, who until now had kept his silence, moaned. "The James ossuary didn't give us enough headaches? And now this? What's next? Jesus's burial clothes?"

"Actually, we may be off the hook there. Remember the Shroud of Turin?" Art sheepishly suggested.

Stifling a snort, Sammy dismissed the idea. "Everyone knows that shroud didn't carbon date to the first century! Enough. Resurrection or no resurrection, you've certainly got something here Art."

Art protested "Well actually last week there was a new study showing that the carbon 14 dating had been bungled because what was tested was a medieval patch sown on the Shroud after the medieval fire, not the original cloth, but . . ."

Sammy interrupted, "Enough already, one proof of resurrection at a time! We'd better head up to Bethany now—I only sent a preliminary team when you called earlier."

"Grace, you'll join us, no?" entreated Sammy.

"Wouldn't miss this for all the coffee at Sarah's." She threw a wink at Art. "Sammy you'll ring Moshe with the request for security? What about the lab team? How soon do we want them up there?"

Sammy sighed. The IAA team was replete with type A personalities. "Grace, dear, we've been through this drill more than few times. You and Art catch up for a bit, and I'll make the necessary calls."

"Before you pick up the phone Sammy, you need to hear this part too. I wasn't joking, Grace, when I said someone sealed me in a tomb this morning. Someone besides Mustafa el Din, the caretaker there, knew I was digging, knew I'd dropped into the mound. No sooner had I translated the inscription than they dragged or pushed a boulder over the opening. Mustafa saved my life this morning. Literally. I think we need to exercise more caution than usual this time around."

Grace's eyes lost some of their laughter and she immediately regretted having given him such a hard time for standing her up. "Art. I had no idea. You know—"

"Grace, relax. I expect nothing less than a good ribbing from you. Thank God, I'm fine. No blood, no foul." He turned back to Sammy. "So what next, Boss?" He knew the Director could get frustrated as the number of cooks in the kitchen grew, as it did with any discovery. "Got a plan?"

"I will by three. Let's meet in the lobby at half past two. And I too thank God for your safe egress from the tomb."

Leaving Sammy to orchestrate the particulars, Art and Grace headed across the street for a quick cup of coffee. He could hear their animated chatter trailing off into the distance as they departed.

# 7

# The Artifacts, and the Art of Living

KAHLIL EL ASAD WAS an imposing figure. For a start, he looked like Omar Sharif with his mustache and big smile, and beautiful olive complexion. For another thing, he was 6' 3" and had a huge booming voice. Last but not least, he was as gregarious as one could imagine. He treated all persons with respect and kindness and so cut quite a figure as a man and as a salesman. He was a Sufi Muslim, a mystic of sorts, and loved the writings of the Egyptian author Mahfouz, and also the Lebanese prophet for whom he was named—Kahlil Gibran.

Largely self-taught, though as a boy he had attended a British school in Jerusalem, Kahlil had developed a great love for history and antiquities over the years and had been apprenticed to one of the best, Mahmoud Sadat, when he was only a teenager. He had learned to develop a good critical eye when it came to discerning the difference between a clever forgery and a real piece of antiquity.

Asad had earned a reputation with all as a fair trader and an honest man, which was increasingly rare in the antiquities business. He had contacts all over the Middle East, and Muslims, Christians, and Jews all traded with him. As Israeli Law required, he kept a scrupulous log of all he had in his shop, which sat about 200 yards from the Damascus or west gate into the old city of Jerusalem. Kahlil, now some 68 years old but as vigorous as a man half his age, was a widower, and his only child Hannah now 40 something helped him run his shop. All in all, he was quite satisfied with his life.

On this morning he had been in a mood to tease his daughter a bit, so when she had asked "Father, how is it with you on this day?" He had replied using the old Islamic proverb: "Today is much the same as yesterday, only more so." She laughed out loud, but quickly covered her mouth, since that was not considered appropriate behavior for a Muslim woman.

Kahlil could tell it was going to be a hot day and so he had stocked his small refrigerator with his favorite fruit juices, particularly Haifa orange juice. He would have a smoke on his water pipe in the afternoon after prayers. Today was a good day to sit quietly in the shop and take inventory. Kahlil's antiquities shop sold all sorts of artifacts, but he specialized in stone objects and coins, unlike many other shops, which focused on clay pots of various sorts. In the morning he had only had a few browsers in the shop, and had sold a couple of small stone cups, but nothing significant.

Much more interesting was the American customer who showed up about four o'clock and wanted some Herodian period coins—the Tyrian half shekel, a widow's mite, some coins of the various procurators, including Pilate, Festus, and Felix. He had had an interesting conversation with this fairly young American gentleman who knew a good deal about numismatics and the good-natured haggling over the coins went on for over an hour while they were sitting on a rug and drinking fruit juice and eating wonderful figs and dates. The young man, whose name was William Arnold, was from Kentucky, and they had talked about horses and horse racing, and a host of other topics, steering away from troubling subjects like the Intifada, terrorism, and the like. Kahlil had no stomach and no sympathy for those he called the "barbarians" by which he meant both radical and violent zealots of whatever religion and no religion. In his view such behavior was a betrayal of the highest and best that all three monotheistic religions had to offer.

Finally Kahlil had said to William with a big grin on his face: "You know my friend, if I do not soon sell you these coins, I shall not even be able to afford to pay for all the drinks and food we have been consuming. Surely, you would not want to shame an old man that way would you, by driving too hard a bargain?" "No" said Arnold, "I know a good deal when I see one, and so I will gladly pay you the $400 we have agreed upon." He reached for his passport carrier to get the money, but all of a sudden there was a commotion at the door of the shop. A short man, quite out of breath, holding some sort of object wrapped in a cloth had burst into the shop. Kahlil could see the man was agitated and impatient and called out from his back room where he and Arnold had been sitting "I'll be right with you in a moment." "Make it quick" the man retorted, "I am in a big hurry."

Kahlil, without rushing took Arnold's money, and Arnold said "I will leave so you can attend to your next customer." "Nothing of the kind," said Kahlil, "Hannah here will carefully pack your purchases and draw up the authentication papers so you can show them to the customs people when you leave the country. Just sit here and enjoy the juice and fruit, and I will be back."

By the time Kahlil had gotten to the front room, the man was pacing the floor at a rapid rate. He blurted out, "I have found something quite remarkable, and wish to sell it. I understand you are the best dealer in town." "First of all," said Kahlil, "I must see this object and evaluate it. Secondly, in view of the Law of Israel, I must ask where you got this object and how long you have had it. If it is something of great value and great antiquity, and you have recently found it, then you must turn it over to the IAA."

This response irritated the little man to no end. "I thought I was told you were the best dealer, and were capable of being discreet!" "Discreet yes," said Kahlil, "but dishonest, no. I will not risk my reputation and my life's work on something suspicious. Nevertheless, show me this object and I may be able at least to appraise it for you."

The man unwrapped the object, which turned out to be a limestone object that looked recently chiseled around the edges, but the surface of which looked quite ancient. Kahlil could not read ancient languages very well, but he could tell this inscription was some sort of Semitic inscription and it looked ancient.

"In my view," Kahlil said, "you must take this object to the IAA, perhaps to Professor Grace Levine first since she is the resident expert in Aramaic inscriptions and their authentication. I cannot take this object off your hands, nor offer you any money for it, I am afraid to say."

At this, the little man ground his teeth, and spat on the floor. "Imbecile, this object is worth millions of dollars. It is a first-century inscription about a disciple of Jesus, and I had thought you could broker it for me with a collector, and we could both make a tidy sum of money. I see that there is a reason why you are still running such a small business in this God-forsaken part of the city." He turned in disgust, and left the shop at once, heading off into the covered shopping area in the old city and in the direction of the so-called Wailing Wall.

Kahlil returned to his back room with a frown on his face. "Well that was as unpleasant as our time together has been delightful. Thank you so much for doing business with me." Arnold shook his hand, and left the shop, shocked at the lack of courtesy of the little man, and apparent lack of familiarity with honor and shame customs in the Middle East.

"Hannah," Kahlil said, "we must have an early dinner, as I am off to see our old friend Art West tonight. I want to talk to him some more about the James ossuary. Some new things have come to light."

Hannah said, "I knew you were going out for some good reason, and so I began the preparing the Shwarma and vegetables already, and of course there is hummus and pita bread. We can eat in a few minutes." Slowly the sunlight was waning in the room and the noise outside in the Cardo, the major market street, was abating. While all seemed peaceful on the surface, Kahlil and Hannah were both uneasy about something indefinable, something just on the edge of consciousness. Why was that little man in such a hurry, and who was he?

# 8

# Mother Lode Missing

SOME THREE HOURS AFTER Sammy began preparations for the trip to Bethany, the team finally pulled out of IAA headquarters. To avoid any implications of impropriety, Art, against every impulse, knew he had to wait and go with the gang. At least with both Sammy and Grace qualified to authenticate the find, he would be several steps ahead of the game when it came to the funding application. Rush hour, well underway, only served to prolong his agony, and the serpentine streets of the Temple Mount added an extra layer of frustration. On the bright side, the interminable ride gave him the chance to catch up with Grace. While he drove, she entertained him with a year's worth of stories and anecdotes ranging from student pranks to senior moments. They'd more than made up for the missed breakfast date. By the time the official caravan reached the church, it was almost five—a full seven hours since he'd emerged from the tomb. With a small shudder, he climbed out of the car and looked to the site.

Motioning towards the church, Art indirectly encouraged Grace to go straight to the tomb without him. Knowing evening prayers had begun, he slipped as quietly as he could into chapel. Not a Catholic, he did not bend to cross himself, but he did pause to once again admire the stunning 12-foot high stained glass depiction of the chapel's namesakes. From the open doors behind him, the setting sun illuminated Mary and Martha, who returned the favor with a cascade of multicolored light upon the high altar. Through a heavy cloud of incense, the priest read the Scriptures in Arabic to the twenty or so parishioners scattered among the front rows. Spotting Mustafa, Art slid onto the olivewood pew beside him.

"Thank you again, friend, for saving my life this morning."

Mustafa turned and grinned. "My honor, Professor. The rest of your day, it was less eventful?"

"Thankfully yes. I've only just returned. The IAA is with me— they're securing the site now. You haven't noticed anyone lurking about since I've been gone, have you?"

"A young couple visited the church just after lunch. But since then, I've been inside, preparing for Mass. Unless someone made a fuss, I don't know that I would have heard anything, and the stained glass makes it nearly impossible to see anything outside these walls."

Wryly, Art agreed. "Could I impose on you just one more time? I need to get up to the tomb. Could we finish this conversation after Mass?"

Mustafa nodded his assent with a smile.

"Thank you, again," Art whispered as he slipped out of the chapel.

The IAA excavation team had wasted no time getting started. In the few minutes Art had spent in the church, they widened the entrance to the tomb—enough to allow for two of them to drop easily into the space. They were just resurfacing when Art joined them. Offering the ossuary to Sammy, they dropped back in to continue their search.

"Be sure to take a ton of pictures of the inscription over the niche!" Art called out after them.

"What inscription?" called back the lead excavator, Ari. "There's no inscription down here."

"The one directly above the niche. It's pretty hard to miss!" Art's stomach began to churn nervously.

"No Sir, Professor West." Ari climbed out to make room. "Nothing here. Come down and see for yourself." Fighting back another wave of panic, he prayed the tomb hadn't already been raided. Rationalizing that any self-respecting looter would not have left the ossuary behind, he sighed, pushed back his sleeves and crawled back into the hollow. Shining his light directly on the spot above the niche, his heart sank in disbelief.

"Impossible!" he yelled with near panic in his voice. "Dear God! Someone's already been here—no way—this is just not happening!" He stopped, denial overwhelming him. Speechless and confused he never heard Grace slip in behind him.

With lips pursed and brow wrinkled, Grace tried to soften the blow. "It's still one heck of a find you know—the ossuary, I mean. And you do have pictures—we know you aren't crazy . . ."

Too distraught to answer, Art rolled his eyes, then scrambled out of the tomb, brushed past an astonished IAA team, and made a beeline for the church.

Skulking in the shadows of the olive trees, a figure added one more note to the day's report.

The inventorying of the shop had tired Hannah as well so she had no objections when her father suggested they close up a little early. Knowing how much he treasured his time with Professor West she skipped the cool shower she usually took after work and instead headed right for the kitchen to inspect what she had just put on the fire.

She reviewed in her mind what she had just done and how long things had been cooking to be sure her timing was right. After lighting the flame on a small grill, she had removed the lamb from the icebox. The marinade of olive oil, garlic, oregano, and her mother's secret touch, a pinch of hawyij—a spicy mixture of pepper, caraway, cumin, saffron and tumeric—made her mouth water. Deftly, she had cubed the meat. Then, alternating it with slices of bell peppers and tomatoes from Sheema's garden, she skewered it. As the kabobs sizzled, she had given some leftover hummus an extra squeeze of lemon and a dusting of cayenne. Her father enjoyed his food with a kick. She replaced the kabobs on the grill with a few pitas, and called to Kahlil that dinner was almost ready. While the meat and vegetables cooled, she filled a bowl with pickled cauliflower, and a small plate with baklava.

"Ah. Hannah. If only my nose could dance! The smells of your dinner demand a celebration!"

She smiled back at him as she set the last of the serving plates on the table. Somehow, each night, he always had a new compliment for her cooking, just as he had for her mother. "Let's celebrate by eating before it gets too cold," she suggested warmly.

Between bites, they mulled over the day's events as they usually did at dinner.

"I wonder who that awful little man was?" Hannah mused. "Perhaps we should have asked Dr. Arnold—just in case that stone was important."

"Don't worry about it, my dear. Should the need arise, I'm sure we can contact Dr. Arnold and ask him then. And by the way, don't think I didn't notice when you nodded at the final price for his coins. Some days I wonder if I shouldn't—"

Hannah cut him off before he could wonder about retirement again. They both knew that he'd wither without his clients, the tourists, and the daily handling of treasures. "I've picked up a thing or two from watching you, Father. But you know I could never run the shop without you."

"Hannah, my little one, you grow more like your mother every day. You, like her, know you can do anything you can put your mind to. You and I both know that you could run the shop with your eyes closed."

"Yes Father. But neither you nor I need worry about that just yet. Would you like me to wrap up some baklava for Professor West?" She usually managed to change the subject before he could start talking earnestly about her taking over the shop. While the idea intrigued her, she couldn't imagine running it alone—after his death. And that was an idea she tried to keep at bay.

"No, thank you child. We've much too much to discuss—no time even for sweets. But that doesn't mean I can't have some now. I'm sure he doesn't know that rumors of the James ossuary are circulating again. The claims that it appeared in one of Mahmoud's shops just up the street from us are completely false. I know the disinformation regarding the authenticity of the inscription has given Art much heartache. I wouldn't want him discouraged any further." Popping the last bit of the syrupy pastry into his mouth, he stood. "With your permission my dear, I take my leave. Thank you for yet another wonderful meal."

Getting up also, she gently suggested that he take his cloak. Despite the intense heat of the sun, the Judean hills cooled quickly at night, and she knew that he would be late—many a night the friends had talked almost until dawn. Coat in hand, he came back into the kitchen to embrace her.

"I will see you soon. Insha'Allah. As Allah wills."

"Good night Father. Take good care."

He slipped into the cool night towards the Shrine of the Book. So eager was he to meet up with Art, he never noticed the man behind him, matching his gait step for step.

# 9

# Harbingers of the Dawn

IN A SPRAWLING HOUSE near Ecole Biblique, a French monastic compound, the Society of the Millennial Dawn (SMD) gathered for their weekly Thursday night meeting. The group usually spent their time looking for correlations between Bible prophecy and modern events. Their roots dated back to the early nineteen hundreds when Charles Scofield popularized a shift away from historic Christianity towards his own, very literal, interpretation of the Bible. Dividing the Old and New Testaments into "dispensations," he believed that the Scriptures contained different messages for Jew and Christian. He believed also in a fundamental dichotomy between Israel and the Church, and in a secret rapture that would precede the Second Coming and save the faithful from the horror of the millennial end-times. Though the literalism touted by Scofield pervaded American Evangelical Christianity, modern interpreters of premillennial signs continued to inaccurately predict the Second Coming. As a result, Dispensationalist Christian groups began to splinter, until most lost all touch with their origins.

The SMD fell somewhere in the middle of the pack. Jamison Parkes Law had started SMD in his own home. Far from the typical evangelical fundamentalist, Law had spent the better part of his post-graduate days as a political activist. With a law degree from Harvard, he'd carefully honed his debating skills and powers of persuasion. He'd also learned that religion more than politics made for strange bedfellows—and set to cultivating a wide array of relationships. His classmates would literally be running the world one day and who knew when the Harvard connection might come in handy.

Armed with his bible college undergraduate degree and a South Texas belief in justice, J.P. easily amalgamated his patriotism with his belief that Israel was in fact the chosen nation of God. Like many of his fellow dispensationalists, Law believed that biblical Israel had been re-established at the end of WWII, and that the Jews had an absolute right to their own country. As a literalist, he had no doubt that Armageddon would occur within the region and that the United States held an obligation to support the Israeli government and its lands.

These views dovetailed nicely with some of those of Rabbi Menachem and the unlikely pair formed an alliance of sorts, vowing to stand vigilant against anyone who failed to embrace biblical Israel—whether Muslim, Jew, or Christian. They'd fallen into the habit of comparing notes at least once weekly, more if something was afoot. This afternoon the two had spent forty minutes on the phone discussing the flurry of activity at a church in Bethany. The rabbi reported that he'd heard a newly discovered tomb had already been raided. Though he knew both Art West and Patrick Stone by reputation only, J.P. agreed that neither could be trusted and promised to handle the situation.

Now, sitting in the well-appointed living room of the house SMD maintained, Law surveyed the thirty members—some sprawled on couches, others cross-legged on the floor—and smiled to himself with pride. Every last one of his disciples had demonstrated the depth of their faith by moving, lock, stock, and barrel to Jerusalem in anticipation of the Rapture. In the time since, the faithful had grown by a handful, and the entire group now waited for J.P.'s benediction.

"It has happened again," he began. "Rabbi Menachem has informed me that someone has raided a tomb up at the Church of Mary and Martha in Bethany. Both Arthur West and Patrick Stone have been seen snooping around up there, and we all know that neither one of them demonstrates any kind of loyalty to our biblical positions on Israel and her treasures. Needless to say, they must be stopped. You know the rabbi and his minyan have no muscle—so it falls to us. I need two volunteers."

Of the half dozen hands that shot up, two stood out. They belonged to a pair of twin brothers whose parents, too old to make the journey themselves, had used their savings to send them to Jerusalem.

Having never left their small Texas community, they had a hard time acclimating to Israeli life. They ate only in Western restaurants, watched only American television, and kept to themselves. However, their faith in J.P. and in the Society of the Millennial Dawn was as solid as their rodeo-conditioned bodies. They would enthusiastically do whatever J.P. asked.

"I want Stone and West trailed—twenty-four seven—until I say otherwise." JP handed each of them the addresses of the professors. "I'll expect no less than four reports a day—if those two so much as wink at a girl in a market I want to know everything about her. Got it?"

"Yes sir!" The boys stood a little straighter with the weight of their assignment as they grabbed their backpacks filled with granola, halva, bottled water, maps, a camera, and a cell phone.

"Now, call me when you find 'em and for Heaven's sake, don't let 'em see you, and don't lose 'em. Am I clear?" Eager nods gave the answer.

"Then go with God my sons."

# 10

# Darkness Falls

THE PREDICTABLE EVENING CHILL enveloped the hillside that led to the Shrine of the Book. Running a bit late, Art fastened the Velcro around the zipper of his Patagonia jacket and leaned into the slight breeze, thinking that in Jerusalem one was always going up or down a hill. The shrine came into view, with its cleverly designed roof that mimicked the curved yet pointed top of the clay casings in which the Dead Sea Scrolls had been found. He couldn't wait to tell Kahlil about the day's discovery. As he silently debated mentioning the attempt on his life he heard a sharp pop. He instinctively flinched and his mind envisioned a gun, but he just as quickly dismissed his overactive imagination and rationalized away the noise as a car backfiring.

Watching his step a bit more closely after the noise, he turned the corner toward the Shrine itself. Entering the park, he quickly came upon their favorite bench, which, surprisingly, was empty. Running late, though par for the course for Art, was unheard of for Kahlil. As he began to wonder about the whereabouts of his friend, he noticed the form on the ground, on the far side of the bench. His gait turned to a trot.

Art thought he was hallucinating when he realized it was a body. Flicking on his flashlight, he gasped. There, in the bright glow of the recharged beam, glistened a crimson profusion of blood, pouring from Kahlil's head and chest. His friend appeared to still draw breath. "Kahlil!

Kahlil! Speak to me! Who did this? Say something! Can you hear me? Hang in there! I'm getting help!"

After fumbling for his cell phone, he dialed 919 with shaking fingers and told the Israeli emergency dispatcher to send an ambulance immediately to the park adjacent to the Shrine of the Book. "A man's been shot! He's alive, but barely. Please. Please hurry."

Ending the call, he turned back to Kahlil. Art had never seen someone fatally wounded—and he'd certainly never seen that much blood spilled. He leaned in close to the body and made sure Kahlil was still breathing. "Hang on Kahlil. Help's on the way." As he debated trying to stop the bleeding from either the chest or the head, Art's flashlight picked up a glint from under Kahlil's left side. Instinctively, he reached for it in an effort to make Kahlil more comfortable.

Immediately he regretted the move. Staring up at him from between his sweaty fingers was a gun—most likely the gun that someone had used to assault Kahlil. Great! Could this day possibly get much worse? Hoping he hadn't smudged any fingerprints left by the true assailant, he set the gun down on the bench that he and Kahlil should have been sitting on together. Instead he now sat there alone, and began to pray over his Muslim friend, "Dear Lord, you are the Great Physician. Please don't let Kahlil die!"

Art was still praying when he first heard the ambulance arrive. He met the medics at the sidewalk and directed them up the hill to the bench. Within seconds, they tore his shirt open and worked to staunch the chest wound. They wrapped his head, stopping the bleeding there as well. With the patient stabilized and secured to the stretcher, they proceeded to the ambulance.

"Where are you taking him?" demanded Art.

"Just to the ambulance for now—we'll get a check on his vitals while we wait for police clearance to head to the hospital. We'll be going to Sinai."

Of course! He'd forgotten that in Israel, the police had to control every bit of the scene and hoped the extra waiting time wouldn't put Kahlil at further risk. Perhaps God had been listening, for no sooner than he'd asked the question, a cruiser hopped the curb and parked haphazardly behind the ambulance. Before the officers could speak, Art jumped in. "Please. Please, officers, release the ambulance so they can get my friend to the hospital before it's too late!"

The officer, not used to being told what to do, started to put the American in his place, until he looked at the patient. "Mr. El Said? That's Kahlil El Said, the antiquities dealer? Everyone knows what an honest man he is—who'd want to hurt him? Go. Take him. Quickly!" Turning to Art he added that he personally would notify the dealer's daughter, Hannah.

Hannah! Art felt sick to his stomach. He really needed to get to the hospital to be there when she arrived. Or should he offer to go get her? No, the police could probably get her there faster. And they'd probably wanted him to answer a few questions. He moved over to the bench and sat down, head between his knees. Now that Kahlil was on his way to the hospital, Art finally had time to realize just how awful he felt. He took several gulps of air, pulled up his head, and after running a hand through his hair, he stood up, offering his hand to the closest officer. "My name is Dr. Art West. I was meeting my friend Kahlil El Said here, and found him like this. What else can I tell you?"

Office Reiss gave him a curt nod. "Why at night? You don't see your friend at his shop? Or at his home?"

"Kahlil and I are old friends. We like the privacy the park gives us to speak freely. It's just been our tradition."

Officer Leibowitz joined them. "Well, either you two weren't alone, or you've got some more explaining to do, Dr. West. What else can you tell us?"

"Did you get hold of Hannah? Is she okay? Does she need a ride to the hospital?" Art ignored the officer's question.

"I spoke with her myself and sent an officer to accompany her to the hospital. She asked about you and I told her that you were the one who reported his injuries—I didn't give her details over the phone—the doctors can do that. Now. Back to my question. What else can you tell me and Officer Reiss here?"

"I was running a few minutes late—I usually am—and when I first got up the hill, I was surprised that Kahlil wasn't here yet. Then I noticed the body on the ground, saw the blood and called 919. I must have just missed the gunman because I remember hearing a noise before I rounded that corner . . . " Art turned and pointed to the garden entrance. "I was just in front of the Museum when I heard a pop, but I told myself it was a car backfiring."

"You sure you only heard one 'pop' as you call it?" Leibowitz pressed, while Reiss scribbled furiously.

"I only heard one. Yes. And like I said, I found him here, called 919, and then tried to make him comfortable until the ambulance arrived. That's when I pulled this out from under him." He gestured towards the gun sitting on the bench. Both officers instinctively reached for their own, but visibly relaxed when Art dropped his hand back to his side. Reiss produced a plastic bag, into which he dropped the gun.

"I know. I know." Art continued, "I shouldn't have touched it. I just wanted to make him comfortable. As soon as I realized that I could have contaminated any prints, I put it down. Maybe the shooter's prints are still on it? Maybe it can help find his attacker?" Art could feel the emotion catching up with him, hear it in his own voice. "Kahlil is perhaps my closest friend here in Jerusalem. Whatever I can do . . . "

The officers knew they'd gotten as much information as they would for the moment, and they needed to do a cursory sweep of the scene before the forensic team arrived. Before leaving Art to collect himself, Officer Reiss asked if Art would come down to the police station with them to give his fingerprints, for elimination purposes.

"Of course, but will it take long? I'd like to get to the hospital to check on Kahlil and wait with Hannah."

"We understand. The tests won't take long. Why don't you sit here for a minute, and we'll come get you when we're ready to leave."

Appreciating the courtesy, Art thanked the officer, and sat back down on the bench, head in his hands, to wait. Nausea rose up in the pit of his stomach and he began to shiver.

# 11

# Departures and Arrivals

THE SHRILL STACCATO OF the phone startled Sara Goldberg as she wiped down the last of the tables in her café. Her stomach dropped with the same weight of the wet rag she let fall to the table as she crossed to the counter to answer. For the past nineteen months, her husband Yacov had been stationed in Hebron, as part of his extended service in the Israeli Army. A late night call could only mean bad news.

"Shalom" she answered shakily.

"Sara! Sara! My father's on his way to hospital. I wouldn't have called so late but I didn't know who else to call. There's a policeman standing here waiting to take me to Sinai but can you meet me there? I'm afraid to be there alone. I'm—"

Hearing Hannah's voice, Sara had started to breathe a sigh of relief, until her words sank in. "Hannah, please slow down. Your father's taken ill? The police are there?"

"No. He's been attacked. He was meeting Professor West in the park. I don't know what happened. Sara, I just can't go to hospital alone." Hannah's voice was hoarse and the tears were still flowing.

Grabbing her purse and keys, Sara had already begun turning off lights in her café. "I'm on my way. Do I need to come get you or should I go straight to hospital?"

Hannah took a deep breath. "The officer's here to take me. I'll meet you there. And can you please call Grace for me?"

"Absolutely. What else do you need me to do for you?"

"Pray, Sara. Pray for my father."

"I'm on my way. I'll meet you in Emergency."

Sara could hear Hannah holding back a fresh wave of sobs as she rang off. Impulsively, she filled a bag with a handful of muffins and grabbed several bottles of juice and water before setting the alarm and locking the shop. This could be a long night and Hannah would need her strength.

Before starting the engine of her worn Accord, Sara dialed Grace. She knew her friend dreaded late night phone calls as well, having received news of sudden death of her father in Boston in the middle of the Jerusalem night. Grace picked up after only two rings.

"Grace, it's Sara. Something's happened to Kahlil El Said and Hannah's asked us to meet her at Sinai." She knew that even if Grace had been sleeping, she was one of those people who sprang instantly into full consciousness with the ringing of the phone.

"Kahlil. What happened? Is it serious? Of course it is, or you wouldn't be calling." There really *is* such a thing as a dumb question, she thought. "How's Hannah?"

"She didn't say much, but it must be bad. An officer came to her door and offered to take her there himself. All I know is that he was meeting Art in the park and now he's on his way to Sinai."

"Where are you? Should I meet you there, or do you want to swing by?"

"I'm at the café. I can probably get there quicker if I go from here, but I can come there if you'd rather not drive."

"Don't be silly. I'll meet you there. Where's Art? Is he with Kahlil?"

"I've no idea. Hannah was too upset about going hospital alone to say much more."

"I'm on my way. I'll see if I can reach him for details."

"I told her we'd meet her at Emergency."

"Will do. Be safe."

"You too. I'll see you soon."

As Sara started the engine and made a quick U-turn towards the hospital, Grace, now in her car, left messages at both Art's flat and on his cell, wondering what he had gotten himself into this time.

～

Ray Simpson tried unsuccessfully to creep about the tiny three-room flat without waking his roommate, Grayson Johnson. He'd been lucky to find someone to share the rent and luckier still that the guy was so laid back he didn't make a nuisance of himself.

Ray's sleep deprivation rivaled that of a medical resident. If he played his cards right though, he'd come out with the same Dr. in front of his name—only it'd be for Archaeology not Medicine. Most days he felt like an indentured servant and didn't look much better. He'd never been an athlete and avoided exercise much the same way he avoided eating anything remotely resembling fresh produce, which resulted in his looking very much like an overstuffed rag doll—softly padded and the color of muslin. No matter. He was basically enslaved to Patrick Stone anyway.

No one else had even applied for the assistantship, and now Ray understood why. But then, his credentials hadn't gotten him much more than a cartload of standardized rejection letters from virtually every major program on both American coasts. Bottom line, they were stuck with each other because they, each in his own way, desperately needed the other.

Ray tried to remind himself that the misery would end soon. He only needed to survive the summer, make enough money to pay for one more dissertation semester, and impress Stone just enough to get a passable recommendation in his file. All *that* really meant was be-ing at Dr. Shrew's beck and call 27 hours a day. He supposed he'd had worse gigs—transferring the school library's card catalogue to disk, for example—than playing step-and-fetch-it for one of Yale's tenured pro-fessors. And he had to admit that the work had, at times, been pretty interesting—especially making replicas of artifacts for Stone's lectures.

Though his eyes burned and his fingers felt like they'd been run-ning violin scales for the last 9 hours, he couldn't settle down enough to sleep. Stone had been particularly irascible this afternoon—so much so that Ray had turned off the ringer on his cell phone and left it to vibrate among the mess of sheets and blankets on his bed. He had more than enough to do for his taskmaster. He'd finally completed the matter of the moment. Anything else could wait until tomorrow.

~

Zeke Johnson looked up from the handheld football game at the apartment building across the street. Still no sign of that Stone guy. He'd changed positions more than a dozen times, eaten through three boxes of Cracker Jacks and beaten his all-time highest score twice since setting up surveillance. This tailing stuff was supposed to be cool—exciting—like it was on TV. The cops on *Law and Order* never made it through a whole cup of coffee before the perp showed up.

He hadn't agreed with his folks at all about moving to Jerusalem for the impending Rapture. He'd been perfectly happy working the rodeo circuit back home in Texas. It'd been Luke who'd convinced him that even if the world didn't end, they might as well get out from under Mama and Daddy's wings and have an adventure or two beyond the interchangeable arenas they'd visited with the rodeo. Trying to rub the pins and needles out of his left foot, he realized, not for the first time, that his big brother definitely didn't know everything.

For starters, the food here made the slop they'd eaten on the road back home look like Mama's Sunday dinner. Even McDonald's tasted funny over here. Then there was football. Around here, football meant soccer—like in England or something—and when they could find the rare game on a satellite TV, it was always pro. No chance of catching the Aggies on any satellite channel in Jerusalem, no sirree. He was ready for some adventure already, but as he'd just reported to Brother Lawes, not a dang thing had happened since he'd struck up his first innocuous pose under the olive tree.

Bored with the football game, he dialed Luke's cell.

"Yo-oooooh" he yawned into the phone as his brother picked up.

"Yo yourself. Man, is this a cool gig or what? I told you coming over here would be better than the Rodeo!" answered a breathless Luke.

"Are you trippin'? I'm so bored I wouldn't mind muckin' out a few stalls right now. This Stone guy ain't nowheres around."

"Well, if he's anything like West, I'd get ready to roll Z, 'cause I've been all over J-town and back this afternoon!"

"You're kiddin' man, right? I mean, no lie, I haven't done anything but eat Cracker Jacks, play football, and cuss the day we got on that stupid seven-four-seven."

"No. I'm not playin' Z, this West guy has been plenty busy. First I followed him down to some official building—the IAA or something—and then I had to haul it up to some church in Bethany, then back down to his place and then over to the park by where they keep the Dead Sea Scrolls—and here's where things got weird. I see the guy go in to the park, and then, like a minute later I see him come running out, and before I can figure what he's up to, an ambulance fires in, and then some cops come right behind 'em, pulling their ride up on the curb! Just like TV, Z!"

"Dude, this is the circuit all over again. I always got the half-dead bull—and you always wound up looking like the Marlboro Man," Zeke whined. "You know, I wish we'd never—whoa Nellie. There he is. The guy really exists. Gotta fly Lu."

He'd spotted his mark weaving down the block towards the apartment building. The dude was muttering and flapping his hands like he was crazy or something—and he kept looking behind him, over his shoulder. Zeke took two steps back into the canopy of the tree's branches and watched while Patrick Stone made his way through the doorway of his building, up the common stairwell, barely visible through the frosted hallway windows, and into his apartment where he systematically turned on all of the lights as he peered anxiously out of his own windows. This might not be so bad after all, thought Zeke, as he traded the football game for the binoculars he pulled out from the depths of his backpack.

# 12

# The Waiting Game

A RT WAS SURPRISED, RELIEVED, and grateful that the trip to the police station had been brief and, as these things go, fairly uneventful. Though he'd never found himself in quite this kind of bind, he had expected to be detained until morning, interrogated mercilessly, and perhaps even denied basic pleasantries like the fresh juice they'd offered. Instead, the efficiency of the Jerusalem Police became crystal clear from the moment he'd set foot in the station.

After Officers Leibowitz and Reiss introduced Inspector Jonah Katz, he in turn graciously showed Art to the men's room so he could freshen up before they began. Returning to the stark hallway, they made their way not to an interrogation room, but to the Inspector's office where he began by asking Art if there was anyone he wished to call before they began.

His first instinct was to call Grace, but he didn't want to disturb her at this late hour. He quickly did some math in his head and decided that whether or not it would come to needing an attorney, he'd best ring his friend Harry Scholer, a D.C. attorney. Paging through his cell phone directory, he found the number and hit talk. After close to a minute the line began ringing through the wind tunnel of the overseas call. After five rings, the lawyer's voice mail picked up. Of course. Harry was probably at the gym or already back and in the shower. Given his audience, he left a brief, matter-of-fact message, minus any of the panic that was steamrolling anew through his stomach. Trying to sound nonchalant, he asked Harry to return the call as soon as humanly possible.

Once he ended the call, he agreed to retell the story to the Inspector. It hadn't changed since he'd reported the evening's events to the officers on the scene, something they solemnly noted to their superior. That done, the Inspector, again, gracious in his tone, asked if Art minded being fingerprinted for elimination purposes, after which he'd be free to leave for the hospital to check on his friend. Art agreed and together he and Reiss headed for the booking area. Reiss was all business while completing the cards, but when they finished the last print, he looked up and smiled. "If you want to wash up, Leibowitz and I would be happy to give you a ride to the hospital, Professor. We know that Mr. El Said will need all the support he can get, while he's there."

Surprised and a little heartened, Art washed up and took the officers up on their offer. It was still close to midnight when they deposited him at the main emergency entrance to Sinai Hospital. He was about to ask the kind looking woman at the information desk for the where-abouts of his friend, when he caught a glimpse of Grace turning the corner at the far end of a hallway.

"Grace! Grace!" he called before he realized he was shouting in a hospital. Luckily no one even turned, much less chastised him. Grace whipped around. "Art? Is that you? What happened? Where have you been? Why didn't you call me? How'd you get here?" she practically shouted back.

He caught up to her, waving a hand in protest. "Easy does it. What are *you* doing here? How's Kahlil? Is Hannah here? How is she?"

"Come. Come. I'll take you to her. She's with Sara in the family waiting room. Kahlil's still in surgery. Hannah called Sara and Sara called me, and none of us, not even Hannah, has been told what happened, so start talking Mister."

"Why don't I wait and just tell the story once, after I check in with Hannah and see if there's any new word on Kahlil. OK?" Art could feel the stress of the day begin to attack his every move. His head hurt, his limbs ached, and his stomach still had that horrible churning sensation.

"Fair enough. They're right in here." Grace opened the door to a small room sparsely furnished with a lumpy couch and a handful of folding chairs scattered around a plastic patio table topped with muffins and bottles of water and juice. Hannah was sitting in one of the folding chairs, blotting swollen eyes, while Sara, kneeling beside her tried to soothe her in low, even tones. They both turned hopefully when the door opened, expecting the surgeon's report. Instead, upon seeing Art with Grace, Sara stood and Hannah ran to him, tears beating a rugged new path down her cheeks.

The message light, beckoning from the kitchen counter, caught Harry's eye as he crossed from the side door to the refrigerator for his post-workout shake. He'd skipped the gym in favor of a quick jog this morning. After twenty years in a lucrative law practice, Harry had decided to fuel his true passion—biblical archaeology—and founded the American Society of Biblical Archaeology. The career shift had allowed for a much needed lifestyle shift, one that now accommodated an exercise regimen and a similar level of intellectual stimulation without the toxic side effects of stress and high blood pressure that had begun to take their toll on his middle-aged body.

Taking a few gulps, he wiped his mouth with the back of his hand and considered the blinking light. It was barely 7 am. Most of his ASBA colleagues kept collegiate office hours—which meant this call, if not a wrong number, probably was for Harry Scholer, Esquire. He pressed the play button and heard his old friend Art West through the speaker. Though he registered the words, he focused more on Art's voice. He didn't sound right—too formal, yet too cavalier. Before the message played itself out, he dialed Art's cell.

Art picked up on the third ring, sounded strained. Harry dove right in, "Art, Harry. What's going on over there? I just walked in and found your message—you don't sound like yourself."

"Harry. Thanks for getting back to me so quickly. If I sound funny now it's because I just finished giving blood. I may be in a bit of a pickle and I wanted to check in with you. How dusty is that JD of yours?"

"You need legal advice on giving blood? Doesn't that fall more into the 'do unto others . . .' category?"

"Well, yes. I mean no. I mean, I'm giving blood because my friend Kahlil El Said—you remember him, the antiquities dealer—was attacked tonight, and I found him. We were meeting for one of our chats and when I got there—what? Oh, thank you—sorry, the nurse just brought me some juice—anyway, he'd been shot and I was taken in for questioning and fingerprinting and—"

"You what? Art, please tell me you didn't say anything without some sort of counsel there."

"Well of course I answered their questions. It was all very amiable. The officers who came to the scene both knew Kahlil, they sent a car for his daughter, and after taking me to the station they even gave me a ride to the hospital. They didn't really interrogate me—we just had a chat in the Inspector's office."

"Arthur. You know better! Where do things stand now?"

"I don't know really. I'm still at the hospital—this only happened a few hours ago. I have nothing to hide, I mean, it's not like the gun was mine or anything."

"Gun? What gun?!" Harry groaned.

"I didn't know it was a gun when I pulled it out—"

"You didn't know it was a gun?"

"No. No. Kahlil was lying on something, I just wanted to make him more comfortable. I—"

Harry groaned again. "Art, for once, words elude me. You bet you're in a pickle. Go home. Now. Stay there. Don't say another word to anyone—especially not the police. I'll catch the first plane over. Try to get some sleep and I'll call you when I land. Will you do as I ask, please?"

Art wasn't sure what exactly he'd done wrong, but he knew that Harry didn't scare easily. "Okay. I will. I just don't know—"

"You're right. You don't know. That's why you called me."

"Thanks Harry. Have a safe flight. I'll see you tonight?"

"I'll do my best, but it may take an extra day. Let me see what I can do."

"I owe you, Harry."

"Yes, you do. But one thing at a time, friend. Hang in there."

"Will do."

Harry hung up the phone and shook his head. He could already feel the blood rising in a way it hadn't in years. Well, he'd been hoping to fit in a trip to the Holy Land later in the summer. He hoped there was a empty seat on the next Jerusalem-bound flight out of Reagan International.

~

Grace's clogs echoed in the hospital hallway as she made her way back to the waiting room. She rarely called in favors, but had taken advantage of her long-standing relationship with Sammy Cohen and woken him up with the request to organize any O-positive donors within the IAA, and had done the same with the academic dean at Jerusalem University. Both men immediately forgave her the lateness of the calls when they realized that the esteemed Kahlil El Said needed not only their prayers, but their blood, and promised to do what they could immediately.

Wondering if she should offer to contact the Imam at the El Said's mosque, her thoughts turned back to Art. She adored the man, she really did, in a collegial way, and she greatly admired not only his fortitude when it came to research, but to his faith as well. As a Christian, Art embodied what she considered to be the most essential teachings of Jesus—an openness of spirit and love. It was these same qualities though, that often gave him a naiveté incongruous with his intellectual wit. Listening to his earlier explanation she'd realized that she'd known him long enough to hear between the lines—there was something big he wasn't sharing and she couldn't wait to drag it out of him.

Reaching for the doorknob of the waiting room, she heard his voice behind her.

"Yes, Bill. That's right. O-positive. We sure do appreciate it. Anything you can do. And again, I apologize for calling so late . . . . Sure will. Thanks again—you're a real blessing. Goodnight." Art looked up as he ended the call. "That was Bill Brown over at the American Institute of Holy Land Studies. Met him while I was in seminary. Hate that I hadn't had a chance to meet up with him yet this trip, but knew that he'd not only rally the troops over there for Kahlil, but that he'd start a prayer chain for him as well."

"Good work. I just spoke with both Sammy and Jack Samuels over at the University. They both send their prayers and said they'd be sure to get some donors over here. Now tell me, what *really* happened out there tonight?"

Before he could answer, they were joined by a tall thin man in scrubs. "Excuse me, please." He motioned towards the door handle

Grace still held in her hand. "Oh! Excuse *me*. Are you Mr. El Said's surgeon?"

"Yes I am. Steven Schwartz. And you are—?"

"Dr. Grace Levine. Friend of the family, as is Dr. Arthur West here. We're both academics." She wanted to be clear about their monikers and avoid any confusion or concern on his part that they might be interfering MDs. "Hannah's inside. We're all anxious to hear your report."

"Very pleased to meet you. After you . . . " He said, holding the door.

This time, Hannah and Sara were not disappointed when the door opened, revealing the wiry, worn out surgeon. "Miss El Said, I'm Dr. Schwartz. Your father's in recovery now, and in a bit, we'll take him to ICU. For the moment, he's doing as well as we can expect. We only found evidence of a single bullet, which entered his body, here . . . " The surgeon indicated his own diaphragm. ". . . it grazed his liver, before it shattered his spleen—which is what caused the majority of the blood loss and is why we sent the nurse down to inform you of the need for blood donations. We removed his spleen—something he can still live a normal life without, by the way—and barring any unforeseen infections, I feel confident that his insides will heal nicely."

Hannah's face brightened with fresh tears of relief and she started to speak. The doctor held up a palm. "Now about his head injury. He seemed to have taken quite a hit on the head—I'm told it may simply have been from falling. In any case, he's sustained a large hematoma, or bruise. We didn't see any collateral damage on the X-rays or CT scans, but there's always a high risk of swelling with an internal head injury. As you know, our bodies have a tremendous capacity to heal, and to protect themselves. That said, I don't want you to be upset when I tell you that he's in a light coma. It's something we expect with this kind of trauma, and right now there's nothing to indicate that this is anything more than a temporary state. We'll keep him in ICU for the next few days so we can watch him closely. You, as immediate family, of course will be permitted to stay with him for as much of the day as you'd like. We do ask that he not have any other visitors for the time being." For the first time since beginning his report, he took his eyes from Hannah's and, in turn, acknowledged Sara, Grace, and Art, with a slight nod. "I can see you have an impressive support system already in place. Once we're sure your father is out of danger, we'll move him to a room where they can visit him without restriction, during the day. Unfortunately, until then, hospital policy only permits visits by non-family members thirty minutes at a time here in the waiting room. Are there any questions I can answer for you at this time?"

This boy must be making a mother somewhere very happy, thought Grace. She didn't know if she'd ever met a surgeon with such a gentle, unassuming manner. He'd not talked down to Hannah, or used a bunch of medical gobbledygook to describe Kahlil's condition, and he'd made it pretty clear by the tone of his voice, that he didn't exactly agree with the hospital's policy towards non-family visitors. She felt good knowing Kahlil's fate lay partially in the young doctor's hands, and made a note to say that later to Hannah.

"Dr. Schwartz, thank you for all you have done for my father, and for being so kind to me. I have only one question—how soon may I see him?"

"I expect we'll be moving him to ICU within the hour. I'll send a nurse for you just as soon as we've got him settled in up there. Anything else?"

"About the blood—"

Grace interrupted her. "Hannah, Art and I have already taken care of that. After he gave his pint, he called Professor Brown over at the Institute and I rang both Dr. Cohen at the IAA and Dr. Samuels at the University. Between the three of them, I expect we'll have the hospital restocked in no time."

"Then, no. No more questions, Doctor. Thank you again."

"I'm glad to have been of help." He handed her a card. "My beeper number is on here—do not hesitate to use it if you think of any other questions. Often this time is so overwhelming that I've found it best to be available for my patients' families. You may well forget everything you've just heard from me, so please, take me at my word, and ring if you have any concerns." He flashed a genuine smile, and with a short bow, took his leave.

"What a charming man. Hannah, I feel very good about his caring for your father," offered Grace.

"I do as well. And thank you all. For being here. Grace, Professor Art, for making those calls—for giving your blood. You are blessings from Allah."

"We wouldn't have it any other way. We'll all be praying for his healing, as will the friends we phoned. You concentrate your thought and prayers on his well being, Hannah."

"Hannah, do you want us to stay with you until you see him?" Grace asked.

"Why don't I stay with Hannah, and you and Art can get some sleep. I don't know how you're still standing after the night you've had!" Sara said, more to Art than Grace.

And she didn't know the half of it, thought Grace. And neither do I. Grace could see Art trying not to look too hopeful when he looked from Hannah to Grace for the verdict.

"Oh! Certainly. Yes. You've both done more than I could ever re-pay. That is, if you don't mind staying a bit longer with me, Sara, just until . . . until . . . " Hannah's voice began to crack again with tears flowing. "I don't know what I'd do without him . . . "

"Hannah. Don't you worry about that just now. You just stay fo-cused on those positive prayers, remember?"

Nodding her assent, she thanked everyone again and ran from the room.

# 13

## Twenty Questions

GRACE ALLOWED ART TO stay lost in his own thoughts only until she'd started the engine of her Honda. Shifting into reverse, she looked at him.

"OK. Time's up. Start talking."

Art sighed, reluctant to start over for the fourth time in as many hours. "Like I said. Kahlil and I were supposed to meet at the park, like always. I was running late and by the time I got to our bench, he'd already been attacked. I didn't see anyone. Coming or going. Harry says I shouldn't say anything else to anyone."

"Harry?"

"Harry Scholer. You know him—ASBA? DC attorney?"

"Harry? You called Harry? What on earth for?"

"Well, while I was at the police station, they asked if I wanted to make any calls, and, having no idea you'd be at the hospital, I didn't want to bother you, and I didn't know how it would go, and . . . "

"Are you considered a suspect?"

"Not really. That's why I agreed to go and give fingerprints—to eliminate myself."

"Fingerprints? From what? The bench? Surely you didn't touch anything!"

"From the gun. I—"

"From the gun? What gun? You touched the gun?!"

Art sighed again. "I didn't know it was a gun when I pulled it out from under Kahlil. It looked like he'd fallen on a rock or something and he just looked so uncomfortable."

"Arthur J. West! For such a smart man, your complete lack of common sense amazes me! I know you'd never do anything to hurt Kahlil—but you're a foreigner in a country that has every reason to be suspicious of foreigners—just what were you thinking?"

"Grace. Cut me some slack. Harry's already given me the what-for. Today's been one of the most trying and, may I add, traumatic, of my life, and while I appreciate that what you're saying is out of concern and care for me, I just don't have the energy to spar right now. I wasn't thinking, OK? I was trying to help our friend and to be cooperative with the authorities. I don't see what's so awful about that."

Grace grimaced. "I'm sorry, Art. You're right. You've had an awful day. Let's focus instead on what you found in Bethany."

"To be honest, I'd almost forgotten. That seems like weeks ago. Who could have raided the tomb so soon after I left? Who would have tried to trap me?"

"God only knows, Art. But let's think about what you did find. You realize that this could make your career—you'd never have to worry about funding again! And Discovery Channel is going to be thrilled—don't you have an exclusive agreement with them for filming any of your discoveries?"

"I think you're putting that proverbial cart before the horse. We still need to get what little we do have left dated, verified, and re-verified. And all I want to do right now is sleep for a week."

They'd arrived at Art's flat. "Join me for a toddy? I'd call it a night cap, but that seems to be sun starting to peak up over the horizon over there . . . ," he joked.

"How 'bout I mix you a drink. I think I'll get you settled and then head to my office. I expect today will be lost mostly to IAA work and I'd like to get a few things off my desk before Sammy calls."

Art started to protest then decided he'd let Grace mother him a bit.

Twenty minutes later, with Art situated, Grace was letting herself out of the front door when she almost ran headlong into a stocky young man with almost iridescent blue eyes. "Pardon me. I've got a special overnight delivery for a Dr. West?"

Taken aback, especially given the hour, Grace pushed the door behind her back open, gesturing inside.

"Why don't you just leave it here where Dr. West will see it when he comes downstairs."

She started to fumble with her bag, looking for tip money. Noticing what she was doing the young courier, who'd dropped the heavy package in the front hall, stopped her. "No need, ma'am. The sender took care of everything. Shalom."

Startled, Grace could only wish him Shalom, before finally closing the door behind her.

# 14

## Stone on a Roll

PATRICK STONE HAD INDEED taken care of everything. He felt positively giddy. In a matter of hours, he'd be 30,000 feet above the havoc he'd wreaked. He practically danced his way between his closet, bureau, and suitcases as he finished packing. Everything was falling into place.

His graduate assistant, Raymond wasn't the sharpest knife in the drawer, as his mother would have said (if she could still speak intelligently), but he did have a gift when it came to forgeries. The poor sap thought that all this time he'd been making teaching tools. In reality, Stone had merely been honing the young man's skills for the day he had known would come. The day that came yesterday, when that dolt, West, had discovered the tomb in Bethany. Raymond had certainly earned his keep—alerting him to the find, and helping him move the boulder over the tomb. He knew West wouldn't stay trapped forever—and the head start on his plans had been eclipsed only by the satisfaction of knowing his arch nemesis was completely helpless.

Stone had stayed out of sight until after that Arab groundskeeper rescued West, and then easily made his way into the tomb to snag the stone bearing the inscription, as well as a jar full of what appeared to be bits of manuscripts. It had taken a bit of chiseling and scraping to remove the stone, but all in all, the block had come out fairly easily. If only he could say the same of the rest of his day.

He couldn't believe what an idiot that dealer had been. Regulations smegulations. He had a priceless antiquity in his hands—something that could have made both him and the old man rich—not to mention famous. Well, it was the old guy's loss—he'd keep all the money for himself, just as soon as he got the original out of the country. He would have settled for some authenticity paperwork—but it became clear even that wasn't an option. That's when he'd moved on to Plan B.

He'd made good time driving it over to the dump Raymond rented and because he'd made sure the student had no life other than to serve his professor's whims, he knew the replica would be completed before day's end, as he demanded. Promising to return later that evening for the original, he'd headed back to the antiquities shop in the hopes of convincing El Said to either play along with him, or, if worse came to worse, threaten the man into secrecy. Finding the shop closed, Stone weighed his options, and was about to leave when, impulsively, he decided to follow the man.

They'd taken a short windy walk up to the park. When the dealer paused at a bench, Stone, hand on his concealed father's antique derringer, had meant to initiate a perfectly civil conversation. Unfortunately, he startled El Said, immediately putting the old man on the defensive. Raising his hands in a show of good faith, Stone had forgotten about the gun—which, now waving wildly from his right hand in plain view, did anything but placate the Arab. El Said reached for it, and darned if the relic didn't actually fire! Tumbling forward, the man caught the bullet in the gut, and, to make matters worse, he'd cracked his head on the bench before landing in a heap, pulling Stone down with him and pinning the gun hand under El Said's head. Panicked, he'd barely managed to pull out his hand from under the stricken man before he caught sight of West through the trees. Ducking back into a grove, he figured he could retrieve the gun when West inevitably went for help. But fate smiled upon him one more time that day. The idiot pulled out the gun before going for help!

Quickly reassessing the situation, Stone decided that he could now make a break for it—the gun would now have Arthur West's fingerprints on it, and by the time authorities moved forward with any sort of an investigation, he, Patrick Stone, would be on his way to fame and fortune on a completely different continent.

He'd taken a labyrinth of alleyways back to his car and sped back to Raymond's flat. When the student had finally answered the door, Stone barged his way in, and seeing that the replica, for all intents, was completed, grabbed the original, and mumbled something about being late for the theatre. Leaving Raymond with instructions to continue aging the faux stone, he promised to be in touch later. The quietude of the drive back to his own flat gave him the final bit of inspiration.

He left the stone wrapped in a raincoat he kept in the back seat and made his way into his apartment, not even aware that his self-congratulatory thoughts had made their way out of his head and into a rapid undertone. The paranoia didn't set in until he reached his door. After checking out the windows and seeing no one on the street, he'd gone first to his desk. Rifling through his Rolodex, he found Art West's address scribbled on a crumpled card. He'd then grabbed a phone book, ordered a courier to stop first at Raymond's and then at West's and then, uncharacteristically, added 20% to the total fee, if they'd guarantee delivery by dawn. It was just money, and he'd have plenty of it soon enough. The best part, of course, he would save for last. One more well-placed phone call and Dr. West's goose would be thoroughly cooked.

# 15

# The Trouble with Harry

S AMMY COHEN COULD SET his watch by his own internal clock. Despite being awakened by Grace's late-night plea for blood do- nors, his eyes opened, right on schedule at 6:18 a.m. No matter that he'd spent more than forty minutes making calls after ringing off with Grace. Living in a city that all too often doubled as a war zone, most companies had established phone trees for emergency purposes—much the same way Amercian Midwestern elementary schools used them for snow closings. By 1 a.m., most of the IAA employees would have been notified that O-positive blood was needed at Sinai.

Donning his *tefillin*, the black prayer boxes devout Jewish men affixed to their arms and foreheads with a series of leather straps, he'd moved methodically and comfortably through his morning prayers, adding an extra *misheberach*, for Kahlil's recovery, before downing his usual Tuesday morning breakfast of muesli and strawberries. By 7:48 he had eased his car into his reserved parking space at the IAA, and by 8:00, on the dot, he was pouring the first cup of coffee from the pot in his office.

Still blowing the steam in anticipation of the first scalding sip, he paged through the emails littering his inbox. The knock at his door made him jump, bringing his coffee dangerously close to landing in his lap.

"So sorry to startle you Sammy! You didn't spill that did you? I can see the steam from here."

"Grace! I didn't exactly expect to see you at my door so early. No my dear, disaster averted—coffee still in the cup. Come in. Can I pour you one? What news do you have? How's Kahlil?"

"Good. Yes, to the coffee, thank you. Sara's not opened Solomon's Porch yet—she stayed on at hospital last night with Hannah. They hadn't moved Kahlil from recovery to ICU when Art and I left around 3. Hannah understandably didn't want to wait alone. The prognosis sounded good though. A charming young surgeon—Schwartz was his name—let us know he'd removed a bullet from Kahlil's diaphragm, removed his spleen and that the coma—"

"Coma? I had no idea it was that serious."

"Actually, he explained that the coma was expected—Kahlil apparently took a nasty spill and conked his head. He has some internal bruising in his head and the coma should help that heal. For as touch and go as we all know the first few hours are after any major trauma, Dr. Schwartz seemed very optimistic. Thank you again for starting that call chain for the O-positive."

"How did Kahlil come to be shot in the first place?"

"Details on that are still sketchy. Art found him—already shot—in the park at the Shrine of the Book, called the police and then wound up at the station giving a statement and fingerprints before joining us at the hospital. You should know, he's put in a call to Harry Scholer, who's on his way here."

Grace took a sip of coffee from the mug Sammy offered her, letting him digest the news.

"Harry Scholer? Harry Scholer! He didn't make enough trouble for us with the James ossuary authenticity report? What would possess Art to call Scholer?"

"There seems to be a little issue with the gun, presumably the weapon responsible for the hole in Kahlil. Art accidentally moved it and while he's not really a suspect they had to rule him out. I think the call to Harry was more preemptive than anything. And you know that he and Art go way back."

"But surely Art knows that after defending Oded Golan and exposing us to months of criticism, Harry's not exactly welcome in these halls."

"I'm sure that if Art had taken the time to think about it, he may have chosen a different attorney, but obviously he wasn't thinking too clearly if he touched the gun at all. In his defense he did have one doozy of a day, yesterday."

Sammy sighed. Maybe he was overreacting to Scholer's impending arrival. He hoped so. He decided to move on. "About yesterday. When we returned from Bethany, we took the ossuary straight to the clean room. After they took the usual photographs they pried it open, and got quite a start when they didn't find bones . . . "

"That's a real shame. So, just an empty box? Not even any fragments? I hope Art won't be too disappointed."

"Quite the contrary, my dear. We found a scroll."

"A scroll? Why would someone put a scroll in a casket?"

"Good question. That's one of the reasons I set up a meeting for 10:30 this morning. Did you know that Andre Chartier was in town for a conference? He's agreed to skip the morning session to join us."

"Well, we couldn't have planned that any better if we tried. Andre's certainly the go-to man for ancient scripts!"

Though recently retired to the south of France, scholars the world over still considered Andre Chartier the leading expert in Herodian period Holy Land scripts. He'd practically transformed epigraphy into an art form. Through the close study of letters—how they're formed, how they're connected, how they're used—a good epigrapher can date a written sample to a particular time period. Chartier raised the bar for his field, not only with his extensive knowledge, but also with unprecedented diplomacy. In any given authenticity dispute, inevitably both sides would call on his expertise. His input at this stage of their investigation could allay any lingering doubts from the James ossuary debacle.

"That he is. Perhaps the tide is turning for our friend Art. This may well turn into the find of a lifetime."

"For Art's sake, I hope so. He could use some good news."

"For all our sakes. If you'll excuse me for a bit, I need to get through my mail. You're welcome to stay and drink your coffee."

"Thanks, Sammy. I think I'll take a walk. I didn't get much sleep and the exercise will do me good. Why don't I just meet up with you at 10:30?"

"10:30 it is. We'll meet here in my office and head up to the lab together."

"Wonderful. See you then."

# 16

## Police on the Prowl

JOHAN KATZ RUBBED HIS eyes and face, aware of the day's worth of stubble building on his chin and cheeks. By the time he'd finished reviewing what little they'd collected on the El Said shooting he'd realized that there was no point in going home for two hours sleep. Shaving kit in hand, he ducked into the locker room at the station.

No sooner had he lathered his face than a young rookie appeared. "Um. Sir. Excuse me? We just got a tip on that shooting last night? I was told to let you know right away?"

Katz met his eyes in the mirror. "Kadinsky, right? Thank you, son. I'll be there as soon as I finish shaving."

The rookie seemed to have grown roots. "Anything else?" Katz waited for a reply, and getting none, turned to face the young officer. "If that's all you've got, you're dismissed."

Kadinsky blinked. "Oh. Yessir. Thank you sir. Sorry sir."

Katz turned back to his stubble. Had he ever been that nervous around his superiors? He hoped not. Wondering what sort of new information might have come in, he quickly finished with the razor and rinsed off his face before heading back into the squad room.

Leibowitz and Riess were waiting for him, looking like he felt. They'd obviously not gone home after their shift ended last night either. "Well men, what do you have?"

Riess fingered a pink message slip in one hand. "We're not sure this has anything to do with the attack, but some guy just called—wouldn't leave a name or contact number—saying that he had it on 'good authority' that Professor West was stealing and forging antiquities. Said we'd find proof at the professor's flat."

Leibowitz chimed in. "Maybe we got it all wrong last night. Maybe Mr. El Said figured out what West was doing and confronted him. We don't have the forensic reports back from last night yet—lab was closed by the time we finished up with the Professor—so we don't know for certain that the professor *didn't* shoot the old guy."

"Ordinarily I wouldn't put too much stock in an anonymous call, but it's a bit suspicious that Dr. West's name pops up so soon after the incident last evening. I think we need to check it out, but we also need to be sure we do absolutely everything by the book. Just to be sure, I'm going to see this through myself. This Dr. West is very well connected here in town. Before we go anywhere though, you two need to hit the showers—you're both looking a little rough. Meet me in my office no later than ten-thirty. Understood?"

"Yessir!" The officers seemed reinvigorated. It wasn't often that the Inspector included the responding officers in his follow-ups. Usually, by this point in a case, he turned it all over to the detectives and waited for the reports.

Art had wasted no time getting to bed. He hadn't objected when Grace offered to let herself out—climbing the stairs to his room as she descended those to the front door. He'd managed to remove his shoes, before taking what would be his final sip of the sweet bourbon and sugar mixture she'd fixed him. Leaning back against the pillows, he'd fallen asleep instantly—sitting upright, fully clothed.

Though sleep came easily, rest eluded him. He dreamed of caves filled with stalactites that, as they hung from the ceiling like popsicles, melted into drops then torrents of blood. The blood then rose in pools around him becoming encrusted, engulfing him like quicksand. Above him he could see a sliver of light that played with the edges of an inscription too dusty to read. The cave became a cell, and as the blood-red sand continued to rise, potsherds and bone began to emerge like small shells and plankton in a tide that rolled not straight against a beach, but rolled in on itself, with him in the midst of what was rapidly becoming a whirlpool. Trying desperately to catch his breath he inhaled a mouthful of tinny-tasting sand. Something—a small rodent—scurried across his right arm. Flinging it off, his hand brushed the ceiling, now rough like limestone. He reached up with both arms and began pounding with every fiber of his soul. Noiselessly he screamed for Kahlil.

It took more than a few minutes for Art to make the journey back from his nightmare to the late morning sun beating down onto his bed. It took a few more, still, to realize that the pounding wasn't a lingering reminder of the dream, but emanating from his front door.

"Open up. Police. Dr. West? Dr. Arthur West? Jerusalem Police. We need you to open the door or we'll do it ourselves!"

Completely disoriented, Art looked at the clock. 11:10 a.m. Why was he still in bed? Why were there police at his door? Why was—it all came back in a rush. The ossuary, the tablet, the trap . . . Kahlil!

Dragging the blanket with him to the window, he raised it and stuck out his head. "I'll be down in just a moment. Sorry, I was asleep—I didn't hear you."

Even to himself he sounded like an idiot. The officers below sounded like they were trying to raise the dead. How could he not have heard them? Then he remembered the dream and blanched. Disentangling himself from the blanket, he splashed some water on his face, ran a comb through his hair and tried to press out the wrinkles in his clothes with his still damp hands, as he ran down the stairs to the door.

Flinging it open, he found Inspector Katz accompanied by Leibowitz, Reiss, and two other officers. "What can I do for you gentleman?" Art exhaled.

"May we come in, Dr. West? We have some follow-up questions for you." Again, Inspector Katz sounded amiable, almost apologetic.

"Of course—" The officers didn't wait for him to finish the sentence before stepping over the threshold. As he started to lead them upstairs, he turned back around. "What's this all about? Did you find out who shot Kahlil, I mean, Mr. El Said?"

Katz started to reply when he was interrupted by an outcry followed by a curse not swallowed quickly enough. They all turned back towards the door. "What is it Reiss?" the inspector demanded.

"Nothing Sir. I apologize. I stubbed my toe on this package . . . " A light could almost be seen going off in the young officer's face. " . . . on this package here. I wonder if this could have something to do with that call we got?"

Art didn't like the way his empty stomach was beginning to turn. "What call?"

Katz ignored him for the moment. "Maybe we ought to have a look." Turning back to Art, he chose his words carefully. "Dr. West, we received a call this morning that gives us reason to believe that you may be, ah, how shall I put this, you may be in possession of some things you shouldn't have . . . may we see what's in this package?"

Something hammered in the back of Art's head. A conversation from yesterday that he couldn't quite recall. "What package?"

Reiss, with some effort, held up the package that had stubbed his toe. "This package sir. From Lo'mi Courier Service."

"I have nothing to hide. I . . . " Again, the officers didn't wait for him to finish his sentence, taking his "nothing to hide" as permission to tear open the wrapping. As the others audibly gasped, Art had to sit on the stair. There, right there in his foyer, stood an officer holding an engraved limestone tablet. He shook his head in disbelief, unable to form the words of protest running at mock speed through his brain.

"Dr. West. I'm afraid we're going to have to ask you to come with us. This is exactly the sort of item we were told we would find here. You can make any calls you need to make from the station." Inspector Katz's tone had changed, the graciousness replaced by authority. Leibowitz reached for his handcuffs but Katz shook his head no.

"Dr. West? I'd like to spare you any embarrassment. If you'll come with me?"

Only then, did yesterday's conversation come back to him. " . . . don't talk to anyone. Especially not the police . . . " How he wished he'd listened to Harry.

# 17

## Stone Cold

Tuesday had been a memorable day—good and bad—for Dr. Patrick Stone as well. On the plus side, he had managed to lead Arthur West into such a quagmire that it should take him days, maybe weeks, to clear himself. He ALSO had in hand a jar with some bits of old manuscript, plus the genuine Lazarus inscription—both of which Raymond had found in the tomb early Monday afternoon. And now he was weighing whether to become more famous by going to the press and creating an international sensation, or whether to feather his retirement nest by making millions.

Stone was the kind of person who got as much satisfaction from seeing West stumble as from receiving personal praise. Praise is ephemeral and not necessarily lucrative. On the whole, he decided it would be far better to take the money and run. But he realized through his experience with El Said that there was no way he could sell the stone here in Jerusalem. The environment was too volatile, and the antiquities police too omnipresent.

But how would he handle the manuscripts? And how would he get the far more valuable inscription out of the country? More to the point, since he didn't want to let the stone out of his sight, how was *he* going to get out of the country *with* the stone? As he drank his cup of hot Nigerian coffee he pondered these problems at length.

As for the downside of the day, true enough, sealing Art West inside the tomb was a nasty prank—but he knew Art would find a way out in short order. Plus, it gave him time to consider options for the rest of the day.

Worse, however, was the episode in the park with El Said. Stone had hoped to talk again, this time more calmly, in El Said's home. However, when he arrived, El Said was just leaving. He followed El Said to the park and confronted him there hoping to threaten him into cooperating or keeping quiet about the inscription. He had taken with him, just as a defensive reflex, an old hand gun that had belonged to his father. But his antique derringer was just that—a conversation piece. Unfortunately, when confronted, El Said had grabbed Stone's hand causing the gun to go off, and El Said to tumble on top of him. To top that off the old man hit his head on the iron park bench.

Stone, frightened, had barely been able to extract his hand (sans gun unfortunately) from under El Said's body, beat a quick retreat, and hide before West showed up. That was a shock! As the devil would have it, things turned out almost perfectly. The one person who could clearly link Stone to the Lazarus tablet was now in a coma, according to the news reports, and Stone's nemesis would surely be implicated. He had not told his doctoral student, Ray Simpson, about the incidents with El Said—plausible deniability. So far as Simpson knew, Stone had simply gone to the theater last night.

Stone ordered Simpson to make the knock off copy of the inscription Monday afternoon. Simpson had a steady hand and experience in making replicas of artifacts for use as visual aids in Stone's lectures. Posting the stone anonymously to West by overnight courier, and tipping off the police were the fun parts. Stone would have loved to hear West try to explain away that copy!

Simpson was sworn to silence and given the rest of the week off. He would leave Simpson some money to stay in Jerusalem for a while to continue his library research and then return to Yale to put the final touches on his thesis. Later today he would call Simpson and explain that his mother was ill and he needed to return home. As a further inducement to silence, he would promise to send a glowing job recommendation to Johns Hopkins. In fact, he would word his message in such a way to suggest that without his silence, Ray would never see a diploma or a job! That should secure Simpson's discretion once and for all. He would be eternally grateful to Dr. Stone.

Stone decided to leave the manuscript fragments in Jerusalem for now. Ray never saw the contents of the clay jar he himself found in the far reaches of one empty niche. He had to think of a way to disguise the manuscripts and hide them for now. Several ideas came to mind.

Stone finally devised a step-by-step plan for how to get the precious object out of the country. Wednesday would be an insanely busy day. He made an abbreviated list on his palm pilot. First, Bethlehem. Second, go to the old Jewish quarter and purchase a form that attested he was only carrying a replica of a priceless antiquity, not the real thing. Third, get the form signed and notarized by one of the shadier dealers in the old quarter. The form would state that the original was in the hands of the IAA. Therefore, the fake would be called the original, and the original identified as a copy. In this way, he could take the object out of the country in plain view as a souvenir, showing it to the authorities with his passport.

So it was off to Bethlehem to do some errands, and off to the old quarter to do some paperwork, and finally back home to pack. He purchased his e-ticket at Gotravel.com for the 10:15 a.m. Thursday flight. Yes, indeed, things were looking up for the man who lived by the motto that looking out for No. 1 was all that was essential in life. Everything and everyone else was expendable.

# 18

# Up in the Air

HARRY SCHOLER HAD HAD two careers and the second one as head of the ASBA was bidding fair to be far more interesting, though far less lucrative than his law career. Scholer had been called many things in his career, but no one accused him of lacking intelligence and insight. He had a real nose for what was significant and what was not, what mattered and what didn't. He also had good friends of all sorts of faith commitments, including evangelical Christians like Art West.

Art had done numerous articles for ASBA's popular magazine *Biblical Artifacts*, which sold hundreds of thousands of copies. While in Reagan Airport, Harry picked up the latest edition of *Ha' Aretz* and was working through the *Jerusalem Post* while on the plane, taking readings on what the temperature would be in Jerusalem in regard to the West arrest. He wanted to use the popular appeal of West and his reputation for honesty to good advantage, especially if this proved to be a big story.

The Alitalia stewardess came to Scholer's seat bringing him another gin and tonic. Scholer only flew first class these days, especially on the long flight to Tel Aviv. The problem was that Scholer himself was *persona non grata* with various people in Jerusalem, including some involved with the IAA. Having defended Oded Golan to the hilt, and shown that the IAA had not done as careful a job as it should have in assessing the authenticity of the James ossuary inscription, he needed to tread lightly while in Jerusalem, and not detract from what general sympathy might be felt for West. He would try to keep a low profile.

Harry pushed the call button again for the stewardess. His palm pilot was the one piece of technology he had proudly mastered. For the rest, he always begged for help.

"Ma'am, do we have wireless access to the internet here in first class?"

"Yes. Did you know the hull of the front part of the plane is actually a huge receptor for wireless signals? Anyway, now that we're at cruising altitude you're welcome to do what you like. Just dial into our AT&T wireless connection number off your laptop to connect to the Internet."

"So simple," said Harry with a wry grin.

He quickly pulled out his Sony Vaio, waited for Windows to come up, clicked on Internet Connection, and typed in the necessary phone number. He was surfing the net within another minute. His Hotmail account was hot indeed—23 new messages in his inbox since yesterday, and another 15 in the junk mail. This was going to take some time. But what he was mainly looking for was access to a file he had lodged on the ASBA website just before he left, which detailed information on whether and to what degree Israeli Law could be enforced on foreign nationals. This was going to take a while, but fortunately he had several hours before he landed in Tel Aviv Thursday morning.

At the Tel Aviv airport, Patrick Stone managed to get through customs with nary a raised eyebrow. His authentication papers had worked like a charm, and now he was going through yet more security checks. He was feeling pretty smug. Soon he would be wafting his way through the friendly skies to London. He had been totally oblivious to the curly-haired gentleman tailing him.

Arriving at Gate 6 with an hour to kill, he entertained himself by examining the pictures in the morning paper showing the notorious Arthur West, who had seemed to be such a nice Christian man. But now, who knew what he was really capable of? Stone allowed himself to smile at all this mayhem.

"Serves that arrogant fool right," he muttered under his breath.

Stone had contacted a Sotheby's agent as well as an old colleague from his Tübingen days who worked in the British Library. He wanted the latter to vouch to the former for the authenticity of the stone, so that it could be properly appraised. The meeting was to transpire on Friday morning. This gave him time to get to London, check into the hotel, and get a good night's rest. Maybe the British Library itself would put in a private bid? Maybe he could leverage that against what he could extract from a private dealer? Maybe he could ratchet up the price to astronomical levels? Such fun, playing on the lust for possessing precious antiquities! What sort of silly persons could really believe that Jesus had raised Lazarus from the dead and that this stone attested to the fact? Stone had enough problems believing in a historical Lazarus, never mind a historical raising of Lazarus from the dead!

The loud speaker at the gate began blaring, "All first class passengers are now welcome to board El Al flight 315 non-stop to London."

"That's me," thought Stone. "Time to get out of town while the getting is good." As he walked down the ramp he realized he would likely never go back to Israel, never set foot in another classroom, never write another scholarly article. Who needs academia anemia? Stone was so wrapped up in his self-centered reverie he never noticed the curly-haired man with the skullcap in the economy line next to him closely watching Stone and the bag he was clutching to his chest.

# 19

## Scroll Down

GRACE HAD BEEN FRETTING ever since Art's call around 11:30. Arthur West had really gotten himself into a jam. He was naive and good and honest, and he lived as though he expected everyone else to be that way as well. Was it just his Christian faith that prevented him from having a healthy fear of danger or from having a wariness of the wicked ways of the world?

Grace knew in her heart he couldn't possibly be responsible for either forgery or attempted murder, but the rest of those connected with the IAA didn't really know the man personally. Besides that, they were now hypersensitive, having already gotten enough bad press from the James ossuary mess. They were going to leave no stone unturned this time in this investigation. After all, they had an object that everyone agreed was a clear forgery, or was it?

The stone could be a fraud without being a forgery. In other words, the stone might be a copy of the original, which would make it a forgery. However, it might just be a fraud, there being no original to copy. West's digital photos showed what appeared to be the original stone with its inscription in situ. Had Art fashioned this stone and placed it in the niche for all to see? No, this couldn't be! There must be an original stone!

And was there any connection between Art's entombment and the grave robbing? Between the grave robbing and the possible murder attempt on El Said? Between the grave robbing and the sending of the forged stone to West? Surely there must be. But Grace could not put all the pieces together in her mind. There was some sort of huge animus that precipitated this chain of events. As a child Grace had loved reading the Arthur Conan Doyle stories about Sherlock Holmes. So far, this was a puzzle he would love, she thought.

It was nearly one o'clock—she needed fresh air and lunch. Her plans to work at the University were slipping away. Maybe a sandwich at Solomon's Porch and Sarah's friendly smile would help get her back on track. And she would ask Sarah if there was anything she could do to help Hannah and her father.

Grace arrived at Solomon's Porch about 1:30. Sarah had already left to be with Hannah, so Grace was finishing her lunch alone when the phone rang. It was Sammy Cohen at the IAA office.

"Oh, Sammy, have you heard that Art was picked up by the police late this morning. And somebody sent him a copy of the missing inscription!? He's probably in some small, dank police cell being interrogated as we speak! It's awful! Part of me wants to call Mr. Golan and ask him what he went through—but I'm not sure I want to know!" said Grace, the words tumbling out.

"Slow down, Grace. Remember, we're partially responsible for Mr. Golan's plight. Anyway, one of our lawyers called from the police station. She's keeping her eyes and ears open. They haven't charged him with anything. I believe this is just scare tactics, however. Art wouldn't hurt Kahlil, and he didn't steal that stone! We don't know much about the forgery though. Try not to worry!"

"You're right. But, after all, they do have a victim and now a forgery to deal with. Who knows what they are thinking? I can't stop worrying right now," replied Grace, her voice shaking.

"What you need is something to take your mind off this problem! Can you come to the IAA building? It's time to scrutinize what we found inside the Lazarus ossuary!"

The ossuary sat on top of the examination table and all the fluorescent lights were turned on. The limestone surface of the box gleamed in the dazzling light of the room, which was enclosed in the middle of the building, had no windows and required keycard access to enter. Most precious antiquities were examined in this special room. Unlike Sammy's office, it was immaculately clean and pristine.

When Grace arrived, already present were Cohen, several other members of the IAA and, surprisingly, Professor André Chartier.

Sammy had invited him to the IAA office this morning. Chartier was one of those rare scholars that would be consulted by all parties in a dispute, so great was his reputation.

Sammy Cohen knew that there could be no rush to judgment, no mistakes, in dealing with the Lazarus ossuary. He still felt the sting of criticism from various factions interested in the authenticity of the James box. When he made an announcement about this ossuary, he wanted to be as sure as is humanly possible he was right about the authenticity of this new find.

What intrigued Grace right off the bat is that no one was looking at the ossuary. Rather, they were all staring at a rather substantial scroll which Chartier had been examining since mid-morning.

Grace interrupted, "What exactly was there in this ossuary?"

Chartier had his magnifying glass out and was muttering to himself, "Extraordinaire! Extraordinaire!"

Turning to Grace he said, "Welcome, Mademoiselle Levine. What we have is a document from the Herodian period, written in clear beautiful Aramaic by a quite literate person."

Grace said, "Why would anyone put a scroll in a casket?"

"A good question. But let me translate a bit for you. Perhaps it will sound strange, yet familiar. There is first of all a heading: 'Memoirs of the One Whom Jesus Loved.' This is followed immédiatement by "A testimony of John when the officials from Jerusalem sent priests to ask him who he was. He did not fail to say, but instead confessed freely, 'I am not the Mashiach' . . . "

Grace blurted out, "This is almost a verbatim quote from the first chapter of John's Gospel."

"Exactemente," said Chartier, who had at one point been a priest and who was well familiar with the New Testament.

Grace spoke again, "But how much of John's Gospel do we have in this scroll? All of it?"

"No, no," said Chartier, "It will take much time to study. Understand, I have only surveyed parts of the document. But, it appears to be, I believe, similar to John 1:19 to 20:31. I did not find the *pericope adulterae*, the story of the woman caught in adultery in John 7:53—8:11."

At this point, Grace interjected, "As far as I know, that passage is not canonical—just traditional. In short, few believe that story is part of John's original Gospel. The oldest texts do not contain it."

"Very true," agreed Chartier. "But there is more to say. The heading of the document is not in the same hand as the rest of the document. Furthermore, I have looked at some parallel passages from John 13–19 where the Beloved Disciple is mentioned. He is not called this in these memoirs. Rather he is called Eliezer! It is interesting that at the point where we find John 11:3 that there Lazarus, our way of rendering the name Eliezer, is clearly identified in indirect speech as 'the one whom you love.'"

Grace asked, "Are you saying that this memoir equates Eliezer with the beloved disciple?"

Chartier replied emphatically, "It is possible. In sum, we seem to have the basis of most of the so-called Gospel of John here. Now, finding this scroll in this ossuary, which seems to be from the Herodian period—well, we may say with a high degree of likelihood that these memoirs were written prior to the fall of Jerusalem in AD 70. Now, if I may be so bold, I can suggest to you some more radical ideas. First, one could say that these memoirs are linked to a Judean disciple who was an eyewitness to some of Jesus' life. And, secondly, this eyewitness, according to these memoirs, was raised by Jesus from the dead!"

Grace's brain was about to burst. "How did the inscription read again? Show me the digital pictures that Art took Tuesday morning."

Cohen picked it up and read it, "Twice dead under Pilatus, twice reborn in Yeshua, in sure hope of resurrection."

No one spoke for what seemed to be an eternity. Finally, André added, "I understand, the police have a copy of this stone inscription. And Professor West took these pictures only yesterday. The original must be out there somewhere. And the original attests that Lazarus died twice during the reign of Pilate, but also that he was somehow reborn through Jesus, and he looked forward to resurrection in the future. In sum, this inscription in the tomb, like the inscription on the James ossuary, bears a testimony to the strong belief in resurrection amongst Jesus' followers."

Again there was silence.

Cohen then spoke: "We know that in early Judaism many Jews, especially Pharisees, believed in bodily resurrection, and we know Jesus and his followers shared that belief. That is indisputable. But this inscription, if not also the scroll, supports the story in John that Lazarus died and was raised from the dead by Yeshua. Those who buried Lazarus had seen him die—twice. They may have been at the tomb when Jesus raised him from the dead, according to the Gospel."

Again silence, dead silence.

Cohen then said carefully, "We cannot allow any leaks of this information to anyone, anywhere, anytime, before we are totally ready to authenticate or discredit the scroll, the ossuary, and hopefully the inscription."

Another IAA official from the legal department added, "The task now is to recover the original stone. It must surface for surely whoever stole the stone yesterday will be trying to sell it quickly. We have already begun interviewing various dealers and brokers. But there are so many ways to get the stone out of the country—it will be difficult to monitor the airport and all the border crossings."

Grace nodded in agreement.

"We need absolute silence in this matter. Let's begin the testing on everything here, even the bones. And don't forget Art and the forged stone. We can vouch for his whereabouts for some of Tuesday. Can we also put out an APB with Interpol to look for the missing stone? And fast?!"

In the corner of the room, Sammy had been talking to Mrs. Dembski, the lawyer who called earlier to alert him of Art's plight. Apparently, Art had been interrogated on and off this afternoon. He would probably be held overnight and questioned further tomorrow. Given that Art was an American citizen, chances are he would be released by the end of Thursday. After hanging up, Sammy called out, "It looks like Art will be enjoying the hospitality of our Israeli police tonight!"

Grace quipped, " I wonder if he likes the standard issue matzoh ball soup they will likely serve him?"

# 20

## The Jailhouse Rock

To say it was hot in the jail cell was putting it mildly. The bottom floor of the Jerusalem police station had a series of cells in it, and this floor of the building, though having the advantage of being below ground, nonetheless had little ventilation, no air conditioning, and no windows. If the police wanted to see their charges sweat, they didn't need to go to any extra effort on a June day in this building. West had not been abused, nor had he been further interrogated, but his cell phone and all other potentially dangerous or blunt objects had been confiscated—even his L. L. Bean walking shoes (must be those dangerous shoe laces). West had only been drinking Ahava bottled water. He didn't trust the food, not even the matzoh ball soup.

West had spent Wednesday afternoon on and off in a hot interrogation room rehearsing the details of yesterday with the police—including the fact that he himself had been stuck in the Lazarus tomb for over an hour. Of course, it was embarrassing to admit he had been in there that long before remembering his cell phone!

He had tried hard not to leave out a minute of his day, which left no room for making or planning some sort of forged stone. No, Tuesday went from excavating a tomb, to getting stuck in a tomb, to escaping a tomb, to examining the tomb with the IAA—a definite repeating theme there! But Tuesday evening was more problematic: dinner alone at home and his meeting with Kahlil. Of course, that meeting led to a dozen more questions. The upside, however, was the fact that the police admitted he had no gunpowder residue on his hands, and no blood splatters on his clothes.

Fortunately, he was given a private cell for the evening. Apparently, more questioning would follow on Thursday, after the police cross-checked some of today's statements. Meanwhile, Art was thrilled to discover that a lawyer, Mrs. Rachel Dembski, who also worked for the IAA had agreed to help him through the legalities. She was a true blessing and during the afternoon had checked the paperwork, reminding the authorities that Art West was an American citizen, well known in his field. The only real downer was having to turn in his passport. Rachel even managed to e-mail Harry Scholer and confirm his arrival at 9:25 a.m. Thursday into Tel Aviv on Alitalia.

Sleep was fitful, and Thursday morning's interrogations were again exhausting. By now, however, he was beginning to realize any case against him was weak. He wished, however, the police would take his complaints about being sealed in a tomb more seriously. No one seemed too impressed.

By Thursday afternoon, Harry arrived at the police station and the police promised to release West on his own recognizance, especially after the Jerusalem police chief received a phone call from Sammy Cohen. Bemused, West thought, "Maybe they'll put a tail on me, hoping I will lead them to the real artifact."

West thanked Mrs. Dembski, walked out of the building into the still blistering heat, turned to Harry and said, "Are you sure you want me to get into that tiny car with you. I am a personal embodiment of that famous saying about Lazarus in the King James: "Lord, he stinketh!"

Harry dismissed the idea of his walking home, and said, "It's a Volkswagen rental car, not a limo!"

West compacted himself into the lemon yellow VW wagon and rode off toward his flat.

"Now Harry, the least I can do is put you up at my place since you came all this way to help me out."

Harry agreed, "Fine for now. I need some real food and sleep, and you need a shower, shave, and some rest. Then we will draw up a battle plan." The two men exchanged tired looks and headed for the bottom of the Hinnom Valley.

∽

In another part of the police station, some extensive testing was being conducted on evidence found at the crime scene—the part of El Said's shirt which had caught on the park bench, his jacket which had been supplied by Hannah, and of course the gun. Also brought in by the police was a stone wrapped in brown paper. In each case the search was for usable fingerprints plus blood or hairs from which DNA could be extracted and matches made. What West had not known is that when he gave blood at Sinai hospital, a few drops had been requisitioned for testing by the police.

The relationship between the antiquities police who worked closely with and almost for the IAA and the general police was an interesting one. There was usually a clear division of labor, but sometimes in the case of a stolen object, there was overlap and cooperation. With a police force as stretched and under siege as the Jerusalem force was they were happy to have all the help they could get from the IAA police. Sammy Cohen called the police station Thursday morning to inquire about Art West but also to check on the lab findings.

"Mr. Cohen," said one lab tech, "I already have one thing for you. There was no gunpowder residue on Mr. West, and no blood splatter on his clothes. But we have taken hair fibers off the jacket of El Said. Some are his own and match what the hospital gave us. But some are not his. There seems to have been a struggle of sorts. There is a fair chance we have something from the assailant on the jacket. We haven't finished our testing yet."

"Good, but what about the stone copy I keep hearing about?"

"Sorry, Mr. Cohen, we are testing the paper for fingerprints. As long as you have clearance I'll keep you posted directly," replied the technician.

Grace had arrived early Thursday morning to continue overseeing some of the testing on the manuscript and the ossuary. She would have worked straight through lunch, but Sammy invited her to go for a ride.

"Grace, I think we need to have a chat about West. Shall we go over to Ben Yehuda Street and have a quiet late lunch?" While this proposal was quite within the bounds of the appropriate, it was also true that Cohen, a widower, had an interest in Levine, who was also single.

Grace looked at him and said, "Fine, a business lunch then." Cohen sighed and shook his head. They reached Ben Yehuda Street in about ten minutes.

Cohen was counting on the upstairs of Sarah's coffee shop, Solomon's Porch, to be quiet by now. Quiet it was, as the two of them ordered lamb kebabs and salad.

"So Grace, why are you so certain that West could not have committed these crimes? He is, after all, a fallible human being, and one with a shortage of money."

"True enough," said Grace. "I grant you both of those points, but you must also agree he's an intelligent man. He clearly did not seal himself in the tomb of Lazarus, and his subsequent actions all reflect a person who cares more about his friends than about his own reputation. He could have called in anonymously to the EMT people and left the scene, but instead he stayed to help, and he even called the police. These are not the actions of a criminal, or even just a person who is in shock. He was doing everything he could to give Mr. El Said a chance at life."

"You are right about all this," said Cohen. "But obviously you are also his true friend, and your pleading might be said to be special pleading."

"You could say it, but it wouldn't change the fact that the logic of what I said stands on its own. I say again, West did not seal himself in that tomb. Somebody was after him, and somebody wanted him not only off the scene, but also implicated in a crime."

Cohen scratched his head, "I agree. I'm just testing. In fact, I already called the police this morning to check on our Mr. West. One of our lawyers was at the station. I suspect Art will be released today."

Grace was relieved and surprised by all these announcements. "But when do we tell Art about what's hidden in the central room in the IAA building? I want to watch his reaction!"

Sammy thought for a moment. He noticed that both of them had been ravenous and had wolfed down their salads. Hard work at a breakneck speed will do that to you.

"I think we should wait on that for a while for both his sake and ours. Let's run our tests. Let him run the gauntlet of the legal process. After that there will be plenty of time to consult with him."

"Changing the subject for a minute, did you see that a whole group of people including some from the Israeli Geological Survey have called for further testing on both the Jehoash tablet and the James box? When will it end?"

"Well this particular mess will end, hopefully, when we get to the bottom of who is trying to frame Art West," said Grace.

As the waitress was bringing the lamb kebabs, Cohen's cell phone rang.

". . . and *alechem shalom* to you as well. What news? Yes. Fine. OK." Sammy turned to Grace, "That was the lab tech again. He confirms that there are absolutely no prints from West on the fake stone. So far in regard to that he is in the clear."

"Which must mean someone is trying to frame him."

"Does begin to look that way, doesn't it? In addition, they did find a partial set of prints from someone else on the stone! Someone was careless. We are sending them to be checked now, and will see if they come back with a match."

"Very good, we are making progress," said Grace. "I think I'll leave the office early and go by the hospital to check on Hannah. Her father is still in a coma. She was hoping to see Art this morning, but obviously that couldn't happen."

Sammy and Grace returned to the IAA and parted company. There was lots of work to do Thursday afternoon. The lab had rung Cohen again.

"Professor Cohen," said the lab tech, "I have some good news. Interpol has helped us find the match on that set of fingerprints on the stone. It belongs to one Raymond Simpson, an American grad student at Yale University, aged 27. Seems he had been stopped for driving while intoxicated in New Haven a couple of years back, and he put up a little resistance so the police took him in and fingerprinted him. That's how we know."

Cohen replied, "Do we know where this Raymond Simpson is?"

"Well, that's a problem for immigration so I will put Samson on the line."

In a second, another voice boomed, "Professor Cohen, how are you! We know Simpson is still in country, but we just don't know where, so we are in process of posting an APB to track him down and bring him in for questioning. The airports, bus depot—the usual—will be watched. We will let you know!"

Cohen hung up the phone and said to no one in particular, "Hopefully, we catch him before he catches on that we are looking for him."

# 21

# Raymond's Folly

AT THAT PRECISE MOMENT late Thursday afternoon, Ray Simpson had just cleared customs and security, and was racing to his gate. The taxi he had taken from Jerusalem had gotten stuck in traffic on the way to Tel Aviv, and he was barely going to make his flight from the new Tel Aviv Airport. After working his way through the security checkpoint and the passport control, he raced through the terminal and sprinted to the gate. They were already boarding. Breathless, he handed the gate attendant his boarding pass, and flashed his passport. The card was run through the scanner once more, and he went down the corridor to get on the plane. He would be able to relax once he was on the plane. Simpson was a person who hated to be late for anything and he was a nervous wreck by the time he arrived for the flight.

The plane pushed back from the gate and taxied out onto the runway. It was fourth in line for take off. Suddenly, off to the right, there was a huge flash of light and an explosion that seems to happen just beyond the edge of the airport tarmac. Something had blown up far too near airplanes for comfort. After a long uncomfortable silence, a voice came over the loud speaker.

"Ladies and gentleman, there has been an incident, perhaps a terrorist incident, near the edge of the airport. So far as we know, no one is hurt, but we are temporally in lock down mode until we get the all clear. We will sit here for a while, and if needs be we will return to the gate if the tower so instructs. Thank you for your patience."

At that very moment an IAA policeman was talking to customs. Holding up a faxed photo, he asked, "Has anyone seen this man tonight. Has a passport for Raymond Simpson been swiped through here?"

A woman at the last booth called out, "Yes, that's the young man who came running through here shortly before his flight was to leave. He was convinced he was going to miss his flight."

The IAA officer joined her to check the records. Ray Simpson, Flight 902.

Suddenly, everyone instinctively ducked when they heard an explosion.

"A bomb!?" someone cried out but not quite sure.

"Well," said the officer peering around cautiously, "if it is, I'll bet no flights are leaving anytime soon! Regardless, I've got to contact the control tower to hold that flight!"

Ray Simpson, as it turns out, was not going anywhere Thursday, except back to Jerusalem. He had a premonition that something was wrong, and since the plane was, according to the captain's announcement, going to try and take off in about an hour, he figured he could wait that long. Almost everyone was standing up talking excitedly, making new friends—except Raymond. He sat glumly staring out the window wishing he were already home. Patrick Stone's phone call was so transparent.

Stone had been "called home"—yeah, right. The good Dr. Stone fled Jerusalem leaving Raymond to deal with the inevitable fallout of taking the stone, making a copy, sending it to Dr. West, etc. etc. Without a word to his roommate, Raymond had made plans to follow his professor out of town as quickly as possible.

The next announcement from the captain was more unsettling. "I'm sorry for the inconvenience, but everyone has been ordered to leave the aircraft. Airport personnel will be available to help you make other travel plans. Please exit in an orderly fashion."

Miserable now, Raymond just sat on the plane while everyone else slowly departed. The attendants looked at him quizzically but didn't bother him yet. Finally, when everyone had departed he reluctantly began to gather up his coat and travel bag.

When the police did not see Simpson get off the plane, they immediately entered flashing their badges. The stewardess got out of the way quickly. The officer in charge, Simon Bar-Elan, proceeded slowly down the aisle to the back of the plane with his hand on his holster gun. Finally he came to a very sad-looking Ray Simpson. One look at the policeman told Ray that he was the target, so he quickly held up his hands and pleaded, "Don't shoot, I surrender!" The men in brown escorted a now thoroughly miserable young man whose head was buried in his jacket off the plane.

# 22

# Hacking Stone

THURSDAY AFTERNOON, PATRICK STONE checked into the Royal Edinburgh Hotel near the British Library, and rang up his old acquaintance, Oliver St. James. Propping his feet up on the bed while sitting in the Queen Anne chair next to the phone and sipping a Glenfiddich, he was determined not to be his usual irascible self. He was going to be the soul of affability so he could get what he needed—authentication and appraisal.

"Oliver," said Stone, "I am looking forward to our meeting tomorrow, and I promise you will not be disappointed in what I have brought."

Oliver, ever the meticulous scholar, said, "We shall see what we shall see. It is a good thing you are bringing this to the labs at the Museum so we can do the patina testing and the like on the spot."

"Right," said Stone. "It should prove to be an intriguing day. Be sure you have your geologist with you as well. I must ring off now and call Sotheby's." As he rang off, St. James pondered the note of excitement, but also anxiety in the voice of Patrick Stone.

"Hello, may I please speak to Mrs. Delia Tidewater, the appraiser, please."

A woman with an exceedingly high voice came on the line. "Halloo, is that you Professor Stone. I am well aware of our rendezvous Friday at the South entrance to the British Library. You did say 10 a.m. sharp, did you not?"

"Yes, and Mr. St. James, whom I believe you know, will be meeting us."

"Quite, see you tomorrow. TTFN."

These British with their abbreviations! The last time he was in England Stone had had a horrible time trying to figure out what the signs with FIY were all about. FYI he understood as an abbreviation, but not FIY. Turned out to be a Fix It Yourself store, the English equivalent of Lowe's! But TTFN—who says "Ta ta for now" in this day and age? Stone was fading fast, and the jet lag was beginning to set in. Best to take a shower and turn in early. Tomorrow would be a crucial day.

Sedek Hadar had had no trouble whatsoever following Stone to his hotel of choice, as Stone was so self-absorbed with what he was doing, but he could hardly afford to stay in such a palace, so he had settled into a bed and breakfast down the street from the Royal Edinburgh. Sedek had been turning over and over in his mind what would be his next move. He had brought his laptop and planned to report in to Rabbi Menachem and perhaps also to the IAA. He had noticed that Stone had brought his laptop with him, and since Hadar, among other things, was a computer geek, he thought of hacking into Stone's hotmail account and seeing what was happening. He had installed on his laptop some conventional spy software and had already managed to both locate Stone's e-address, and had even decoded his password—YALEPROF. He was thus set to listen in to what was going down, provided of course Stone actually used his laptop while in London.

The email he had perused so far was boring in the extreme, except for a curious memo sent to someone with an e-address of simp3@archeolog.net reminding him not to forget to await Stone's phone call about the nativity set! What could that be about? In any case Sedek figured that something was going to go down tomorrow, and so he would simply stay locked in to Stone's account all the following day and wait and see what happened. Unlike Stone, Saddiq would spend most of the night pacing the floor, and wondering what to do next.

# 23

## Deal of the Century

A T 10 A.M. FRIDAY morning, the door to the south end of the British
Library swung open and Oliver St. James welcomed both Delia
Tidewater and Patrick Stone, carrying his satchel with its priceless content. A light rain was falling, so they put their umbrellas in the stand
in the hall. Stone muttered to himself, "The only nation in the world
that has umbrella stands in the entrance to every public and private
building."

The long, narrow, corridor was old, as was the museum, and the
lighting in this part of the building was poor, creating an eerie effect.
Stone felt like he was walking down a corridor in a maximum-security
prison. At the end of the hall Oliver turned right and then another immediate right, and took his guests into a laboratory where three other
persons, dressed in the white frock coats so favored by European scientists, were waiting.

"Let me introduce you," said Oliver. "First we have Professor
Soards of Leeds University. He is one of the leading geologists in the
country, with a specialty in the geology of Israel." At the end of the line,
a tall man with wavy white hair nodded solemnly.

"Then we have Dr. Pamela Thistlewaite, a geochemist of note from
Oxford, who will be checking the stone in regard to composition and
patina." She smiled briefly.

"And Professor Ian Baring-Gould, an expert epigrapher for the
New Testament period who will be examining the script on the stone. If

it is likely that this stone is what you claim, we should be able to render a preliminary judgment later today. Which brings me to Mrs. Delia Tidewater from Sotheby's. She will aid us with the appraisal—Professor Stone invited her expressly."

Stone took the tablet out of his satchel and laid it on the table in the center of the room. He had some qualms about handing it over to anyone, but he knew that if he showed hesitancy it would indicate a lack of trust that would likely endanger the possibility of selling the object immediately.

The office of Oliver St. James looked like a hurricane had recently come through. There were not only files everywhere but also pots on the floor, wilted plants on the window ledge, two worn Queen Anne wingbacks in one corner, a pipe on a tea table between them, file cabinets bursting at the seams, and two banks of fluorescent bulbs—some not working. Taking piles of files from several folding chairs, St. James said to his guests, "Please forgive the clutter, it can't be helped. Grab a chair and do sit down."

St. James was spry for his seventy-four years and had been with the museum for almost fifty. He had struck up an acquaintance with Stone the last time Stone was in town and had given a lecture at the museum on Ancient Near Eastern archaeology. St. James found Stone a bit off-putting and arrogant, but nonetheless a fine scholar and lecturer. He was not totally surprised to hear from Stone, but he was certainly surprised to hear what he had to say.

"Naturally, Professor Stone, we will need some assurances that this tablet has not been illegally obtained. What documentation have you brought?"

Stone opened his satchel again and brought forth the two documents he had purchased Wednesday afternoon on the black market. The first document, dated May 17, attested to the authenticity of the stone and claimed to be from the Israeli Geological Survey. The dealer had brought up a photo of a genuine Israeli Geological Survey document that he cut and pasted into a document. After the blanks were filled in, he printed the fake document on paper designed to look quite old, signed it with a real ink pen, and notarizing it complete with an embossed stamp. There was no easy way to tell the difference between this document and a genuine one from the Israeli Geological Survey.

The second document had been easier to produce. This document stated that Stone had bought this tablet in the dealer's shop in 1972—in other words, well before it became illegal to own such precious objects. This second document was, in fact, genuine, but Stone had paid the dealer enough money to make the date read 1972, not 2004.

St. James looked over the documents carefully one by one, and then handed them to Delia Tidewater. "These papers seem to be in order, and since we are all familiar with the Israeli law about precious antiquities that come to light after 1978, this object would seem to fall well within the legal limit for purchase by a collector or a museum. What is your assessment, Ms. Tidewater?"

After a moment she concurred,

"Yes these papers seem to be in order. Of course, let me add that Professor Stone could not have left Israel without the authorities seeing the tablet, checking the papers and passing him through the security and customs checkpoints. The very fact that he is here in London would seem to speak for the genuineness of these document."

"Quite so, a good point," said Oliver. "Miss Tidewater, you are free to go now."

"Certainly," said Delia, "I have some more research to do if I'm to come up with some dollar figures this afternoon."

St. James closed the door behind her. He invited Patrick to enjoy the comfort of the old chairs in the corner. Oliver lit up his pipe. Settling down into his chair he said to Stone, "Now Patrick, you must tell me how you came to have this tablet, and why it is that just now, if you have had it all these years, you have come to us with it."

"It is not a difficult tale to tell Oliver," said Patrick. "Back in 1972 after I was in college, a group of us visited Jerusalem. I bought all kinds of trinkets, and this stone from a dealer. According to the notes I made at the time, it had been found in some Jewish graveyard at the bottom of the Kidron valley near the Pool of Siloam, but closer to Bethany. The dealer said some poor Palestinian who found it on his own property had sold him this item. I think he said the man lived in Silwan. In any event, when I returned home, I put the stone in my attic along with my other souvenirs, and only recently rediscovered them all. So, here I am at the end of my career, a man in his 60s. I am tired and would like to retire. Maybe this tablet can help make that an easier process."

Stone was quite pleased with himself. He felt he had come off as genuine as one could manage, considering it was all a pack of lies, except the bit about wanting to retire on his nest egg. He knew it would be tough to explain why a man of his training would not have seen the significance of the stone much earlier in his career. He hoped he had been believable. He wasn't sure, and he was trying not to sweat.

Oliver looked intently at Stone, which made him squirm. He tried to keep his composure as Oliver said evenly, "I know what you mean old thing. If I hadn't the security of my Old Age Pension, or the O.A.P. as we like to call it, I reckon I would be looking to do something like you are doing if I could manage it. Your social security system is certainly dodgier than ours. Well, shall we go and see how the testing is progressing?"

"I thought you'd never ask," said Stone as he too quickly jumped from the chair and moved to the table. He could barely contain his excitement.

St. James thought to himself: "Here is a man who is hoping for a sudden windfall at the end of his career. It is sad what happens to American teachers as their careers wind down. I can't blame Stone for hoping for something grand. Perhaps we can help him."

# 24

## Limits of Law and Success of Stone

JAMISON PARKES LAW WAS pacing the floor having just read his email from his main contact within the Sons of Zion—Sedek Hadar. Something bad was about to go down and it seemed to involve both Patrick Stone and Art West. This puzzled Law, as Law knew these two men to be rivals, and he had even had some congenial conversations with Art West once or twice. What could they be up to? Could West really be involved in some sort of shady antiquities scam? Sedek had promised to send more information as soon as he knew it, but what would Law do with the info? Would he go to the press? Would he call up the IAA? Should he involve Rabbi Menachem more directly? He couldn't decide just yet.

Law had become increasingly agitated when his two disciples had reported to him that West had been taken into custody, apparently for forgery, and possibly for assault on El Said. But this made no sense to him, in view of the fact that Hadar had already communicated with him that it was Stone who had gone to El Said with some object and then later that evening had met with El Said in the park before West had arrived. Hadar had not been sure in the dark who had fired at whom, but El Said had ended up being shot.

Could West really be in on such immoral actions? Yet, he had showed up on the scene almost immediately after El Said had been shot. The clock was ticking, and Law's legal sensibilities and conscience would not leave him alone. What to do? He prayed and then decided to await the further revelations of the day before doing anything. One thing for sure, it would reflect very poorly on conservative Christians in Israel if West turned out to be a criminal. Law would need to have incontrovertible evidence before blowing the whistle on West.

〜

For three hours the British Library's finest tested the Lazarus tablet. After a break for a late lunch all the parties reassembled in the lab. Oliver convened the session with the words, "Colleagues, what have you to report?"

Pamela Thistlewaite spoke first, "We have run all the appropriate tests on the stone, and we have found no reason to doubt this is a first-century stone, with a first-century inscription."

Professor Baring-Gould added, "And as for the inscription itself, not only did it have ancient patina with no signs of modern tampering, but the script itself was of one hand, all likely executed on just one occasion."

Thistlewaite added, "This is clearly Jerusalem limestone, but it is not from the Mt. Scopus region, but rather further down the ridge where the limestone is of poorer quality. Perhaps from the region of Silwan or Bethany."

"So, then, it is your judgment that the stone is a genuine artifact of the Herodian period?" said Oliver.

"Yes," said Pamela. "We are all in one accord on that point. We see no reason to have any doubts about the antiquity of the object or its inscription."

"Jolly good," said Oliver. "You may go home early today in view of your exemplary work on this project."

They all smiled and moved off towards the cloak room to take off their professional garb, and head for the nearest underground station, quite pleased with themselves.

Oliver beckoned Stone and Delia Tidewater to sit in chairs next to the examining table, and he handed her the stone. "Delia, the stone is now literally in your hands. What is your appraisal?"

Delia did not hesitate, but spoke up in her high voice, "We have in our business a term—commensurate appraisal. We appraise an object on the basis of what other similar objects of equal historical importance and of equal antiquity would fetch at a public auction. This artifact is unique in that it has a unique inscription on it, and it is entirely the inscription that makes it so valuable. Therefore the most crucial part of the testing was the patina test and the epigrapher's analysis. I gather the ultraviolet test showed absolutely no signs of modern tampering as well, which is good to know. Taking all things into consideration, especially the rather unique claim of the inscription to refer to a person who had died more than once, and taking Professor Stone's word that this comes from the very region where according to historical record Lazarus was buried, I would judge that this item would bring no less than about forty million US dollars on the open market. Of course what you two negotiate is your business entirely, but now at least you have a general figure to guide the discussions."

"Thank you, Delia, I will be sending your cheque along in the morning with thanks," said Oliver. The weak sun had finally peeked through the clouds outside the window as the afternoon was drawing to a close, and Oliver sat in thought for a moment.

"Well Professor, I hardly know what to say. Were the museum to acquire this object I have little doubt it would cause a sensation and draw paying customers to the museum for many years. If we placed it in the room with Codex Sinaiticus in its own secure temperature-sensitive case I am sure many millions would eventually come to view it. You have told me that time is of the essence, and I take you at your word, and you have also told me that you have a collector prepared to pay market price for this object in Tübingen. Is that still the case?"

Stone cleared his throat and responded, "Yes, but I am prepared to bargain with you in a fair manner, in exchange for a consideration."

What consideration would that be?" asked Oliver.

"I would like this negotiation to be in complete confidence—I have no desire to deal with the publicity. The records must be sealed."

"That is quite extraordinary. Any lesser man would bathe in the glory of such a find. I admire your dedication to pure scholarship."

"Thank you, Oliver. You told me on the phone that you are prepared to strike a bargain today, and do the wire transfer tomorrow morning. Is this still the case?"

"Yes, the trustees of the museum are quite in a dither about this find, and they have given me a figure we are prepared to pay."

"Very good. And what indeed is that figure."

"We are prepared to pay twenty million pounds sterling, that is, thirty five million dollars, drawing on our Barclay's account, in order to acquire this artifact."

Stone knew that he did not want to go through a long negotiating hassle with a collector. He replied abruptly, "Oliver, it is a pleasure doing business with you, let us shake on it. We have a deal."

The two men arose, smiled and shook hands. Stone then added, "I presume I can store the stone safely in your vault here?"

"I had anticipated this request. Shall we go and place it out of harm's way together? Then you can work with my secretary on the paperwork including, of course, your Swiss bank account number. I expect that we will do the transfer Saturday morning at approximately 9 a.m."

"Oh, and one more thing. I want one million pounds transferred to a Jerusalem account to further the archaeological work there."

"That should be no problem, just give me the number now."

Stone wrote out the number of the Jerusalem checking account of Dr. Arthur West, though St. James had no way of knowing whose number it was. Stone saw this as his master-stroke. Sooner or later the police would be checking West's account balances to see if there were any dramatic changes. When $1.7 million dollars suddenly showed up in West's account, he would be in even further hot water.

Stone had obtained West's account number in the most unobtrusive way possible. He had had Simpson follow West to the bank one day, watch him right out his deposit slip on the usual desk blotter in the lobby, and when West left, not paying any attention to Simpson, Simpson simply highlighted the place on the blotter where West had written down the number with a yellow highlighter, bearing down hard, and the account number had magically appeared. Simple and effective. West was about to be in a world of hurt.

St. James and Stone walked to the end of the hall, this time turned left and walked into an inner room boasting a very large safe. St. James turned two dials on the combination lock, placed the stone on a shelf, closed the safe, and escorted Patrick to the office of the Museum Director.

The director and his secretary were sitting at a conference table— all the paperwork neatly laid out and ready for signatures. The business was transacted calmly and efficiently, and the director congratulated

Stone on making such an important contribution available to the museum rather than a private collector.

On their way out, Stone said to Oliver, "Shall we go celebrate with dinner somewhere? I am glad to buy!"

"Why not?" said St. James, "I know just the place. The Boar's Head is not two blocks from here, and has an excellent wine list, and wonderful cuisine."

"Fine," said Stone. He was now feeling like he had pulled it off, and he wanted to leave a good impression tonight on St. James. They walked down the boulevard together, happy men for very different reasons. Neither one of them paid any attention to the young man standing in the doorway of the B+B which they passed on the way to dinner. Following them at a distance Hadar planned on eavesdropping on their dinner conversation. Little did he realize what indigestion that meal conversation would produce.

# 25

# Patrick's Scapegoat

THURSDAY NIGHT FOUND RAY Simpson sitting, not in a plane, but in the very jail cell where West had spent the day. He had already survived one grueling round of questioning, and he barely managed to keep his cool. He had demanded a lawyer, but was told that under Israeli law they had every right to interrogate him if they chose. No charges had been made as yet, and even if they did press charges, they could hold him without bail. Ray Simpson soon realized that the law of Israel was indeed very different from what he expected. Could torture be involved? Thursday night produced very little sleep.

Raymond's Friday was certainly not going as well as Patrick Stone's Friday. At nine o'clock in the morning, no less than four IAA police agents came to his cell. They trotted out the brown paper that he had used to wrap the forged Lazarus stone. They showed him the evidence of his fingerprints on the forgery.

Detective Shimon spoke, "Mr. Simpson, we know from this piece of paper that you have a connection with a stone inscription found Tuesday in Bethany by Dr. Arthur West. The fact that you made a copy indicates you have some knowledge of the original—which is still missing. Further, we believe that a man answering to the description of Dr. Patrick Stone probably brought the original to the shop of Kahlil El Said on Tuesday afternoon, the same El Said who was attacked Tuesday night. We also know that you are a graduate student currently working with Dr. Patrick Stone. Unless you tell us right now where the original

Lazarus stone is, and where Professor Stone is, you will be charged with attempting to steal antiquities, forgery and, if we find you had anything to do with the shooting of Kahlil El Said, attempted murder as well. So, Mr. Simpson, where are the two "stones"—the man and the rock?"

Simpson had begun to sweat. He thought to himself, "I guess I won't be getting out of this cleanly just by stonewalling, so to speak. I have to give them something and I have to tell them at least some of the truth." From the line of questioning so far, he realized there was plenty they didn't know.

Clearing his throat Simpson rehashed most of last night's answers.

"I'm just Patrick Stone's teaching assistant. We have been here in Jerusalem doing various sorts of research, and buying a few things. Professor Stone called me Wednesday saying he was called away on family business. I presume he left Wednesday night or maybe Thursday for New Haven and then his home in Tennessee to see his ailing mother. He told me I could stay in Jerusalem and continue my research, but I decided to go home for a visit."

"As for the inscription, yeah, I made that cheap copy and sent it by courier to Dr. Arthur West at Stone's request. Professor Stone gave me a blown-up picture to make the copy. Really, honestly, I don't know where the original is! Perhaps Professor Stone can tell you, but I don't know."

So far, he was telling the truth—not all the truth—but the truth nonetheless. However, he finally lied, adding, "I've never seen the original!"

Ray started getting more defensive and sarcastic. "To my knowledge it's not against the law to make a copy of something ancient. Right? I wasn't trying to pass it off as anything real. You have the package—you know that there's no request or demand for payment or anything like that. Finally, I have no idea at all what you are talking about in regard to the shooting of Kahlil El Said. I was in the apartment with my roommate, Grayson Johnson, watching basketball and eating a late supper Tuesday night."

"We will be checking your alibi by talking with Mr. Johnson. Meanwhile, we will be tapping your phone in case Professor Stone calls. We think you know a lot more about the original stone, especially since Dr. West claims to have seen the original stone Tuesday morning in a tomb in Bethany. He also claims he was mysteriously sealed in that tomb for a time! Do you know anything about that?"

Raymond looked up sheepishly but said nothing.

"As I said, we think you know a lot more. For the time being you will be held in custody for further interrogation and possible charges. Calling the American Consulate will do you little good, given the nature of the charges. So I suggest you make your one phone call a more profitable one." With this, the officer turned on his heels and left the room. Raymond was taken back to his cell.

Shimon said to the other IAA police, "He is probably telling the truth to an extent. I'm convinced, however, it's not the whole truth. Check customs and flight manifests for Patrick Stone. We need to find him quickly."

# 26

## "Born on a Mountaintop in Tennessee"

AMONG HIS OTHER DUTIES, Detective Hoffner was in charge of one key piece of evidence—the weapon. Surprisingly, it was a 19th century derringer, a one-shot weapon that could be concealed in the palm of a man's hand. Probably made in the US, the gun was too old to have a serial number. Hoffner narrowed his search to cities where Patrick Stone had lived, beginning with his birthplace, Johnson City, Tennessee.

The Internet is a wonderful thing. Even if you connect in outer Slobovia, you can still find out the name and phone number of the local antique and gun shops in Johnson City Tennessee or New Haven Connecticut. Hoffner had been calling numbers for a day now. Finally, he came to Marvin's Gun and Ammo Shop. Hoffner was in no way prepared for the conversation he was about to have. Worlds and cultures were about to collide here, even worse than if Bonnie and Clyde had paid a visit to the Bedouins in the Judean desert.

Marvin's Gun and Ammo shop was sort of the Wal-Mart of gun shops—one-stop shopping. The neon sign blinked irregularly; figures hand-painted on the windows ranged from Wild Bill Hickcock to Annie Oakley to G.I. Joe to Johnny Reb. The building was the sort of place no sane woman would ever enter. It was strictly a man's domain. Not only were there guns and ammunition of all sizes and descriptions, there was all sorts of Army surplus stuff ranging from uniforms to canteens to medals. Shoot, there was even an old howitzer and a small tank in the front parking lot!

The floors in the store were concrete for the very good reason that they need hosing down once in a while due to the spitting of chewin' tobacco here, there, and yonder. Right next to the cash register there was Red Man chewin' tobacco, Skoal dippin' snuff, a revolving display of Army patches, and even canned possum. Marvin's had it all, except of course for a computer. Marvin had not yet had a close encounter of the first kind with the computer revolution. His son set up his website and monitored it from home.

Hoffner calculated that he was a good seven to eight hours ahead of Johnson City time, so he would wait and call late Friday afternoon. Dialing up the number in his small cubicle in the police station it took a while for the phone to ring, and even longer before someone picked up. A gravelly voice finally rang out, "Yup, this is Marvin's, whatcha need?"

Hoffner swallowed and answered, "My name is Detective Hoffner. I am calling from the police station in Jerusalem. Do you know anyone by the name of Patrick Stone or Leroy Stone?" There was a pause. Avi could hear some arguing going on despite the fact that someone's hand was probably over the receiver.

In truth, things were a bit confused at Marvin's store. Marvin was sharing the conversation with the boys playing checkers.

"Jerusalem? Jerusalem Tennessee? Ain't that over near the border with Kentucky?" said Charlie, the best player around.

"Yeah, maybe, but this here caller wants to know if we know'd someone named Leroy Stone."

The next thing Hoffner heard was laughter. Finally Marvin was back on the line.

"I reckon so. Leroy used to be the mayor of this place. His son Patrick's a big shot, but he visits his mama sometimes."

Hoffner tentatively ventured another question. "Did either one of them ever buy a gun from your shop? In particular, an antique hand weapon?" Again laughter broke out at the other end of the line.

"Feller, it's clear you ain't from around these parts. Nobody around here would dare call a firearm an antique hand weapon. That'd be bows and arrows around here."

Hoffner tried again, "I believe it is called a derringer, and it came with a pearl handle."

"Now you're talkin, let me go look in the books." When Marvin said look in the books he meant he would go back to his cluttered office, get out the sales receipts for the years when Leroy was living and start leafing through them. This could take forever. Ten minutes, later, Marvin picked up the phone again.

"Records take too long. Now Vernon's here right now, and he saved me some trouble. He recollected that Leroy did buy himself a little derringer just after he became Mayor in 1950 something, on account of he figured he was a VIP now and could afford antiques. It was a Civil War gun carried by some officer in Braxton Bragg's army. Didn't have much velocity and no percussion at all. Only works at really close range. Don't do much damage. May I ask now why you are askin' these funny questions?"

Hoffner had begun to make some sense of this particular brand of southern American dialect, and he decided that the best thing to do now was beat a fast retreat before he got in any deeper. His mental picture of the man he was talking to didn't come close to matching the reality of the codger at the other end in bib overalls and a Braves hat.

Hoffner bravely continued, "I am engaged in some police work involving Patrick Stone who seems to have taken possession of the gun at some point."

"Uh huh," said Marvin. "Doesn't surprise me, seein' as how that boy went off to some fancy university up north, became an educated fool, and went atheist on us. That boy in some trouble now? His mama's poorly you know."

"You could say that; we are going to be questioning Dr. Stone," Hoffner replied, "but let's not frighten his mother with rumors. One more thing, what is your full name?"

Marvin spat and responded proudly, "Marvin Moon, the gun expert."

"Thank you kindly for your assistance," Hoffner said and hung up.

About then the chief of police walked by. "Making any progress on tracing the gun?"

"Yes sir, but you wouldn't believe the person I just talked to. I don't think we could coax him over here for the trial. Nobody would understand his testimony anyway. He sounded like those fellows in that movie, *Oh Brother, Where Art Thou* with George Clooney. Let's just say, the gun did originally belong to Leroy Stone, the father of Patrick.

Getting proof, on paper, will probably be impossible. Plus, it's not registered. I'll try to get some sort of signed affidavit."

Sedek Hadar had not slept a wink the previous night. The conversation he had overheard in the booth next to his own in the Boar's Head Restaurant had so turned his stomach that he could barely restrain himself from attempting to do something violent. He knew from the conversation that not only had Stone sold the Lazarus stone to the British Library for a considerable sum, but Stone intended to disappear into retirement as soon as he left London. The trail might suddenly run cold. Without question Hadar would have to do something in the morning and he had heard the reassurance from St. James as they got up to leave that the wire transfers would take place about nine in the morning. "Why transfers, instead of just a single transfer?" wondered Hadar. He formulated in his mind a plan of action just as soon as he had monitored Stone's emails that were likely to go out sometime between nine and ten the next morning. "All Sheol is about to break loose in Jerusalem," said Sedek and he grimaced.

# 27

# Parole without a Life

HANNAH HAD BEEN VERY touched by Grace's visit Thursday after-noon. She had only met Grace once before in her father's shop, although both she and Grace were friends of Sarah and she had seen Grace on occasion at Solomon's Porch. Grace had brought Hannah up to date on Art's overnight stay with the police. She reminded Hannah that the police were interested in finding not only her father's assailant, but also the stone's forger. Apparently, the police still felt that Art knew more than he was telling them, but the police were planning to turn Art loose Thursday night.

Hannah had loudly expressed her attitude right there in the ICU lounge. "That's ridiculous! Art and my father are best of friends! He was right here giving blood to save his life before he was arrested. Of course Art didn't shoot him!"

All of that anger and frustration against the injustices done to her people by Israeli police and armed forces welled up in her. Of course she knew that her own people, indeed her own former husband, had also committed atrocities, but it was hard to keep a balanced perspective when one had experienced great loss personally.

Friday morning Art had made a brief visit. For a while, Harry and Hannah, old friends, talked about all sorts of recent finds in Israel. Art just stood by rather amazed at the depth of Hannah's knowledge about Israeli antiquities. Hannah even gave Harry a key to her shop so Harry could peruse some things at his leisure.

It was now Friday evening. As Hannah sat by her father's bed reciting again and again the basic Islamic prayer in Arabic—"There is one God, Allah, and Mohammed is his prophet"—her heart had other words in mind, asking the Almighty to save her father, a good man. She was kneeling on her prayer rug facing Mecca and praying so intently that she hardly noticed that there was another sound in the room, the sound of very soft moaning. She stopped praying and realized the sound was coming from her father. She leapt up and went to his bed turning her ear in the direction of his mouth. Yes, he was moaning, now even more audibly. Could he be coming out of his coma? At once she pushed the call button for the nurse.

Grace finally arrived home from synagogue, with her mother Camelia in tow. Camelia had moved from New York to Jerusalem at the insistence of Grace, as she had no close relatives in the United States anymore to look after her. What Grace had not counted on was that her mother was still just as formidable and domineering as ever. She had moved into Grace's apartment and immediately rearranged everything, including Grace's own bedroom!

Her mother was like a runaway freight train, and Grace was constantly looking for the brakes. Camelia's latest tantrum occurred at the local grocery store after learning they did not carry her favorite brand of gefilte fish. She harangued the storeowner for so long that his wife called up Grace and told her to come and take her mother home! Grace was mortified and apologized profusely for her mother's overbearing behavior. Of course, she was forgetting that she too could sometimes be very pushy and get in people's faces. It's funny how we wince at the behavior in others that we are oblivious to in our own lives.

Once home Camelia put on the kettle and again set in on her usual litany with Grace. "You realize that if you keep turning down the overtures of Sammy Cohen and others that you will end up sad and alone. Far be it from me to tell you how to run your life, but I am just saying it would be nice to see you find someone before you are as old and gray as I am."

Grace practiced the art of "selective hearing loss" and went about getting on her pajamas and getting comfortable before bedtime. It had been a long day. Finally, she returned to the kitchen.

"Mother, thank you again for your concern for my life, but I am really quite happy and fulfilled just as I am. I love my work. I have numerous friends. I enjoy the socials and services at our synagogue. And you are here with me. Really that's more than enough."

Grace was attempting the kill-them-with-kindness approach. In actuality Grace felt like she had received a sentence of parole without a life. There was a deeper part of her that really longed for love and permanent companionship, but Grace kept suppressing those feelings.

Grace turned on the 10 p.m. news and was immediately accosted with follow-up stories about the bomb that blew up outside of Tel Aviv airport Thursday night.

"This country has turned into a terrorist's workshop. Practice here what you hope to make perfect when you export it to Europe and America. Why is civility and friendship so impossible now between the various religious and ethnic groups in this land?" She found herself arguing with the TV.

Her mother just listened quietly from the kitchen and shook her head. She could not understand why in New York a thousand races could live side by side and survive without totally destroying each other's way of life, but here in Israel, even just two or three ethnic groups and faiths couldn't manage to get along and share the land and its blessings.

But there was another person on the other side of town who also felt like he was on parole without a life. Art had been released Thursday night. He and Harry had spent a quiet evening at his flat, especially since Harry needed food and rest.

Fortunately, he had not been charged with a crime, and therefore had not been required to post bail when he was released from jail. Yet he had been stripped of his passport and told not to leave town. In short, he was still under suspicion. Art began to understand how Oded Golan, owner of the James ossuary, must have felt, living in some sort of twilight zone, waiting for the ax to fall. West decided, however, that he was not going to let the situation get the best of him. He was not going to hang his head and hide—he was going to be proactive.

Friday, Art relaxed and toured some of Harry's favorite spots. Late morning they visited Hannah, which turned out to be a lot of fun for

Art as he watched Hannah and Harry together! Harry's enthusiasm for his work and antiquities in general was just the medicine the doctor would have ordered—for Hannah!

On Saturday, Shabbat, Harry spent the day at Kahlil's shop. When Hannah left for the hospital, she gave Harry a crash course in making a sale. But there were few customers. He had the day and the shop mainly to himself to examine every piece.

By Saturday night Harry had settled in nicely in the guest bedroom and spent most of the evening attending to e-mails. He made a few phone calls to Mary Minor and Sam Feldman, two of his editors at *Biblical Artifact*. Plus, Harry had begun drafting an amicus brief, just in case he had to go to court on behalf of Art. Of course, Art would need an Israeli lawyer as well, since Scholer did not know all the ins and outs of Israeli law. He planned to consult with a local firm and take suggestions on who could best represent Art.

One thing Harry did know however—normally Israeli trials were trial by judge, though there was a provision for trial by jury if the defendant was from a country where that was the normal practice and it was requested. Harry was hoping for a trial by jury for sure. The judges he knew in Jerusalem were hanging judges with a low tolerance for possible antiquity thieves, much less potential murderers. Too many years of having to deal with the fallout from the Intifada had hardened them and their approach to such matters of jurisprudence.

"It is going to be an uphill battle," Harry said under his breath, as he prepared for bed.

# 28

# Flower Child

GRAYSON JOHNSON WAS QUITE the young man with a rather amazing pedigree. The son of the cult leader Charles Johnson, and a graduate of Fruitland Bible Institute in California, he was a blond hippie for Jesus. He sported a nose ring, a tongue stud, and more tattoos than one might think safe. "Israel is real, but Jesus is more real," read his favorite t-shirt which he wore constantly. Grayson Johnson was Ray Simpson's roommate, sharing an apartment near the Scottish Presbyterian Church in Jerusalem.

Grayson supported himself by working at the Jerusalem YMCA and a health food store. Whenever he could, he hung out with various conservative Christian groups in the city including attending from time to time the Society of the Millennial Dawn's public seminars. He was a vegetarian, a pacifist, and someone profoundly interested in the correlations between archaeology and the Bible. This latter interest had led him to attend worship services at the Garden Tomb not far from the Damascus Gate in the old city.

An avid reader of *The Left Behind* series of Timothy LaHaye and Jerry Jenkins, Grayson figured the world was coming to an end soon, and he wanted to be in Jerusalem when Jesus came back. For that reason, Grayson also kept up with the local news. Wednesday night, the headlines in the *Jerusalem Post* included the story about West's arrest on suspicion of not only assault but also forgery—something having to do with an inscription and a limestone block. That sounded familiar! Friday morning's news included a story about a bombing at Tel Aviv airport.

Grayson's morning granola was interrupted by a knock at the door. The police searched Raymond's room and talked to Grayson for about an hour. Grayson related all he knew about Raymond's activities that week—including the fact that he was indeed home Tuesday night.

He knew Ray was up to no good, but he couldn't quite figure out what to do about it. At the American Institute of Holy Land Studies, he had heard Professor West lecture on various occasions. One could say that West was in a sense Grayson's hero, being in his eyes the man most responsible for helping the world to see that archaeology backed up the New Testament's claims about history and Jesus.

He knew a lot more than Raymond could ever imagine. He knew 1) Ray had snuck out Monday and Tuesday mornings very early; 2) Ray was furiously chiseling an inscription into a limestone block Tuesday afternoon in the back courtyard; 3) Ray had returned to the apartment Wednesday afternoon very agitated; 4) Ray packed his suitcase, grabbed his laptop, and left Thursday; and 5) Ray spent entirely too much time with that crabby old professor from Yale instead of getting his research done.

After work Friday afternoon, Grayson walked around the old city seeking guidance from the Holy Spirit and muttering, "Principalities and powers man, principalities and powers. Somebody has got to help Doc West."

He remembered an afternoon recently when he and Ray took a short trip from the bus station out to a local dig site. Before leaving, Grayson saw Ray checking out a locker. When Grayson asked him about it, Ray said it was for personal belongings, and he should mind his own business. Grayson was no Sherlock Holmes, but he suspected that if Ray was hiding something, it might be in that locker. He decided to search for the key!

Sunday morning provided a glorious blue sky, and Grayson was off to the Garden Tomb for worship. He loved the outdoor worship service, the singing, the preaching, the communion service. He called it the Adam and Eve praise service. Grayson knew from last Sunday's bulletin that Art West was scheduled to preach. The text for the day was, "You are the light of the world. A city set on a hill cannot be hid" (Matthew

5:14). Grayson sang lustily at the service, drawing a few stares, but settled down to listen intently when Arthur West took the pulpit.

West stressed in his sermon how important it was for Christians to be honest and open about their faith. In Israel, of course, it was against the law to proselytize Jews or other non-Christians but one could indirectly be a good witness by living a truth-filled life, and always helping the truth, of whatever kind, to come to light. Grayson had found the message powerfully convicting, and had decided he would be brave enough to go up and speak with Dr. West after the service.

As the worshipers were gradually filing out of the Garden and passing through the gift shop on the way out to the street, Grayson deliberately got at the back of the line of those who were shaking West's hand. Being rather shy despite his love for singing, it took Grayson some doing to be brave enough to speak directly with his hero. As he came up to West and shook his hand, these words came tumbling out:

"I'm Grayson. For sure that was a good sermon Dr. West, and it reminded me that I need to be totally honest so that gnarly dude the Devil doesn't win any victories because of me being shy and quiet. My roommate Raymond Simpson is not walkin' the straight and narrow, to say the least, and he's been hanging out with the wrong crowd. Thursday he packed his bags and split—but he didn't get far! Yesterday, I found a key on a nail behind Ray's bed. I know it goes to a locker at the Bethlehem bus station. In the rush, I guess he had a 'senior moment'—uh, sorry Dr. West for rattlin on!"

"No offense taken!" laughed West. This young man was an enigma, but he could see Grayson was very sincere. "What has this locker got to do with me?"

"I don't know man," said Grayson who then continued with the world's longest one breath sentence: "But the police searched Ray's room Friday and talked to me all about the mess with the stone and all, and some guy named El Said, and you being accused of bad stuff, and Ray's in jail now, and I know Ray hid stuff in that locker and maybe the rock's there—wow, think of that!—but I figured you being an archaeologist and all, you could check it out cuz' I've been praying for you what with all your troubles of late, and I figured this is what God wanted me to do."

West looked deeply into the young man's blue eyes and saw a simple soul who really did want to help.

"Tell me your full name again," said West still staring.

"Oh, I'm nobody compared to you, I'm just Grayson, Grayson Johnson. This is about my roommate Ray Simpson. Like I said, he up and left me all of a sudden Thursday. He was hanging with the wrong crowd—to say nothin' of that Stone character."

"You are certainly not nobody," said West. "You are a precious child of God, and who knows—what you've done may shed light on many problems."

Grayson blushed and said, "Thanks man for makin' it real, the Bible I mean." West thought to ask, "Could you give me your address and phone number? At the very least I owe you lunch—and I'll need to return this key and let you know what I've found!"

Grayson turned in amazement.

"You mean it? I don't have a cell phone, can't afford them plus I hear they mess with your brain, the signals I mean. But my apartment phone is 783-4242."

West took out his palm pilot and entered Grayson's address and phone number. "I promise to be in touch as soon as I've learned something. God bless you." Grayson waved and went out through the gift shop.

Now Art was eager to share the morning's excitement. He headed for one of his favorite sidewalk cafés in the Jewish quarter to have brunch with Grace.

 Walking quickly through the Damascus gate, he passed right by Kahlil's shop, which reminded him to visit with Hannah later in the afternoon. Going through the bazaar, the crush of people was huge. Sunday, of course, was just a normal workday in Israel for the vast majority of people.

West strolled through the Cardo Maximus, the remains of the old Roman street and shops from not long after the period in which Jesus lived. He often thought about which of the early Christian figures might have walked down this same street. Just beyond the Cardo was a nice Italian pizza parlor. Grace was already waiting there sitting under an umbrella sipping something cool.

"Man, I've had a weird morning, so much to tell, but let's order first!" he exclaimed.

# 29

# Out in the Clear?

S AMMY COHEN'S PHONE HAD been ringing off the hook on Sunday morning. The lab tech kept calling with new revelations. First was the fact that neither West's nor Simpson's DNA samples matched the DNA from the hair fibers on El Said's coat. Then came the news that the prints were neither Simpson's nor West's. Both the prints and the hair samples were being checked against those found in Stone's apartment. Of course, the police still had Ray Simpson in custody charged with producing the forged stone. And Sammy knew the police were also looking for Patrick Stone especially since the gun belonged to him!

"Any way you cut it," said Cohen to no one in particular, "West cannot be charged with assault, nor, it would appear, with the forgery either. I had better call him."

Art had put his phone on voice mail so he could have an uninterrupted chat with Grace. He told her all about the morning service at the Garden Tomb and the unusual Grayson Johnson.

"What will you do next?" she asked.

"If it's legal I plan is to go to the Bethlehem bus station, but that means going through a check and there is that horrible wall around the city now as well. But I probably should take Sammy and Harry with me. Meanwhile, I want to talk to Mustafa again, and I really should visit Hannah."

Lunch had been going very pleasantly with their sharing a kosher pizza and some drinks, but Art could tell that Grace seemed a bit withdrawn. She wasn't really listening to all his plans. She kept bringing the conversation back to his personal state of affairs.

"Art, if this all gets cleared up pretty soon, then what will you do? Will you go back to the States?"

"No," said Art, "The digging season is far from over, and I hope to at least make a start in the excavations in and around the tomb. I'm going to have to draft one or two volunteers to help me, but since it's a small, self-contained site, it won't require a lot. I have an idea for one person who might help me."

"I am glad to hear this. I think it is important that you stay here," Grace replied emphasizing the last two words.

"Well, I can hardly do otherwise at this juncture. Your police have my passport you know!" reminded Art.

Art did not press Grace, but he could tell she was being somewhat evasive.

In truth, Grace was trying to make sure her friend didn't plan to leave. She was bursting to tell him about the contents of the ossuary! But Sammy hadn't given her the go ahead yet. Art's name had to be cleared before he would be allowed anywhere near that ossuary.

As their Sunday lunch was winding down, Art flipped up his cell phone and discovered he had two new messages. The first was from Harry: "Hey, Art, give me a buzz as soon as you can." The second message was from Sammy in his best professional voice: "Professor West. I am pleased to tell you that we now have sufficient evidence to exonerate you from the crimes of attempted murder and probably of forgery. You will probably be able to retrieve your passport at the Jerusalem police station next week sometime. They need to track down a couple of final details before releasing the passport."

Art let out a yelp—"Hey, looks like I am going to be cleared. Sammy was pretty definitive about the matter of assault, and seemed confident about the forgery and theft allegations."

Grace looked up shocked. "Who called you—Sammy?"

"Yes, which must mean they now have some firm leads that point in some other direction. Boy is that a load off my mind. Now if *Ha'Aretz* and the *Jerusalem Post* will just print that news in as prominent a spot as the original story about my arrest."

"I will see what can be done," said Grace laughing.

Grace headed home—her mother had made "not to be dismissed" plans for her this afternoon. Art lingered long enough to enjoy another cold glass of lemonade and return phone calls to both Sammy and Harry. Sammy was feeling kindly toward Art and heartily agreed that the search should be conducted officially. He promised to go with Art to Bethlehem with the proper papers. Harry was definitely up for the treasure hunt, and Art promised to swing by the flat and collect him within the hour.

# 30

## Pilgrimage to Bethlehem

HARRY AND ART PASSED easily through the security check point on their way to Bethlehem. The bus station was rather nondescript. Made of the same limestone as everything else in the area, the one-story building was off-white in color. The lockers were on the far back wall of the ground floor. Within minutes, Art and Harry were joined by Sammy and Officer Avi Hoffner who had followed them in another car just to make sure all went well at the checkpoint. Pleasantries were exchanged quickly—Sammy and Harry were still keeping their distance. Each person was provided with gloves to prevent any fingerprint contamination.

West headed straight for locker number 666, and with Sammy's go-ahead nod, put the key in the small lock and opened it without a problem. In the locker were two objects. The first was a leather bag, a tool kit of some kind, with chisels and pointed instruments. The second was a cardboard box, covered with brown paper, which appeared to have been taped properly at one time, opened, and resealed hastily. Officer Hoffner held the package carefully while Sammy peeled back the layers of paper. The cover was removed. Lying among wads of tissue paper were several olive wood nativity figurines—Mary, Joseph, and the three wise men. West was allowed to pick up one of the figurines and examine the bottom—a red and white label read, "Three Arches."

West mused aloud, "I've been to this shop on several occasions—the owner is quite reputable. Why would Ray Simpson hide nativity figures in a locker?"

"Keep looking, maybe there's some paperwork," chimed in Harry.

West poked around in the box and found a mailing label with a name but without a return address. The name he immediately recognized: "Dr. Patrick Stone."

"Looks like the good doctor did some souvenir shopping, that's all. But we don't know where he planned to send the figurines," mused Harry.

"Well, maybe there is more here than meets the eye. An olive wood piece like this should be heavier," commented Sammy as he weighed one of the figurines in his hand. At that point he gave the figurine a vigorous shake. Something moved up and down within the statue. Under the label, he noted a wooden plug. Looking at the bottom of the other four statues, the same was the case with each of them.

"Well, there are certainly more surprises in store," laughed Harry.

"Yes, but we should open these back at the IAA office—not here in a bus station. And I'll get a team in here to thoroughly inspect the locker," promised Hoffner, the resident expert in forensics, as he flipped up his cell phone.

"I suggest on our way back to the IAA office that we stop first at The Three Arches. Avi you stay here and secure the area," ordered Sammy. All were in immediate agreement, especially Harry who had promised to bring back a few quality items to his family.

The Three Arches was a popular tourist spot for those looking for early Christmas presents. Situated only a few blocks down the street from the Bethlehem plaza and the Church of the Nativity, it was usually packed with browsers in June. The wall erected around Bethlehem however had put a damper on business and there was only modest business being transacted. The three men walked in the front door and West immediately saw Ibrahim's daughter, Hagar, dealing with a customer at the main counter.

Art smiled and waved to her when she looked up, and asked, "Where's your father?" She pointed to the office door and replied, "He's in there with a friend working on his third Turkish coffee of the day."

A knock and a call of "Enter!" allowed the men to peer into a cramped little office. Seeing the impossibility of them all squeezing into such a small space, Harry immediately agreed to do some shopping. Art and Sammy stepped into the office where Ibrahim was sitting at his desk drinking coffee with a fellow Palestinian. Ibrahim smiled and offered the usual greeting, "*Salam Alaykum!*"

"And to you," said West, well versed in the proper protocol.

"Ibrahim, this is Mr. Samuel Cohen of the IAA. We have some very important business to discuss. But I see now is not a good time for you—may we come back soon?"

Ibrahim's friend arose and bowed.

"I have been honored with my friend's company long enough—it is a good time to continue my business elsewhere." Turning to Ibrahim, he nodded, and left graciously.

Art continued, "I must ask you to remember something, something which seems to have taken place some time ago, though I don't know just how long ago—perhaps within this year. A customer seems to have come into your shop, bought carvings of Mary, Joseph, and the Wise Men, and then asked you to hollow them out so they could contain something, and then after the insertion be plugged back up by your artisans. Do you remember any such transactions? Surely one like this would stand out." Ibrahim pulled on his beard and said thoughtfully, "To tell you the truth, I do not remember something like this, but as you know I do not handle the small day-to-day trade any more, I am more the negotiator for sales in bulk. Let me call my daughter Hagar to come and speak with us privately."

Ibrahim left the office. There was a lull in the activities in the shop and Hagar was merely arranging bills in the drawer. He said to his daughter, "Hagar, my dear, please come with me to the office. We must have a private word with you."

"Certainly, Father, let me ask Kalitha to take over here," she replied dutifully.

After Hagar was seated in the office, Art repeated the question he had asked Ibrahim, and Hagar got a very excited look on her face.

"Oh, yes, I remember. That transaction occurred only in the last week—Wednesday morning I believe. A small, older, nearly bald man came in, picked out the carvings he wanted, then asked if we could safely hollow out the statues. He said he wanted to put some surprises in them as additional gifts for his family. We thought that was fair enough and so we did the work quickly, boring out the statues very carefully but making sure the plug in the bottom would be secure. He came back about mid afternoon, and paid cash for both the product and the labor, no questions asked."

"Did he give his name?" Sammy asked.

"No, in fact, he did not really say much at all."

"Would you know him if you saw him again?"

"I think so, and in any case, he spoke with an American accent."

"Thank you, Hagar, I think that is all for now. You have been a great help to us." Hagar smiled and left the office. Ibrahim stepped in with cold drinks for his guests. "I presume you do not want Turkish coffee!" he said smiling.

Art laughed, "You know us well, Ibrahim! Thank you for your hospitality. Now I must find my friend."

Back in the shop, Harry was enjoying himself. Art cautioned, "If you are buying something there is not much time for haggling. We've got to squeeze ourselves into the Mini Metro and get back to Jerusalem."

Harry smiled and said, "Well, OK, but perhaps I can come back next week. They do quality work here."

Sammy joined them.

"It is getting late, gentlemen. I am going to return to the IAA office with the tool kit and figurines we found in the bus station. Art, if you want to be there for the grand opening, you may join us. We *will* be working late tonight!" explained Sammy with authority.

"Yes, indeed I do want to be there if I can. Let me drop off Harry at my flat, and we can rendezvous about 5 p.m. How about calling Grace and inviting her to join us—if her Mother will let her? I think Grace is eager to hear about our Bethlehem pilgrimage."

"Agreed," said Cohen. "Five o'clock then."

As Art drove off, Harry turned on the radio to listen to the 4 p.m. local news report. The radio crackled for a moment and then they heard, "A young American named Ray Simpson was taken into custody Thursday night at the Tel Aviv airport. He has now been charged with forgery. The police are looking for an alleged accomplice."

Harry and Art looked at each other and said simultaneously, "Patrick Stone!"

~

At that same moment Jamison Parkes Law walked into the offices of the Jerusalem Post. "I have a story for you," he said to his contact there, the senior editor Shlomo Glickstein. "Hear you have evidence of a very large wire transfer of moneys into the account of Arthur West from the British Library as of yesterday morning. We all know that West was lacking funds for his dig this summer, and we also know that he has been under suspicion in regard to theft and forgery involving the Lazarus Stone. It looks to me as though West and some accomplice have now sold the stone to the British Library for a huge sum of money."

Glickstein looked at Law eagerly and said, "If this pans out, it will be sensational news. How can we check out this story?"

Law replied, "You see the email address for the British Library, there. Why not just send them a message asking for confirmation about the transfer of funds?"

Glickstein paused and said, "Well they may deny it, unless and until they are prepared to go public. I think I will just fax this document over to Sammy Cohen at the IAA and ask him to comment before pulling the trigger on this story."

Law was looking a little chagrined. He said, "You need to understand the urgency of this matter. If we do not act fast, Israel may lose another precious piece of its own heritage, precious to both Jews and Christians."

"Alright," said Glickstein, " I will fax this right now and follow it with a phone call after a bit. Thank you Mr. Law. I will call you for further comment and a full interview shortly."

"Remember," said Law as he was leaving, "Time is of the essence now."

# 31

## Christmas Comes Early

SEATED AROUND A LONG conference table, Grace, Art, Sammy, and Avi peered at the booty collected from the locker in Bethlehem. Officer Hoffner began removing tools one by one from the leather bag.

"You see these tiny little chisels with narrower than usual blades, and some with points on them? These are indeed the tools of a forger. No one would be doing the plastering or repairing of a wall or tiles in a bathroom with this equipment!"

"If I'm remembering correctly, the forged stone is made of Mount Scopus limestone, right? Can we check and see if there's any residue of that precise sort of limestone?" inquired Art.

"Yes. As a matter of fact, the stone is now in our possession. The police sent it over for inspection after you were released from jail," informed Hoffner.

"And now the part we've all been waiting for—our Christmas presents!" smiled Art turning to the figurines.

"These gifts just keep on giving. Each one seems to contain something that rattles or shuffles around a bit, without being heavy."

With gloved hands, Avi Hoffner carefully removed the wooden plug from the bottom of the Joseph figurine. A digital camera flashed. With forceps he grasped the edge of a piece of paper and slowly but surely pulled out a tiny scroll. The camera flashed again. As he laid the scroll on a piece of glass, everyone instinctively leaned forward.

Grace was the first to break the silence, "I recognize the script. It's definitely Aramaic. And if I'm not mistaken—it sure looks like . . ." she stopped short and looked at Cohen not knowing whether to proceed. Art, after all, had still not seen the manuscripts recently found in the ossuary.

Sammy's expression and head shake discouraged her from continuing.

"It sure looks like . . . some other first century manuscripts I've seen recently."

"What other manuscripts?" asked Art, shooting a quizzical look at Grace.

"Well, that's a long story, my friend, a story we will NOT get into right now," began Sammy holding his hand up to stop any further comments along those lines. "Right now, let's find out what's in the other figurines."

Outranked, Art bit his tongue. For the next hour, each figurine was carefully opened, each manuscript was carefully removed and laid out on glass slabs, and each leaf was meticulously photographed. The real work of examining the manuscripts would begin tomorrow.

"We really have no proof that these manuscripts are genuine as yet, but I'm willing to guess that they have something to do with the Bethany tomb. My staff will get to work on them right away. Art, did you see anything like this when you were in the tomb?" asked Sammy.

"I just saw the ossuary and the inscription. Of course, darkness descended if you remember! I looked around with my flashlight while I was temporarily entombed, but I wasn't really paying much attention to every nook and cranny. If those manuscripts were in the tomb, they weren't just lying on the floor, I'm sure! And if they were in the tomb then they were removed with the stone inscription. And since they were found in Ray's locker, it sure looks bad for Ray—unless he's being framed like I was," reminded Art.

Everyone was looking tired, and everyone agreed it was time to lock up for the evening and head home. Art was invited back Monday morning with a promise to explain all, if he promised not to ask questions until then.

Art, who preferred to be in charge, really didn't appreciate being left out of the loop, or so it seemed. But more and more, Art was learning to appreciate his cell phone, and he now took a moment to check his recent messages. Sure enough, Hannah had called. He said to Grace, "I've got a message from Hannah and I'm sure she wants me to visit tonight. Do you want to get something to eat and come along with me?"

"Sure, let's go outside and give her a call," agreed Grace.

Once outside, Art quickly punched in the numbers.

"Arthur, Arthur, some good news," exclaimed Hannah breathlessly. "Father is regaining consciousness. I'm sure of it. Today he opened his eyes. He saw me! This is a good sign!"

"Excellent! God is working. Grace and I are here—we can eat quickly and come right over. Can you arrange for us to come up to his room? I promise we'll be brief. I suspect the police will also want to talk to him when he's fully conscious."

Hannah replied, "Yes, the police check in regularly. And yes, of course, I will make sure you can come into his room tonight."

Hannah adjusted the sheet over her father's chest and sat down to read for a while. Like her father, she loved a good novel and was currently enthralled by the works of Naguib Mahfouz. Today she was reading *Midaq Alley*. In 1988, Mahfouz became the first Arabic writer to be awarded the Nobel Prize in Literature. Sometime after that honor two Islamic militants stabbed him in the neck, but he survived. Hannah took some comfort in that fact. So absorbed was she in her reading, she didn't even notice when the doctor slipped in and began to check her father's pulse, IV, and general condition.

After the examination, the doctor pronounced, "This is all good. He is making progress. The fact that he opened his eyes briefly and spoke to you this morning signals that he is beginning to come out of the coma. You should take a little encouragement from his vital signs, which are all stable and steady."

"Thank you doctor. I do appreciate your taking such good care of my father. I don't know how we will ever pay the hospital back," said Hannah with a worried look on her face.

"Well, things have a way of working out, and you need to concentrate on being there for your father and not fretting about other things you can't control. Please, however, talk to our business office soon," instructed the doctor.

At this moment, Grace and Art peeked into the room.

"Come in," invited the doctor. "You are welcome to keep Hannah company for awhile; I am on my way out."

Without warning, Kahlil began stirring and trying to turn over. Hannah rushed over and spoke excitedly, "Father, father, can you hear me?"

There was a long pause. Finally in a mere whisper the words came, "Hannah, Hannah, I am so tired."

Tears of joy came streaming down Hannah's face. Her father had spoken her name clearly and distinctly. He had understood what she was saying. "Yes, I know, Papa, you may go back to sleep. We will talk later."

Kahlil never opened his eyes, but he smiled and drifted off again into sleep. Hannah remembered the line from Shakespeare: "Sleep which knits up the raveled sleeve of care, sleep the best medicine." But just those few spoken words were medicine to Hannah's soul. Her father was back in the land of the living. Grace and Art respectfully drew near the bed.

"Like Lazarus come back from the dead—do you know the story Hannah from the Christian New Testament?" asked Grace.

"Yes," replied Hannah, "Jesus was a great prophet."

"Perhaps more than that, Hannah," said Art softly. "Perhaps also the giver of life itself."

Meanwhile back at the IAA office, as Sammy Cohen was finally trying to get some paper work done, one of his secretaries raced in. "Mr. Cohen this fax just came in marked urgent from the Jerusalem Post. You are to read it, and then call Shlomo Glickstein at once."

Cohen read slowly through the fax, and just started moaning, "Oh no, surely not! Oh no. Now the police are not only going to charge West, he will become a prime suspect in this matter." With a heavy heart Cohen dialed the number at the Jerusalem Post.

# 32

# A Credit to His Account

SATURDAY MORNING, THE SUN rose over the Royal Edinburgh Hotel. Stone rose early and packed his bag. Nine o'clock couldn't arrive quickly enough. The dining room was gorgeous, complete with a huge chandelier and elegantly appointed tables each with a flower arrangement of roses and pansies. His breakfast had consisted of eggs and stewed tomatoes with toast points. As a treat, he insisted on an order of fresh strawberries and Devon clotted cream—hardly proper for that time of day.

Full of himself, he was prepared to be told he was very rich indeed. At 8:45 he went back to his room to await the call from the British Library. Stone sat on the bed. He no longer believed in praying, but he was concentrating on thinking positive thoughts. Nine o'clock came and went. Stone sulked. Finally, the phone rang.

"Hello, this is Oliver St. James. At precisely 9:06 a.m. the funds were transferred into your account and the other million into the Jerusalem account. Are you sure we cannot persuade you to attend Monday's press conference?"

Stone's pride was such that he was sorely tempted to do so, even if he had to sit in the back row. However, when someone in Israel finally figured out what had happened, which he hoped would not be soon, then he might be labeled a felon or worse, unless of course they blamed it all on West.

"Sadly," replied Stone, "I cannot do this. I am flying back to the States today to be with my mother. But I wish you the best. At this juncture I would like to enjoy the beginning of my retirement and privacy without a lot of paparazzi bothering me."

"Just so," said Oliver, "I understand entirely, and would want it this way if it were me. You can count on us being discreet. Farewell, and thank you."

St. James rang off. Before Patrick headed to Heathrow, he went to the business center, connected to the Internet, and keyed in his account number with Banque Suisse. After a brief pause a huge number came up on the screen: 35 million 312 dollars.

Stone began to laugh uncontrollably.

"Those fools really gave me all that money. They're as gullible as West and all those true believers like him." He then sent an anonymous email message from a hotel computer to Shlomo Glickstein at the Jerusalem Post: "Check out Arthur West's Jerusalem bank account." Checking out of the hotel, he went straight to the curb and hailed a black hansom cab. He hopped in the back and heard the dulcet tones of the Cockney accent: "Where to guvner?"

"Victoria Station," said Patrick truthfully.

"Too right," said the cabbie. And they were off.

Sedek Hadar, having monitored Stone's internet activity in the morning had immediately sent a full report to both Rabbi Menachem and Jamison Parkes Law, including forwarding the verbatim of the message Stone sent to Glickstein. But what was he to do now? He looked out the window just in time to see Stone leap into a hansom cab and drive off in a hurry. He had not been prepared for such a sudden exit. Apparently Stone had his bags packed and simply made a quick trip to the business center at the hotel before leaving. Now he would never catch him . . . unless of course he emailed someone soon about his whereabouts. He would stay in London for the next day or so, and continue to monitor Stone's email account.

# 33

# Viva La France

Patrick's trip took him further and further from home—first by train to Paris, and then by car over miles and miles of country roads through miles and miles of stunning countryside. He enjoyed a long and circuitous route paid for with cash and never by credit card. Patrick Stone covered his tracks as best he could given his limited knowledge of being a potential fugitive.

As luck would have it, the dealer who had supplied him with the fake documents, had also offered him a fake passport. Unfortunately, that counterfeit cost more than the other documents! He had used his real passport only to get to London. From there he hoped his trail would go cold. By Monday night he arrived in Cannes and checked into L'Otel de Roi.

The beautiful south coast of France, known as the Côte d'Azur, is one of the most expensive and exclusive places to live in all of Europe. As the local tourist brochure for the area says:

> Originally, the French Riviera was a winter retreat for European and Russian aristocrats fleeing from the fog, cold, and damp. Then, in the Roaring Twenties, sunshine became all the rage— albeit with parasols and stripy cover-up bathing suits, and it was then that the Riviera's towns kicked into higher gear as fashionable summer resorts. Thanks to fun-loving Americans Scott and Zelda Fitzgerald, the Murphys, Isadora Duncan, and other celebrities such as Picasso and Chanel, this seasonal switch acted as a catalyst to the Riviera's year-round development. But more

recently, another switch was thrown, this time to diversify the region's activities from tourist playground to high-tech, clean industry, congress, seminar and convention center. Today, outside the summer season, one of every two trips to the Riviera is business-related.

In short the old cliché is true: "If you have to ask how much something costs—on the French Riviera or in nearby Monaco—you can't afford it." Stone was enjoying a glorious sunrise, sitting on the balcony of his hotel room, drinking a rich red wine from the Loire Valley. He was slowly reading the local brochures, and had to laugh at the fact that the Riviera had become a hub for business. Not as far as he was concerned! "To life's finer pleasures!" he toasted as he raised his glass to the sky.

Tuesday's *London Times* carried a press release outlining a major new purchase by the British Library. The press conference had apparently drawn a lot of attention, including from AP, UPI, Reuters, and others. True to his word and their contract, St. James had made sure there was no mention of the seller. Patrick hoisted his glass for a second toast: "Here's to you, Oliver!"

No doubt, news of the British Library's purchase would travel to Jerusalem quickly. One thing he was sure of—it would be very difficult to get the French to extradite someone to Israel. France did not exactly have a close relationship with the current Israeli government. The French government had regularly sided with various Arab and Palestinian causes through the years, in part because of the high Muslim population in France.

"Viva la France!" was his third toast of the morning. His spoken French was a little rusty, but he read French just fine. He would adapt. Today he would find a bank, look at cars, visit a realtor, and he should send a message to his mother via email to see how she was doing. That would set his new life in motion. Maybe tonight he would go to the local jazz hot spot, Club Noir, and hear one of the great jazz legends, Oscar Peterson and his Trio. It appeared to Stone that the world was his escargot, to rephrase a cliché, and he was ready to consume it.

# 34

## Oh, Lazarus, Who Art Thou?

M ONDAY MORNING ART FOUGHT the Jerusalem traffic to pickup Grace and arrive at the IAA office before nine o'clock. Art was never late—he considered being ten minutes early being late. He was actually irritated to see that Grace was standing by the curbside waiting.

"Well, Arthur, I have some good news, and then some shocking news. Which do you want first?"

Art smiled. "Your choice—but make it a good one!"

"The good news is that the ossuary has been authenticated, there are no problems with the inscription. Its patina is just fine; it passed the ultraviolet test, and it's made of the right sort of limestone. There are no real bones in the box—just some shards, maybe even first century shards—but that takes time to determine."

"OK. Now give me the other news."

"Be patient," commanded Grace, "and drive slower; go around a few extra blocks. There's more to tell. When the IAA examined the shards they noticed a few hairs attached to one piece, perhaps the ointment poured over the body preserved it. In any case, they are running DNA tests—that should confirm our skeleton is a male of middle-eastern descent if nothing else. But what the scientists are guessing now is that our man may have had leprosy."

"Wow!" said Art. "Boy does that fill in a few gaps in the biblical story. It explains why grown daughters and sons in a particular family were still single and living together. It also explains why in the earliest Gospel account in Mark we are told that Jesus was anointed by a woman in the house of Simon the leper while he was in Bethany, yet the Fourth Gospel says this took place in the home of Lazarus, Mary and Martha. These two stories are speaking of the same house and the same family, only Simon, as the ossuary inscription suggests, is the father, and Lazarus or Eliezer is the son."

"Very intriguing," said Grace trying to hurry along the conversation. "But you haven't heard anything yet. We found something else in that ossuary besides bones, Art!"

"I take it you're about to divulge the shocking news, the sooner the better," urged Art.

"Well, I would, but there's the IAA office. You'll just have to wait a few more minutes." said Grace, enjoying every minute of Art's frustration.

Once in the IAA building, Grace led the way to the examining room. As she opened the door, she blurted out, "We found a scroll in the ossuary as well!"

"What? What are you saying? Was it a death certificate or some sort or a will?"

"Well," said Grace as Sammy joined them around the table, "you could say, in a manner of speaking, that it's a last will and testimony. In fact, it's an Aramaic telling of the Gospel story that we now call John's Gospel, only the heading says it's Eliezer's memoirs."

Art started laughing, "You've known about this for some time now—I guess having my name cleared allows me into the inner sanctum now. Grace, you almost slipped up Sunday afternoon when we were looking at the fragments in the figurines, didn't you?"

"Yes, that was close. Sammy here wasn't too pleased."

"True," piped in Sammy. "I was still waiting for the official paperwork, even though I called you Sunday morning! Keeping secrets is not Grace's strong suit; so let's get to work! I should tell you that Prof. Chartier has already looked at this scroll."

Grace and Art both put on the latex gloves used for examining any large and precious samples of papyri. Then Art was allowed to roll open part of the scroll. It was written in an absolutely beautiful hand. Some of the letters had the more cursive shaping, some more squared off, but that was typical of Herodian period Aramaic lettering. Art thought of all the time and care it took to write all this out. Perhaps Lazarus, because of his disease, had a lot of time late in his life to write these stories down. Perhaps he spent a lot of time alone.

"Well," said Sammy, breaking the silence. "A propitious moment, don't you think? We rarely see such complete manuscripts, in such a well-preserved condition. I have examined many Qumran scrolls, but this text is exquisite. Prof. Chartier has already examined parts of the scroll. He believes it to be first century—dating is not certain yet—it could be a copy of a copy. He, of course, wishes to head up a committee to study the text; however, plans have not been finalized. Any chance you wish to be involved?"

"Oh, yes," exclaimed Art emphatically, dismissing Sammy's teasing tone, "in *any* way possible. Just looking at this manuscript takes your breath away. Do you know what this means? We have a Gospel written from the perspective of a person whom Jesus raised from the dead! Now that sort of miracle could really change your worldview! Scholars have been debating for centuries why this Gospel is so different from the other canonical Gospels. And the dating! This is the earliest Gospel, an eyewitness testimony of a Judean, not a Galilean disciple! Is the entire Gospel on that scroll?"

"Apparently not," said Grace a bit cautiously. "According to Prof. Chartier, the beginning of the Gospel, the material before John 1:19, is missing. Like Mark it begins with John the Baptist. Also missing is John 21, and the famous passage about the woman caught in adultery."

"Well, most scholars say that the Fourth Gospel is a collection of texts, but the core material is attributed to the Beloved Disciple," explained Art.

"And that, brings up one more thing. In the part of the text that tells the story of Lazarus's illness, it calls him 'the one whom you love.' I think that's John 11. But where we normally have the references to the Beloved Disciple there is instead the name Eliezer."

"Now let's think about this," said Art now pacing around the room. "If the Beloved Disciple is Lazarus . . . Wow, this solves so many puzzles about the Fourth Gospel. For one thing, scholars had always thought it unlikely that a disciple of Jesus would run around calling himself the Beloved Disciple if he wrote this Gospel. Now we have evidence that he didn't do this. Rather, whoever translated this document into Greek likely made the changes, and perhaps he was also the one who added the beginning and end of the story."

"So, the beloved disciple is Lazarus—interesting hypothesis," mused Sammy, "And what do we do with the story of the woman caught in adultery?"

Art took up the story, "No one thinks that wonderful story was in the original Gospel. It shows up in too many different places in the Greek manuscripts of John, and in one manuscript of Luke you also find the story. Clearly it's a story looking for a home. Various scribes loved the story, and kept sticking it into various manuscripts! You've gotta admire their persistence!"

Grace was feeling like a super-sleuth again. "Try this out, everyone. If John's Gospel was actually written by a Judean disciple, a southerner, doesn't this explain why all but two of the northern Galilean miracle stories found in the other Gospels are missing in this Gospel?

"Sure it does. Plus, having a Judean author explains why all the special stories about the Twelve, about the three, about even the Zebedees are not found in this Gospel. It is *not* by a Galilean disciple! Our author just didn't spend any time with the boys in Galilee," laughed Art.

Sammy, after taking all this in, raised his hand and added, "I was born and raised in Jerusalem. For me, this explains why our author knows so much about Jerusalem, and knows so much about Jesus' ministry in that city and its vicinity, things the other Gospel writers do not know. John's Gospel just has the sound of a local author. But the long-standing tradition opts for a John of Zebedee, correct?"

"Well, that's a later tradition," explained Art. "The Greek labels on the Gospel documents were added later, and nowhere in the text of this Gospel is John of Zebedee equated with the Beloved Disciple. Holy Smokes . . . these finds are going to change the face of Johannine scholarship, not to mention raise a bunch of questions about the reality of resurrection!"

Grace could tell how passionate Art was about all this. As for her, it merely confirmed that some early Jew was brought back from death. Maybe he was healed by Jesus, maybe he revived in the cool of the tomb, but in any case that resurrection didn't prevent him from dying again. Extrapolating from this case to the case of Jesus would be a stretch. Though Lazarus was raised, he obviously didn't get the same resurrection body that Jesus is supposed to have gotten. But still . . . it was a remarkable miracle. It raised again the question about whether and how such things happened. She had to admit this shook her up a bit.

Grace was a thoroughly modern person in the sense that she did not expect to see miracles happen, though she could not absolutely rule them out. So now she had a big question mark in her mind. How should she interpret these findings without seeming to try and explain them away?

Quiet pervaded the room for some time. Each scholar's thoughts lost in the first century—each imagining a man named Eliezer carefully writing down his memoirs in an oil-lamp-lit Judean room in Bethany.

Sammy had decided, knowing that West was coming to the IAA office anyway, to simply play dumb for a while and see if West showed any signs of being a duplicitous person when shown all these treasures. He could detect no such signs, so either West was very good at masking his real intents and behavior, or some one was truly trying to frame Art. He decided that now was the juncture to drop the bombshell about the money in the bank account. He would show him the report of the bank deposit and watch closely his reaction.

"Art," said Sammy, tentatively, "would you by any chance have a bank account in the Jerusalem Bank which has this account number?"

West looked at the paper on which the number was written, and said, "Yes, but how did you get this number, and why are you asking?"

"Well either you've been playing the Israeli lottery and got very lucky in the last couple of days, or you've got some serious explaining to do, as it appears the British Library has deposited over a million dollars in your Jerusalem account."

"What!!" said West and Levine in unison.

West was showing all of the signs of being totally dumbfounded.

"Grace," said Art, "I know you told me there was some shocking news but I was not prepared for this!"

At this juncture Sammy handed Art the faxed evidence of the wire transfer of funds into his account. Art stared at it incredulously. "Someone is going way out of their way to try and frame me Sammy," Art finally said in a hushed stunned voice as he broke into tears.

Sammy wanted to believe him, but the evidence of the fax seemed very damning. "Sorry, Art, but I suspect the police will be here in a few minutes to charge you with theft and illegal selling of antiquities. I would like to believe you are innocent of all this, but I am hard-pressed to explain this evidence. How did someone at the British Library even know your account number?"

"I don't know," said Art, and now he was shaking.

Sammy turned to Grace. "Grace you must absent yourself from Art's problem for now, lest you and the IAA somehow be tarnished as well, and in any case there is so much work to be done. And then there are the fragments from the figurines. How do they fit in? Do you have time to study those little manuscripts after lunch?"

"I'm certainly up for it," Grace replied, "but I shall not be abandoning my friend Art."

There was a knock on the door. Detective Shimon was standing there. "I am sorry Professor West, but we must take you in once more for questioning, and it seems likely you will be retained in custody as you will be charged with a crime before the end of the day."

Art looked at Grace and said, "Please call Harry at once, and ask him to meet me at the jail." Grace nodded and said, "Hang in there Art, we'll get to the bottom of this." Right now, thought Art, I seem to be in free fall with no bottom in sight.

# 35

## The Sleeper Wakes

Hannah was just leaving the antiquities shop, having spent the last two hours catching up on paperwork, when Grace called. As Grace arrived in the fifth floor visitor's lounge, she was met by an entirely different and more upbeat Hannah.

"Father is actually talking now Grace. In fact, at lunch he asked for you. It's so wonderful, like he has come back from the dead!"

"Yes," said Grace nodding. "Art would call this the Lazarus Effect." Pondering how much to tell Hannah, considering the delicate state of Kahlil's health, Grace said quietly, "Hannah there is something I must tell you."

"Yes."

"Our friend Art has just been taken in a second time by the police and this time it looks quite grave. They found evidence that he was sent lots of money by the British Library; apparently for something he sold them. Now I am still not convinced he has done anything wrong, but the evidence is pretty damning at this point and so we need to keep Art in our prayers, and equally importantly it will be wise not to tell Kahlil about this most recent shocking news for awhile, during the time that he is mending, lest he have a setback. Are we agreed on this approach?"

Hannah's demeanor had gone from cheerful to profoundly worried once more, but she shook her head and said, "Yes, for now his re-arrest had best be a secret, as Father is only beginning to regain his strength."

The two women entered Kahlil's room in a more somber mood than they had hoped to do in view of Kahlil's improvement.

Kahlil was sitting up in bed drinking his favorite Haifa orange juice and complaining to his nurse that he needed *more* food. This was a good sign! Still bandaged about the head and across the chest, Kahlil looked like he had been through the war, emerging bloody but unbowed. "*Salam Alaykum*," boomed Kahlil when he saw Grace coming. Grace came right over to the bed with an "Also to you," and smiled at Kahlil.

"I would greet you less formally, but I imagine physical contact's still forbidden due to your injuries. What's the medical report?" asked Grace.

"I no longer have a spleen, but apparently I can do without it. My liver is mending itself as we speak, and as you know I have always been hard-headed."

"So tell me," urged Grace, "What do you remember about last Tuesday night? Can you talk about it—have the police been here?"

"Slow down, my friend," said Kahlil. "The police are coming later this afternoon. Unfortunately, I remember very little about some things. I remember sitting on the bench in the park, then standing because someone said something to me. I turned and then . . . I remember nothing."

"Wow, amnesia! I've never met anyone with amnesia," mused Grace. "What about earlier in the day. Anything stand out?"

"Only that a small angry man came into the shop and had a heated argument with me over a stone tablet. I sent him away dissatisfied, as he wanted money too quickly and under suspicious circumstances. Hannah saw him briefly from behind the safety of her desk, as did a Dr. William Arnold from your United States. But neither of them saw the stone tablet he was carrying."

"OK, first the man. Did you know him?"

"My memory is a bit fuzzy. However, I do not believe I have met him before, nor do I care to meet him again. Come to think of it, Dr. Arnold recognized him, but we did not speak of the man."

"But do you remember anything more about him—more than what Hannah saw?"

"Yes, he was quite short compared to me, I would say in his 60s, an American by accent, and with a rather impatient nature. Oh yes, also nearly bald."

"Would you recognize him again if you saw him?"

"I should think so, but let's talk about Art for a moment. Is he out from under the dark cloud Hannah told me about this morning?"

Grace chose her words carefully. "No, not entirely, but we live in hope. The police do not appear to suspect Art had anything to do with your attack. But the stone being missing is another matter. Art photographed a stone inscription last Tuesday morning in a tomb in Bethany, but it was stolen Tuesday afternoon before he went back to the tomb with the IAA and me. A copy of that same stone arrived at his apartment Wednesday morning. We don't know where the real stone is! So tell me about the stone you saw in your shop."

Grace sat down in a chair next to Kahlil, and Hannah stood beside him, while Kahlil carefully described the very stone that Art took pictures of inside the Lazarus tomb. There could be no doubt.

"So we know for sure this stone really exists. That is important news," said Grace.

"A man named Raymond Simpson has already been arrested for making the forgery. He's the graduate student of one Dr. Patrick Stone who fits your description perfectly. So there's no doubt that he and Ray Simpson are involved in stealing the inscribed stone. The question in the mind of the authorities is whether Art is also involved. Did Hannah tell you Art was temporarily sealed up in that very same tomb?"

"No, no, what is this? Did the ghosts of the cemetery try to frighten you off?" exclaimed Kahlil.

"I'm embarrassed to admit it took Art awhile to realize he could call out and get help! Mustafa the church steward rescued him. Maybe someone followed him. Maybe grave robbers are everywhere. Maybe it was just a local prankster. But it gave him a scare nonetheless. And by day's end the ossuary was safe with the IAA but the inscription stone was gone."

"Ossuary, what ossuary? I've been asleep too long!" sighed Kahlil.

"I'm sorry, Kahlil, I know there is much to tell you but some of these stories must wait while you rest. Hannah will slowly catch you up on all the excitement, and I promise to come back and share wonders even Hannah doesn't know about. Trust, me I've already had an interesting day!" said Grace.

Hannah added, "Poor father, when he gets back to the shop, he'll be overwhelmed with work, too—we have lots of new items to catalogue!"

Finally, Grace asked gently, "Are you sure you don't remember who shot you?"

"No, but I think the memories will come. I see a vague form already in my mind, and I pray to the Almighty for clear thinking on this," sighed Kahlil.

"I'm sorry if I am being too pushy. Would you mind if I said a little prayer of thanksgiving to the Almighty for your deliverance and that Art may be cleared?" Hannah and Kahlil both smiled, and Kahlil said, "Of course not, we also pray to the Ineffable One you know."

With a tear in her eye Grace prayed, "Gracious God of all peoples and nations, I thank you so much on this day that Kahlil is going to be alright. I thank you for the healing you have brought here. God, a grave injustice has been done to Kahlil, and I pray that the truth will come out. Give us strength through these days. Help us all to continue to live in the light, and be honest and true persons who live according to your will. Amen."

Monday afternoon was warm with heavy clouds as Grace left the hospital, and her heart, while warm, was also heavy. Art would have said God really does work all things together for good for those who love Him, but right now Grace felt circumstances were about to put that idea to the ultimate test.

# 36

## Mass in the Morning

WEST WOKE UP AT seven o'clock Tuesday morning, refreshed for the first time since the excitement began a week ago. He dove into the shower, toweled off, pulled on a khaki shirt, long pants, and his comfortable sandals. He was ready for breakfast and church. Though the authorities had taken Art in Monday evening, Harry had been right there with him, and had immediately posted bail. Art would not get his passport back any time soon he figured, but Harry was an excellent lawyer and he had already proved his worth Monday night when he came to the rescue.

When his toast popped up, Harry wandered into the kitchen, and said, "You're up and about rather early."

"Yes, I'm off to church in Bethany and to have lunch with one Grayson Johnson. And you are welcome to come. By the way I saw you watching *Law and Order* reruns on the tube last night. What do you think of that show?

"It's the best. I love it," admitted Harry. "Most of the time Sam Waterson gets his man—or woman as the case may be. You realize that show is a huge hit over here. In fact, the ultimate compliment was paid to one of the lawyers at the firm I contacted on your behalf. Their point man, Benjamin, is called 'Mr. Law and Order' here!"

"Interesting, plus it's a big improvement over *Beverly Hillbillies* so far as the image of Americans is concerned," laughed Art. "I gather you are getting a good deal done here for articles that will go into *Biblical*

*Artifact.* I promise you an exclusive interview about the Bethany tomb, the ossuary, the inscription, and—oh yes, did I mention we found manuscripts?"

"I know about the small scrolls in the figurines you found Sunday. Are you saying there's more?"

"Oh yes, much more! When the dust settles, and the IAA is free to make all its announcements, I guarantee you'll be filling your journal with stories. And I'd like to see you and Sammy Cohen work together, despite past differences. What do you think?"

"Yeah, I obviously want to work with them as well—having *you* to plead *my* case would be an interesting role reversal! But I gather they will not be fraternizing with you for a while until you are cleared in regard to this latest shocking news. How do you think that money got into your checking account here in Jerusalem? Any theories yet?"

Art just shook his head and said, "I never want to believe the worst about a person, but the only thing I can think of is that someone connected to Ray Simpson is trying to frame me, and that someone would seem to be the ever elusive Patrick Stone."

"My thoughts exactly, but proving it is another matter!" said Harry. Harry was a great guy, and it seemed he was enjoying having some more quiet time here in Jerusalem talking to archaeologists, visiting digs, generating stories and the like. Art liked having a congenial roommate, but he liked his legal acumen even better.

Patrick Stone was sitting in an internet café in Cannes composing a note to his mother. Little did he suspect someone was reading his outgoing and incoming mail! The message said:

> Dear Mother,
> Through an incredible turn of good fortune I have been able to come into a significant amount of money, and would like you to begin thinking about coming and living with me in Europe so I can look after you more properly. I realize that would be a big move, but they have the best health care imaginable here in southern France on the Côte d'Azur, far better than in Kingsport, and I am now able to make it possible for you to have

the surgery you have needed for such a long time. I hope you
will consider this request and get back to me soon.
Love, Patrick.

Stone knew that his nephew Randy would be reading this and then
reading it to his Mom. She would then make an oral reply that Randy
would type in an email message. He hoped to hear from her soon.

Sedek read this message with some relief, and immediately for-
warded it to both Rabbi Menachem and Jamison Law. They would
know what to do with this evidence, and perhaps they could alert
Interpol. It was time for him to return to Jerusalem before his funds ran
out. He had noticed in the *Jerusalem Post* that morning a small article
about West being further questioned, this time about a wire transfer of
money. Sedek licked his chops and said, "We are going to nail this ring
of bandits who are stealing our heritage. Finally I am doing something
for the good of the cause."

The Church of Mary and Martha is beautiful in its simplicity.
Apart from the stained glass windows there is very little color in the
place, but the semi-vaulted ceiling makes for a great echo chamber if
one is inclined to sing. Art was definitely a singer, always had been. He
had sung in church choirs and loved all kinds of music, both highbrow
and lowbrow. His CD collection included everything from Tchaikovsky
to James Taylor, from John Coltrane to Allison Krauss, from the Bee
Gees to the Beatles. Lately he was enjoying jazz, and regularly went to
the club off Hadassah Street—Le Jazz Hot.

To many conservative Christians, West was something of an
enigma. He was orthodox in his theology, but had no problems as a
Protestant attending Mass and benefiting from it. The Mini Metro
seemed raring to go as it raced down the serpentine road along the
Hinnom Valley towards Bethany. He would get there in plenty of time
for the service. Parking in the back of the church he walked in the door
and was immediately welcomed by Mustafa who handed him a missal.
Putting something of a damper on things was the fact that the police
had told him he would be followed wherever he went. Nevertheless,

saying a prayer, Art tried not to let this get him down when he saw the police cruiser pull up and park next to his own vehicle.

Art whispered in Mustafa's ear, "I must speak with you afterwards." Mustafa nodded and ushered him to a pew. There were only twenty-five people in the church, which held perhaps a couple of hundred. The Catholic service involved a good deal of liturgy with a little bit of singing, all in Arabic. The service was only forty-five minutes long, with a ten-minute homily. West's spoken Arabic was not great, but he got the drift of the sermon, which was about loving your neighbor, even your Jewish neighbor, as yourself. How very odd, thought West, for a Palestinian to use a Jewish text to obligate Palestinians to be neighborly to Jews! That's just like God, thought West. What did Paul say? "In Christ there is neither Jew nor Gentile . . . but all are one."

The service concluded with communion, just the bread, not the wine. The cup was reserved for the priest. There was a final benediction, which surprisingly enough was in Latin, and then the passing of the peace. West found himself nodding and smiling towards a diminutive Palestinian woman of about eighty.

Walking out the door, West was followed by the unflappable Mustafa.

"Mustafa, my friend," said West slowly as Mustafa's English was not great.

"I need to figure out what happened to me that day sometime ago when I was trapped in this tomb back here. Did you see any one loitering around here that Tuesday or on Monday when I was surveying the tel? Anyone strange who didn't seem to belong here?"

Mustafa answered, "There are many tourists who come here to see the traditional site up the road where Lazarus was thought to be buried. Of course, it is only called the *traditional* site. Now we know better! Yes? But I saw a few people that day wandering around the church and looking out back during that time. One was a short man, an American I think, though he had someone younger with him. Come to think of it, I may have seen the younger man on Monday also. The IAA have questioned me about this already."

"This man, was he rather bald, rather short?"

"Yes that describes him. I did not have time to inquire what he was doing as I had so much work in the church. And I don't think he saw me at all. The two were busy taking pictures and looking around. Thank goodness you had a cell phone or you might still be in that tomb now, resting peacefully with Lazarus!"

"Don't remind me. Can we have one more look in the tomb? I realize that the IAA has it cordoned off, but I have permission to look though I can't take anything away from the site. Apparently the robbers found the small manuscripts in a clay jar, or maybe they were in the back of another niche."

"Of course, let us go together," said Mustafa, back to his usual serious self.

Sliding again into the tomb and pulling out his flashlight West peered into the various niches. "Here, you are smaller than I am, Mustafa, can you crawl in and see if you see anything at all."

Mustafa examined a number of niches. At one point he shimmied in so far that all one could see were his two legs dangling out. He rolled over and looked up at the top of the niche. "Yes, there is a writing on the roof of this niche."

"Can you manage to photograph it with my small digital camera?"

It took a minute or two for Mustafa's eyes to adjust and for him to focus on the inscription. He realized that when he took the picture the flash would go off and blind him, so holding the camera very still he looked through the viewfinder, aimed, closed his eyes, and shot the picture.

"Take two or three if you can," said West. A minute or two later Mustafa emerged with the camera.

"Let's get out of this humid place, Mustafa, and get some air."

When they emerged from the tomb West was already checking the pictures on the back of the camera as they came up. One shot was especially clear and complete. There was an inscription all right in Aramaic . . .

*Martha, asleep in the Lord, lies here, awaiting resurrection.*

Here was further evidence that this indeed was a family tomb of Lazarus, Mary, and Martha. Art had no doubts now that the Eliezer in question was the same person mentioned in John 11. As he walked back to the church with Mustafa he queried,

"I wonder where the ossuaries of Mary and Martha went?"

"Ah," said Mustafa, a man of wise words, "we must be thankful for what we have found, not complain about what we have not."

"Amen to that," agreed Art as he climbed into his car for the short ride to Jerusalem and his lunch date at Solomon's Porch. Right on his bumper was his new Israeli shadow, Officer Shimon.

# 37

# Headline News

GRAYSON JOHNSON WAS WAITING on the bench staring at the passers by who, in turn, were staring at him. He hopped up as soon as Art approached. "This is great, man, I love this place. Sarah's a neat lady—she always waits on me," exclaimed Grayson.

Art enjoyed telling Grayson about all the excitement on Sunday at the Bethlehem bus station. He related how they had found the tools and figurines in the locker. The key to the locker was still with the police, and his roommate Ray Simpson was still in custody.

Grayson enjoyed telling Art about his visits in jail with Raymond. "I've been telling Ray all about the Lord. He's scared, man, so he's really willing to listen."

"So you really did see Raymond working out in the courtyard with rocks and tools on Tuesday afternoon?" asked Art.

"Yeah, he was making a racket with the chisel. He had on goggles and all—stone was flying, man. He was in a rush. I've seen him make stuff before for Dr. Stone's lectures. He's pretty good at it."

"Did you see the stone that he was copying?"

"No, I think he just had a picture—a good picture."

"And you're quite certain that Ray was at home with you watching the TV between seven and ten last Tuesday night?"

"For sure. The dude wouldn't even let me have the remote once so I could check my favorite Nature Channel show once in a while. I can't vouch for Monday or Tuesday morning, but he was working away after lunch, and lounging around eating Cheetos and drinking Maccabee beer most of the night. Not a healthy diet if you ask me."

"Did you ever see Raymond with the statues of Mary or Joseph or the wise men?"

"Not me, man. I knew about the locker, but I don't know who put those fancy figures in the locker—or when. The police are hoping Dr. Stone will call and ask to have those figurines sent somewhere. Then they can catch him! And none too soon, if you ask me. But what I don't get is why Ray's covering up for that Dr. Stone. He must have some hold over my poor roomie. But you know what the Bible says, 'God is not mocked. Whatsoever a person sows, that shall they also reap.' That's sort of the spiritual version of what goes around comes around, if you catch my drift."

Art laughed, "Yeah, Grayson, I like your Cotton Patch version! I presume you are going to stay around for the summer?"

"Oh yeah, I like my jobs, especially at the Health Food Store, and Sarah says I can work here anytime. This will be the happenin' place to be when the Lord returns!"

Just then, Sarah came hurrying over, and handed Art the daily papers, with a breathless, "Have you seen this, Dr. West?"

> Priceless Artifact Obtained by British Library
> Press Conference Reveals Ancient Inscription

Below it, and mercifully in smaller print there was the article entitled, "West questioned about money transfer from British Library."

Grayson, looking over West's shoulder, opened his mouth in amazement, checked himself and then said "Principalities and powers man, principalities and powers. Time for some serious prayer Doc."

"You are right," said Art, "why don't you pray for us before we eat." Art would be finding out who his real friends were now. Things were about to take another turn in an unexpected direction.

# 38

## Love Feast

GRACE HAD LEFT HER mother fuming in the kitchen because the vegetable soup had too much water in it. Camelia's memory of the recipe called for six cups of water, but it was obvious that four cups were plenty. Now Camelia was contemplating starting over, but she hated to waste anything. So Grace had thin soup for lunch and then announced that she was off to the IAA for the afternoon.

Camelia retorted, "Mazel tov."

While Grace sometimes drove her mother's Honda, her own car was a rather flashy one for a teacher and part time IAA operative. It was a Mazda Miata ragtop, bright red. She figured she deserved a little fun in her life. Zooming down the hill towards the IAA building she passed the Knesset and the Shrine of the Book, and kept right on going.

Parking across the street was Art West, who saw her red car flash into the staff parking lot. Grace was a lot of fun to be around, always the life of the party, that is, when she ever had time to go to a party. Like Art, Grace was a workaholic.

Art waved a newspaper in the air, as he raced toward her. "Grace, come on, let's go find Sammy!" he yelled, grabbing her arm and rushing her into the building. The two of them nearly collided with Sammy who was talking to a secretary.

Sammy turned quickly and called out, "Did either of you see today's papers?"

"I've got a copy of the *Post* in my hand. Grace you won't believe this!"

"Come on, let's go into my office," said Sammy. "It seems that our Lazarus stone has turned up sold to the British Library." He deliberately avoided mentioning the other article on the front page of note—the one about Art. Sammy kept telling himself—"He's innocent until proven guilty."

"What? Are you kidding?" cried Grace in response to Sammy's audible comment.

"See for yourself," said Art handing her the front page of the *Jerusalem Post*:

Priceless Artifact Obtained by British Library
Press Conference Reveals Ancient Inscription

The British Library press release included a picture of a man named Oliver St. James, and the article detailed how the Museum had bought the limestone inscription after careful authentication. Despite repeated questions from the press, neither the seller nor the price tag were revealed. In conclusion, the report stated that the British Library looked forward to displaying the stone in the room with Codex Sinaiticus.

Sammy was fuming. "Do you two have any idea how hard it is to pry a stolen artifact from the clutches of those who run the British Library? You know that they still have never given back the so-called Elgin marbles, the friezes from the Parthenon, even though Greece requested them to be returned several summers ago in time for the Olympic games. What a mess!"

"Well, the inscription stone has been found, but Patrick Stone wasn't mentioned. Mustafa told me this morning that he saw Patrick Stone at the Bethany site. Even though Simpson isn't giving him up, it's obvious he took the stone. Did he give it to a broker to sell, I wonder? Did he take it to London himself? Did he shoot Kahlil? Are the police tracking him?" Art wasn't running out of questions, so Sammy interrupted.

"Yes, well, the police are looking for Dr. Stone, and yes, Raymond Simpson is still withholding evidence, and now they're thinking you are in cahoots with these other two ne'er-do-wells also. I guess Simpson's praying that Dr. Stone won't roll over on him!"

"Enough with the stone jokes," laughed Grace. "The police can do their work. How hard can it be to track a short, nearly bald man in his sixties—unless he's a master of disguise!"

"With plenty of cash and maybe even a false ID," added Art.

"You two watch too many detective shows. But, yes, even the most amateur felon can elude the police for some time. Meanwhile, did I hear you say you were in Bethany this morning, Art?" asked Sammy.

Glad to add to the news reports, Art said, "Yes friends, I have a little surprise for you. Lest anyone argue that this Eliezer is someone other than the biblical Lazarus, I crawled back into the tomb with Mustafa. And guess what? There are inscriptions in the roof of one of those niches. Here's a picture that Mustafa took."

Grace playfully snatched it from his hand and looked closely at the Aramaic. She translated: "Martha, asleep in the Lord, lies here, awaiting resurrection." "So this was truly a family tomb, and at one time Martha and presumably Mary were also interred there."

"Which brings us to the other manuscripts, the small ones found in the figurines. Some of our technicians are working with the fragments right now. I suggest you both look in on them. I have some phone calls to make—to London," said Sammy with a deep frown.

Minutes later, they joined some of Grace's coworkers examining the fragments. So far all of them were pieces of John's Gospel. The workers were attempting to put them in order.

"Look familiar?" Grace asked as she handed Art a fragment ready to be translated. He read a line in the Aramaic: "Jesus stooped down and started to write on the ground with his finger." "Well, no doubt this is a copy of the story of the woman caught in adultery. Do you know what are in the other fragments?"

Anna, one of the other workers, a graduate student from Cornell spending her summer studying Aramaic texts, explained, "More of the same story, and a couple of others from John 21."

Art turned to Grace, "So Stone found these fragments in the tomb after I managed to get out last Tuesday morning. It's a good thing the ossuary was too big for him to get it through the hole. We already know Stone had the figurines made. I'm sure he put the manuscripts inside. He probably gave them to Ray to hide for the time being in his locker. It's possible Raymond didn't even know the manuscripts were inside. Grayson said he never saw the figurines at the apartment."

At this point, Sammy entered the room. "London promises to return my call. Sure, and it might rain in Jerusalem today. Sorry for the sarcasm. Are you talking about the figurine manuscripts? Raymond Simpson has finally admitted that he stored the figurines for Dr. Stone, but he swears he had no idea that the manuscripts were inside. He remembers Dr. Stone picking up a jar from the tomb, but he never saw what was inside the jar. My guess is that Dr. Stone had no intention of sharing this find with Raymond. But I'm also hoping that Dr. Stone will eventually get in touch with Raymond in the hopes of having them sent by mail somewhere."

"Yes, I had lunch with Grayson," said Art, "he mentioned you were tapping his phone. Do you think Stone has any idea that Raymond has been arrested?"

"No, I don't think so. Raymond has an answering phone in his apartment, so we are tracing all incoming calls. So far, nothing. Our Mr. Stone might not call for some time. He thinks the figurines are safely stashed. Detective Hoffner is monitoring the calls with one of his favorite gadgets. Of course, there are some perks. Hoffner is getting an education from Grayson in Tofu burgers, Christian rock music, tie-dyed t-shirts and, my personal favorite, the art of tongue piercing! And they say that working for the IAA is tedious and boring!" laughed Sammy.

Everyone in the room turned to listen to Sammy's uncharacteristically long speech. Sammy obliged them by continuing, "We have to do the press conference tomorrow to counter the press conference in London. Wouldn't we all like to know how much the Museum paid for our stone! Anyway, I need you two to walk with me to discuss the details. Let's head down to the room where the ossuary manuscript is laid out. I'm sure you want to see it again."

Sammy had decided that for the time being the best way he could finally make up his mind about whether Art was actually involved in some nefarious way in these matters was to continue to proceed as normal and watch West's reactions to the various developments. Art West did not strike him as a person who could readily conceal his feelings about matters that he was passionate. He also noted the absence of defensiveness on the part of West thus far. He had informed the police of his modus operandi in this matter and suggested that they remain cordial, but distant while they were observing and following Art. Thus far, they had agreed that was the way to go, perhaps on the theory that at the worst Art might lead them to something that would make a difference in the case.

Art, Grace, and Sammy left the workroom still staring in silence. On the way through the halls, Sammy continued, "Art, we need you to put on your game face and emphasize that you found the inscribed stone on Tuesday, June 1, on site, and therefore the British Library has been lied to by the seller. Obviously, you can't mention the name of Stone. You can save your lengthier explanation of the significance of this find for next week. We'll have another briefing then for the press, and you can talk to your heart's content. And if I were you I would also forestall a lot of questions by stating flatly what you have told us—that you have no idea how that money got in your checking account."

"And," said Art, " I have decided the best thing to do is to turn that money over to the police forthwith to avoid even the appearance of ongoing impropriety."

"Good idea," said Grace, feeling a bit relieved to hear Art say this, "but—be matter of fact when you say this. Don't be defensive."

Sammy interrupted, "By next week we hope to have located Stone, and to so embarrass the British Library that they will at least talk about returning the stone. I am sure they have insurance, so they can probably recoup most of their financial loss. Now I am going to leave you and Grace alone with the manuscript for a while as I must arrange the news conference. Behave yourselves."

Art rolled the scroll open and found the story he liked to call "Nick at Night," one of his personal favorites from John 3. Jesus' dialogue with Nicodemus reminded him of some of his chats and debates with Grace about the early Jews who were followers of Jesus. He read out loud in Aramaic John 3:16–17, then he translated,

> For in this way, God loved the world, that he gave his only natural Son, in order that all those believing in him might not perish but have everlasting life. Because God did not send the Son into the world in order to condemn the world, but in order to save the world through him.

Art fell silent for a moment. "You know, it's hard to understand how anyone who reads this could not realize that God loves everyone, not just the so-called elect, not just one ethnic group or another. Don't you think this text means that it's God's desire for everyone to be saved and have everlasting life? And, the essence of the mystery which brings about redemption is this self-giving of the Son. This is the way God loved a lost and dark world. But, at the same time this does not help us unless we respond. It is not just about God making a decision from before the foundations of the world. We must believe in him, we must engage freely in the relationship and trust God."

West stopped. "I'm sorry, Grace, I didn't mean to start preaching, but this is the beating heart of it all, that which most reveals God's character and our dilemma. Whenever I come to this text, I feel like I'm finally standing on solid ground with all the saints who have come before us, including Lazarus. He, above all persons, could understand that love is a transforming force that could change the world and stop the cycle of violence. Tom Robbins once wrote, 'There are many things worth living for, there are a few things worth dying for, but there is nothing worth killing for.' Can't anyone in this country stop Palestinians killing Jews and vice versa?"

Grace had just let him go on. It was rare when he really shared this deeply what he believed, and it helped her understand his credo.

"Not meaning to trivialize what you just said, but it sounds rather like the plot of the movie, *The Fifth Element*, where love is the fifth element which can save the world. In that movie, Leelu yearns for love, and Dallas learns that only true love can overcome evil."

"Yes, love conquers all. But for me, the gospel message is even more profound—Jesus, the personification of love, conquers all."

"Well," teased Grace, "let's put your theory of love to the test. My mother, a person to be reckoned with, can probably be won over if you love her cooking. Are you game to try? Would you like to join us for supper?"

"Yes, I'd be delighted to join your love feast!" laughed Art. But Grace had more than dinner on her mind.

# 39

# Call and Response

A WEARY SEDEK HADAR arrived safely back in Tel Aviv armed with new information—Stone was in the south of France. As he was riding in the taxi back to Jerusalem he pondered whom to share this information with. Should he just tell the authorities? Should he call Sammy Cohen at the IAA? Should this be anonymous or should he go public now? He decided that since he did not trust all the authorities, and trusted the IAA even less, filled as it was by Jews who were hardly ultra-orthodox, that he would leave an anonymous tip with the police.

Dialing up Jamison Parkes Law first, while riding along, he heard the phone ringing and ringing. Finally Law picked up. "Yes," he said.

"This is Sedek; mission accomplished. The stone was indeed sold to the British Library, Stone sold it, and he then went off to the south of France. The question is whom, other than you and Rabbi Menachem, should I actually tell about this? How did your interview with Glickstein go?"

Law paused and said, "Fine, although West made bail, and the IAA seems to not be all that worried about the money put in West's account. Perhaps they are stringing him along and giving him enough rope to hang himself or reveal his real role in all this. I am still thinking we are dealing with two Protestant scholars out to make some money quickly, although I am reluctant to believe this about West."

"Yes," said Sedek, "but how else do you explain the payment into West's account? Stone doesn't strike me as a generous man wanting to support the archaeological work of the good Dr. West. To the contrary, he has always been a rival of West. There must have been some sort of deal struck."

"Unless of course Stone is so malicious that he wants to mainly pin the rap on West, and get away scot free."

"I suppose that is possible, but again who do I tell this news about Stone to? It looks like your going to the press didn't produce instant confessions or results."

"You're right, you should call Shimon at the police station, but use a pay phone that can't be traced to you. Trust no one other than the Sons and the Society—do you hear me?"

"Right," said Sedek, "Shalom," and he rang off. Once he got to Jerusalem, Sedek would make the call at the bus station on the north side of town where he had asked to be dropped off. The traitors to Israel had to be smoked out.

And there was something else really worrying Hadar. If West was exonerated and was able to use the Lazarus Stone as a platform he might be able to make a compelling case for the earliness of the idea of Jesus' divinity, since he was someone who could actually raise the dead. Then West could argue by connecting that miracle to the creation of the Fourth Gospel that the earliest Gospel, written by a Jew, had affirmed such a notion. And knowing West, he would stress that affirming Jesus' divinity actually comports with the Jewishness of that Gospel!

For Sedek such an idea was anathema; it was heresy and blasphemy; it was an idea that would lead even some faithful Jews astray. And as a zealot for true Judaism, Sedek could not allow that idea to prevail. Rabbi Menachem had stressed that this idea was an extreme violation of Jewish monotheism and if necessary, it required an extreme response.

The Mashiach had not yet come to earth Sedek told himself, and so such Christian ideas about Jesus as a divine messiah should not be made appealing to Jews, especially not to a Jerusalem audience. West above even Stone, must be stopped as a promulgator of blasphemy, one guilty of besmirching the divine Name and nature. Sedek got furious just thinking about it. If the police didn't discredit and stop West, something else would have to be done before long.

Sedek could tolerate working with someone like Law because Law believed in leaving Jews alone, he believed in a two track model of salvation, of peoples of God, of prophecy and the like. But West was much more troubling and dangerous because he affirmed that Jesus had come to create only one people of God—Jew and Gentile united in Christ. Like a modern version of Saul of Tarsus, Sedek was on a mission of zeal to stop the mouths of those who blasphemed God in the Holy Land. How far he was prepared to go on this mission remained to be seen.

# 40

# Seek and Ye Shall Find

INTERPOL HAD BECOME MORE and more efficient over the years, but it was by no means infallible. Finding Patrick Stone was proving difficult on several counts. In the first place it appeared that, unlike Ray Simpson, Stone had never been fingerprinted, nor were there any mug shots of him. He seemed to have stayed on the good side of the law throughout his life, so far as one could tell.

All the evidence that the IAA and the Jerusalem police had amassed so far indicated Patrick Stone had taken the stone inscription from the tomb, arranged for the copy, smuggled it out of the country, and sold it to the British Library under false pretenses. He also took some small manuscripts from the tomb—manuscripts that ended up in a bus station locker.

Finally, the derringer was a Stone family antique. Plus, the hairs found at the scene of the crime matched those found in Stone's apartment. Stone's passport had been tracked to England but there the trail went cold. He hadn't used any credit cards. He was now wanted for stealing, forgery, selling stolen goods, and attempted murder—a one-day crime spree from a seemingly unpretentious American professor!

Everyone agreed that Ray Simpson was withholding information to protect himself and Dr. Stone. West's role in all this was not yet clear. Patience was now the plan. First, the police hoped that Stone would eventually call Raymond about the figurines—the phone was already tapped. There was no reason for Stone to suspect that Raymond had tried to flee the country—the small news article on Simpson's arrest had not made the front page of any major paper. Secondly, if Stone tried to use his real passport or a credit card, they could track him quickly.

Meanwhile, Patrick Stone was oblivious to all the ruckus he had caused. He really hadn't given Raymond a second thought. Right now he could not care less about the small manuscripts—he had a friend in Germany who would love to have those papyri. No, right now he had no rainy days on the horizon. Tuesday he had visited the bank, a car dealership, and a realtor before collapsing on the beach in the late afternoon. He never made it to the jazz club.

Having established a bank account with Credit Lyonnais in Cannes, he transferred €10 million from his Swiss account and withdrew €200,000 cash. The bank official was cordial but hardly impressed. In fact, he conveyed the impression he had already handed out more money to other individuals that very morning. Stone had certainly landed in the lap of luxury.

The first real purchase Stone made was a car—a car with class—a Mercedes-Benz CL55AMG. This car had more power than anyone could use, and a sound system that could make one go deaf rather quickly. Stone was enthralled with its ease of handling, the way it hugged the road, its leather, and polished wooden interior. He had paid over one hundred thousand Euros cash in the Cannes show room, and the dealer had not even blinked. There would be no obvious paper trail.

So, on a sunny Wednesday morning, Stone was house hunting. Everywhere by the sea and in the hillsides there were enormous homes, and he was wondering what in the world he would do with all that space. Of course, he would have his ten-thousand-plus-volume library shipped over from New Haven, and his personal effects, but that would hardly fill up even a third of some of these homes. He delighted in the idea that his mother could stay in such a palace rather than a nursing home in Tennessee. He could afford 24-7care for her now.

The road to Monaco was filled with tourists and residents enjoying the sunny summer weather. Driving down the highway, Stone finally came to the border with Monaco. He had in the seat beside him his two passports and an appointment to see a house. The realtor had shown him a number of homes from the listing book—homes so large that it would be gauche and unnecessary to list the prices. This annoyed Stone, but he realized he had to play the game by the rules. They narrowed down the choices and his realtor was able to make one Wednesday appointment—in Monaco.

The winding narrow road up the cliff was interesting to drive, and Stone remembered once seeing an auto race on TV that went through Monaco on these very roads. There had been no problem at the border checkpoint. Stone thought he looked rather chic with his Gucci leather loafers, expensive open-collared shirt complete with cravat, golf shorts, and Ray-Bans. The fact that he looked something like an over-dressed lobster, due to a severe sunburn from sitting on the beach Tuesday, never occurred to him.

The house was elegant, overlooking both the beach and a nearby castle. Best of all, however, it came with furnishings and a staff who spoke three languages! He would instantly be in business and wouldn't have to go through all the falderal of shopping. The house, pompously called Chateau Puissant, had been owned at one time by a French Duke and a Texas oil baron, but recently by an English rock star who had fallen on hard times.

Stone drove up to the huge iron gate. A voice came over the speaker box saying, "Chateau Puissant. Identify yourself, *s'il vous plait*." He took a deep breath and answered boldly, "Patrick Stone. I have an appointment."

The gate swung open and Stone drove into the most gorgeous estate he had ever seen. The lane was flanked by huge Lombardy poplars. The lawn was meticulously manicured and rolled so that there were symmetrical patterns in the grass. As he rounded the last bend, the house came into view. It took Stone's breath away. He stopped the car for a moment and just stared at the mansion partially draped in purple bougainvilleas. The old saying "Seek and ye shall find" came to mind, though doubtless Jesus, who in the same sermon had also said, "Blessed are the poor," would not have agreed with Stone's use of the text. What did Stone care now? He had landed in the lap of luxury and he meant to enjoy it—for the rest of his days.

# 41

## Meet the Press

HARRY AND ART WERE both up bright and early on Wednesday, press conference morning. Art had showered, shaved, and put on his best suit, usually used for lecturing or attending church back in the States. Harry for his part had put on his lawyer attire except that he was wearing a bright red bow tie. Harry was something of an expert at holding press conferences in Washington to announce major archaeological finds. Over breakfast, he was coaching Art.

"You need to be clear, concise, and definitive," Harry was saying. "Don't go wandering off on the importance of this, that, or the other. Make the main point the MAIN point, if you catch my drift. And by all means, defer some questions until the next press conference, which you can announce today. Has Sammy arranged for next week's press conference?"

"Yes," said Art, swigging his orange juice. "What about questions about Patrick Stone if there are any?"

"'No comment' is your answer, since he hasn't been arrested for anything yet. And keep your remarks about the money in your account to a bare minimum."

"OK, I think I've got the basics covered in regard to my own involvement in these matters. Sammy's opening remarks will include a clear statement that a person is innocent until proven guilty, and that I have not formally been charged with anything yet, hence it is OK for me to speak at this news conference."

"Good," said Harry, "you stay away from being defensive. You are to be definitive, not defensive, at this press conference—by the way, relax. I've heard you speak, you'll be fine."

Art was indeed a first-rate lecturer but he knew he could be a bit pompous and prone to exaggeration especially when he got revved-up. He would need to be on his best behavior today. Art had put together a PowerPoint presentation using his digital pictures of the tomb, the ossuary, and the inscriptions. He already had the printout, but hopefully, there would be time before the meeting to check out the laptop and run through the slides. Technology was great . . . when it worked.

The public announcement in Monday's papers, *Ha' Aretz* and the *Jerusalem Post*, would guarantee a highly professional, demanding crowd. The pressure was on. Art received a call late Tuesday night from Sammy saying all was in readiness—even the PowerPoint show was running smoothly. Golda Meir Lecture Hall on the campus of Hebrew University was ready. Art felt good about using the university setting—his natural turf.

The ride to Hebrew University was a short one, situated as it was northeast of the old city walls on Mt. Scopus overlooking the city. By the time Harry and Art got there at nine, an hour before the press conference, the parking lot was already packed full of vehicles. Fortunately, the IAA had reserved Art a space, and equally fortunately he was driving a Mini Metro, which could be shoehorned into almost any opening. The sun was climbing in the sky, and all kinds of things were about to be brought into the light of day.

Entering into the lecture hall, Art was immediately waylaid by Grace. He waved goodbye to Harry, who gave him the thumbs-up sign.

"Art, several important points before we start. Sammy has asked me to speak to the authenticity of the materials in question, in particular in regard to the Aramaic. I may have failed to tell you this but the inscription, and the script of the scroll was authenticated by no less than André Chartier."

"Yes, you told me, but that makes it a slam dunk," said Art brightly.

"This means that you need not belabor the authenticity question. Just concentrate on the time line issue, and that you were the person to discover the Bethany tomb."

"Grace, we've been over this. Please relax, even if I can't," he urged truthfully.

"Remember," said Grace slightly exasperated, "no remarks about Stone, and no more than ten minutes of questions. You are our clean up hitter, so hit a home run." Grace, like Art, was a big but long-suffering baseball fan, having grown up loving the Boston Red Sox. Thank goodness they had finally won the World Series!

"Right," said Art, his stomach beginning to churn. "You know I was once told that the only cure for nervousness before public speaking is embalming."

"None of that today, even though we are talking about the twice-dead Lazarus. Be your lively self, nothing stuffy please." With that remark they reached the platform and were met by Sammy Cohen who had been running around getting everything in order. Sammy looked a little disheveled. Grace tidied up the table while Art exchanged pleasantries and tried not to look awkward.

Grace returned and fussed over Sammy: "Straighten your tie and put on your coat and comb your hair. This deal will be on major networks in the US. Let's make the IAA look good and competent, shall we?"

Sammy blushed and straightened his tie. He wasn't going to argue with Grace when she was in "master and commander" mode. The cameras were being positioned just to the right of the stage, and huge banks of floodlights were being set up on the left, so the participants would be well-lighted but would be looking slightly to their right into the camera and away from the lights. Careful thought had gone into this entire event despite the limited time.

The next thing Art, Grace, and Sammy knew they were sitting on the podium. The IAA banner had been draped over the lectern. Sammy looked at his watch and the cameraman gave him the high sign. It was show time.

Sammy rose first, went directly to the lectern, and started slowly. "I want to first thank the Hebrew University for allowing us the use of this hall on such short notice, but in view of the fact that we are dealing with a major news story, the choice of venue was important. I also wish to thank Professors Grace Levine, André Chartier, and Arthur West who have helped the IAA in many ways since the onset of this matter. The IAA believes that Professor West should be deemed innocent until proven guilty of some crime, though we are mindful of the recent allegations, and needless to say we would not have asked him to speak today, and represent the IAA today, if we did not believe West was a trustworthy person."

"This brings us to the matter at hand. We are announcing today that the tomb of a New Testament figure, Eliezer, also known as Lazarus, has been discovered behind the church of Mary and Martha in Bethany. This discovery must be credited to Professor Arthur West who will be speaking to you about this matter shortly."

Sammy summed up with the following surprise announcement.

"I must also announce that the tomb was indeed looted Tuesday, June 1, shortly after its discovery. The original inscription over the ossuary of Eliezer was removed, and then illegally sold to the British Library. You have perhaps read of the news conference held by the British Library on Monday. It is good to know that the inscription stone is in safe hands. Unfortunately it is in the wrong hands, for the law of Israel is perfectly clear—any precious antiquity found from 1978 on becomes the property of the state of Israel and shall not leave the country, except for touring exhibits in museums which have the proper security. In short, we will negotiate with the British Library for the return of the inscription stone. The police are currently investigating the case, and hope to prosecute the perpetrator or perpetrators to the full extent of the law. I cannot comment on the investigation at this point. I will now turn things over to a leading expert in ancient Aramaic inscriptions who is both a professor at this university and works with the IAA. Will you please welcome Professor Grace Levine?"

Grace arose to a round of applause and marched directly to the podium carrying her portfolio with her. Wearing a trim gray suit with a colorful red scarf she looked professional yet classy. No rumpled academic here. Grace adjusted her red glasses and began.

"Along with the two Aramaic inscriptions in the tomb, we also found one complete document and a number of fragments of a document, all in Herodian period Aramaic. Both Professor Chartier and myself are in complete agreement that these are genuine first-century documents of inestimable value for the study of early Judaism and the rise of the Christian movement. Both the carbon dating and the epigraphical evidence are clear—the script is pre-70 Common Era Aramaic, written in a beautiful hand. All the materials are in the same hand, except the heading to the longest document. As for content, we have an early and Aramaic form of parts of the Greek Gospel of John.

I will defer to Professor West to speak more directly to the significance of this for New Testament Studies."

Grace turned and nodded to Art before continuing.

"Let me stress that these documents are the earliest Jewish-Christian documents of *any* kind, dating to before the end of Pontius Pilate's reign, which is to say before 38 of the Common Era. The IAA intends to properly house and protect these documents. A building similar to the Shrine of the Book could display the ossuary, the manuscripts, and the Lazarus stone when it is recovered and returned to its rightful owners, which, if there is any justice and fairness, will happen soon. Thank you."

Applause rang out throughout the room, and leading the charge was Grayson Johnson. He kept saying, "Go, Dr. Levine, go," under his breath. Grace Levine's word was considered Gospel when it came to her areas of expertise.

As soon as Grace was seated, Art moved to the podium, grabbed the mouse, and the first PowerPoint slide picturing the Church of Mary and Martha came up on the screen.

"Friends, I am here to tell you the story of a remarkable discovery, which unlike most such discoveries did not come after weeks of hard labor digging in the ground. On the contrary, this discovery was made on the very first day I was inspecting a tel behind this church, the Church of Mary and Martha in Bethany."

Click went the mouse.

"Here you see the tel itself. Let me be perfectly clear that this mound had not been dug at anytime before June 1. Any claims by anyone to have seen or owned the inscription stone of Lazarus before that date are clearly false. This means that the stone in question, which now is housed in the British Library, was first stolen and then sold to them. To be fair, the British Library would not have bought the stone unless they believed the accompanying documents were bona fide.

"Now we are inside the tomb and you will notice various niches in the back wall, which usually contain ossuaries or bone boxes. We do not know what happened to the bone boxes of Mary and Martha; they were not found in the tombs.

"This next slide shows an Aramaic inscription found on the roof, if you will, of one of the niches. I am indebted to Mustafa el Din, the church caretaker, for managing this excellent shot. According to this inscription, Martha was interred here in hope of the resurrection. The practice of using ossuaries for burial has to do with a strong belief in the afterlife, such that it was felt the bones should be kept together in hope of bodily resurrection. I will say more on this matter at my press conference next week.

"And here is the already famous inscription originally carved right into the limestone above the niche. Here," Art continued with another click of the mouse, "is the close-up of the stone and its inscription which reads in Aramaic, 'Twice dead under Pilatus, twice reborn in Yeshua, in sure hope of the resurrection.' It is a remarkable inscription in many ways. First, it attests to the fact that Lazarus died twice, which is to say he was raised from the dead as the Gospel story tell us, only to die a second time.

"Secondly, it attests with the 'twice reborn' reference to his spiritual rebirth through discipleship to Jesus. This is certainly the earliest attestation to early Jewish Christian beliefs about being born again. Outside of the Gospels there is nothing comparable in the works of Josephus, Philo, or in other early Jewish or Christian works that date to the first half of the first century AD. More on this next week.

"I have purposely enlarged the bottom corner of this slide that has the inscription in full view so you can see the date on it which the camera automatically stamps on the slide—notice the number 06-01-2004. This stone was still an integral part of the tomb when I took this picture Tuesday morning. Just a little aside, here. While I was in the tomb Tuesday morning, someone managed to seal *me* in the tomb for awhile. Thanks to a cell phone and the aid of Mustafa, I was not buried permanently with the saints that day!

"Anyway, here for comparison is a picture taken late Tuesday afternoon by the IAA. As you can see the stone inscription is gone. Someone stole the inscription on the very day I discovered it!

"Moving along, this is the simple ossuary of Lazarus which has a traditional patronymic inscription—Eliezer son of Simon. The name Eliezer is the ancient form of the name Lazarus—notice the similarities in the consonantal radicals or letters—L-Z-R. We know beyond reasonable doubt that this is the Lazarus of the Bible. How? First, because his tomb is located in Bethany. Secondly, because in this very same tomb we found an inscription about the burial of Martha. The chances of those two names being juxtaposed in the same tomb from the early New Testament era are slim at best."

He pushed the clicker again. "Here is the scroll which was found, not by me, but by the IAA when they took the ossuary into protective custody.

"And now we have a close up of the scroll itself, written in a beautiful linear hand in that interesting mixture of formal and cursive script that characterized Herodian period Aramaic inscriptions.

"As Professors Cohen and Levine have already stressed, we have overwhelming evidence that the Lazarus stone belongs here in Jerusalem with the other artifacts found on this site. We hope and trust the British Library will see fit to do the right thing. Thank you. We will now take approximately ten minutes worth of questions."

A lanky man with a decidedly French accent and an *International Herald Tribune* badge arose and asked, "Are you suggesting that this find attests to, or provides authentication of a miracle, the raising of a dead person?"

Taking a deep breath, Art replied, "I can't speak for my colleagues, but yes, that would be my conclusion. Now, having bone fragments of Lazarus makes clear that his resurrection was not of lasting duration. The New Testament does not claim that was the case for anyone prior to Jesus. Only Jesus received a resurrection or permanent body, but more of this next week. Next question."

A lady from the third row asked, "Do we know when these artifacts will be put on public display?" Sammy Cohen joined Art at the lectern. "Given the amount of work that needs to be done, I hesitate to predict a date."

A man from the *London Times* arose: "Has anyone contacted the British Library yet?" Sammy again answered, "Yes I have, but I cannot comment on the progress of those talks, yet."

A reporter from the *New York Times* called out, "Professor West, why were you questioned about the forged stone in the first place and would you please explain how all that money got into your bank account if you were NOT involved in selling the stone to the British Library?"

"Wednesday morning, June 2, a copy of the original Lazarus stone arrived at my door, anonymously, by courier. The alleged forger, an American named Raymond Simpson, is now in custody. As for how that money got in my bank account, I honestly and truly do not know, but I am announcing today that however it got there, I am now turning the million plus dollars over to the police. In my hands I have a banker's check," holding up the check for the camera to focus on it, "and I am now handing the full sum over to Officer Shimon of the Jerusalem police." Art walked over to the wings of the stage, and handed the check to Shimon who had been standing at the far end of the stage for security purposes. With a stunned look on his face and with his hand extended but visibly shaking, he accepted the check.

"I want nothing to do with ill-gotten gains, wherever they may have come from."

Before any more questions could be raised Sammy leaned into the microphone. "On behalf of Professors West, Levine, and the IAA, thank you for coming today. A formal press release is available."

Sammy, Grace, and Art sat looking at each other with silly grins alternating with sighs of relief. Harry approached the stage. "Well done. That will not merely preach, that will litigate."

"Spoken like a true lawyer," said Art.

Grayson rushed up gushing, "Y'all were like totally awesome. I just want to shake all your hands, and then I have to go back to the flat to keep Detective Hoffner happy. He's waitin' for that phone call, you know. Dude's bored! I play my music for him—some praise songs, Led Zeppelin, some praise songs, Boston—I think he's gettin' into it!"

Art stuck out his hand and said to Grayson, "Ah, you have a devious mind! You know, brother, I'll need someone sharp like you at the Bethany dig once all this commotion settles down. Would you be interested?"

Grayson lit up like a Christmas tree and exclaimed, "I'm there in a heartbeat!"

But another figure standing behind the cluster of lights on the right, was experiencing a far different emotion. "West is actually going to get away with this," he muttered to himself. "But he must be stopped before he goes any further in testifying to Jesus."

# 42

# Justification

PATRICK STONE HAD BEEN frankly overwhelmed by the beauty and elegance of Puissant Chateau. The staff seemed cordial, even relieved, at the prospect of having a "normal" owner as opposed to a heavy metal rocker complete with groupies. He toured every room, but fell in love with the library. For an hour he just sat in one large leather chair imagining a life in this home. Francois Boule, the agent, understood human behavior well enough to see that Stone was hooked. He busied himself with business online on his laptop until his potential buyer finally agreed to stay in town for the night.

Stone spent the rest of Wednesday relaxing in one of Monaco's finer hotels, daydreaming about life in this seemingly idyllic country. He turned off his cell phone—he didn't read the papers—he didn't watch the news. Sitting on the balcony overlooking the ocean he tried to minimize all the events of the past ten days—and nearly succeeded. It all seemed so unreal. Surely, now that the inscription was safe at the British Library all would be well. Finders keepers, after all. The British Library is brimming with artifacts from other countries. The transaction was confidential, wasn't it? And his money was protected in a Swiss bank, wasn't it? And sealing Art West in the tomb—well, any prankster could be blamed for that. Who would know other than Raymond? And the incident with El Said—well, that was just an accident. A misunderstanding. I'm sure he's recuperating just fine. And the manuscript fragments—he would return those—he didn't need the money after all.

All would be forgiven. By late Wednesday, Stone decided to become a homeowner.

Stone returned to Chateau Puissant to meet with Francois at nine o'clock Thursday morning. Once again he sat down in his already favorite leather chair in the library—a library that had bookshelves two stories high complete with moving staircase on wheels. Trying to remain cool, Stone said to the agent, "I am prepared not only to make an offer on the spot, but also to transfer the money. My banker at Credit Lyonnais is awaiting your call to authorize the immediate transfer."

"Very good, monsieur, and what would that offer be? This dream home is *tres cher*, to say the least," smiled Francois wryly.

"I am prepared to offer two million in US dollars," said Stone, his heart pounding.

"Yes, but my client needs a bit more. I am authorized to accept no less than $2.5 million and I will guarantee that the transaction can be completed swiftly and discreetly. You may have the key today."

Stone thought for a moment and concluded that he was so rich it would be beneath his dignity to haggle. He heard himself say, "I agree."

"*Trés bon*. Shall we have a celebratory toast?" Francois turned, clapped his hands and the butler came at once.

"*S'il vous plait*, two glasses of the best champagne in the cellar."

The butler nodded and left to fetch a maid. Francois continued.

"Yes, this house comes complete with a wine cellar, and well stocked I might add. The last tenant, if I may say so, was a pig who drank only cold beer. He had no palate for wine, and so the cellar has for the last four years gone largely untouched. This is a special gift to you," he said, as he popped a bottle of Moet et Chandon champagne.

The maid brought tall-stemmed dark blue glasses which were soon brimming with bubbly. "To a momentous decision," smiled Francois.

"*Salut*," answered Stone feeling tipsy even before he took a sip.

"Now let us go to my office, sign the papers and make the calls to transfer your money. I must also tell you that in order to finish the business of the day we must visit the office of the duchy, and at the same time have you sign papers making you a resident of Monaco. Citizenship can be applied for, if desired, in another year."

Stone was so numb by now that he simply followed along docile as a lamb. Hours of paperwork followed before he slowly drove back to Cannes in a daze. In the passenger seat laid a huge folder with paperwork claiming that Dr. Patrick Stone was now the proud owner of Chateau Puissant, Rue d'Rivoli, Monaco, 3PL 1XZ.

Thursday evening, after a wonderful meal and a glass of wine, Stone felt revived. Reviewing everything he had mulled over the night before, he decided to call Raymond for updates, and have him return the fragments to the tomb. No sense in being too greedy. The phone rang twice, and Grayson picked up. Avi Hoffner hovered in the background monitoring his recording equipment.

"Hello, this is Dr. Stone. I need to speak to Raymond."

"Ray's not here just now, but he left an important message for you. He wants to know your current address so he can send some kind of statues. I don't know what statues he's talkin' about," said Grayson, going along with the charade.

Stone replied, "I am surprised Raymond discussed the figurines with you. But in any case, I have decided *not* to have them sent. I wish to give Ray instructions on *returning* them."

Grayson was frantic. This conversation was not going as planned. Hoffner just encouraged him to keep talking. "Well, Ray said the figurines came from The Three Arches. Is that where you want them to go?"

"No, no! Not at all. It's far more complicated than that. I must speak with Raymond. When will he be home?" demanded Stone getting more than a little irritated and worried about the manuscript fragments.

"Relax man, Raymond's been a busy boy lately. My roomie hasn't been home much! But he sure has a bunch of stuff here he wants to send you. Where are you, if I can be so bold to ask?" replied Grayson with some creative flourishes.

"He can send my personal effects to my home in Tennessee—and business mail to Yale—he has the addresses! I have no desire to continue this conversation," replied Stone rudely.

"Don't have a cow, Dr. Stone. I'm just Grayson, the middleman. You two can work it out!" Grayson was still stalling the conversation while Hoffner traced the call. Stone, however, abruptly hung up.

What the trace revealed was an American cell phone number belonging to one Patrick Stone, not a location. Hoffner had gotten the entire conversation on tape, a conversation that clearly linked Stone to Simpson, to the statues, and to the papyri fragments. In other words, this was very damning evidence indeed for the inevitable trial. The snowball of justice had been pushed down the slope a bit.

# 43

## Mending Walls

PRECISELY AT ONE O'CLOCK London time, Wednesday afternoon, the phone rang at Oliver St. James's office in the British Library. Oliver's secretary sang out, "Halloo, St. James' office, how may I help?"

Sammy Cohen replied, "This is Professor Cohen of the IAA in Jerusalem. I need to speak with Mr. St. James please, it is urgent."

"He is in conference watching the news. Do I really need to fetch him at this moment or could he call you back?"

"We need to talk at once please," insisted Sammy. There was about a five-minute silence on the line then finally St. James got to the phone.

"Hello, this is St. James. Is this indeed Professor Cohen of the IAA?" Sammy replied in the affirmative. "I presume you are calling about the Lazarus stone. We have just finished watching a BBC copy of your press conference. I can only say that I am more than a little mortified by these revelations. We had various experts authenticate the stone, albeit quickly, and we bought it from a known academic. We checked his past before dealing with him. In addition, we have here the *bona fides* that the stone is genuine and that he purchased the stone in 1972."

"Well, unfortunately, your seller's greed has led him to commit various crimes, not the least of which is lying to you by supplying forged documents. Very cheeky, as you would say."

"Our press conference was Monday—you could have called us with a warning about what was to come. Your briefing was a bit challenging you realize. I will have to consult with our trustees and lawyers about what is to be done next. You are certain that the stone and its inscription are genuine—correct?"

"Absolutely," insisted Sammy. "But yes, you are right about one thing. We could have worked together on this. But this matter must be rectified as soon as possible."

"Remember, the terms of the agreement included protecting the identity of the seller. Again, until I hear from our lawyers . . . "

Sammy interrupted, "From our end, we believe the seller was Dr. Patrick Stone, or possibly an agent working for Stone. And our Dr. Stone would now be a millionaire, am I right?"

At that St. James actually laughed. "I can't confirm or deny! But yes, the seller pocketed a tidy sum. We have insurance, of course. What we recoup is another matter. The insurance company will only cover so-called unrecoverable sums."

Sammy pushed on, "It is imperative that we turn over the seller's name to the authorities as soon as possible. I presume funds were wired directly into an account. Can those numbers be made available to the police soon, very soon?"

"Yes," St. James promised. "The account numbers are with the confidential documents. But I will release them as soon as possible. And, I believe, the account was in a Swiss bank. That will pose some problems in terms of accessing the account and freezing the assets. But there was also some money wired to a Jerusalem bank."

"As for the Jerusalem money we have already recovered it, and are prepared to send it along in exchange for the stone. I'm sure you will do your best," said Sammy cordially. "I have no wish to spoil relations between our agencies. It is an unfortunate matter. One man nearly died, and another's reputation has nearly been ruined. But when all is said and done, we have, I believe, a wealth of fabulous artifacts to share. Maybe at some point a tour will find its way to the British Library!"

"That would be honorable end to a dishonorable beginning," said St. James.

After hanging up, Sammy thought of something more. He knew Oliver St. James to be an honest man who, like himself, was coming to the end of his fine career. This would be a humiliating way for it to end. Perhaps he could convince the IAA to give St. James something in exchange for all his trouble. Perhaps it would help to rehabilitate the image of the IAA, if the IAA engaged in an act of pure generosity.

Perhaps the IAA board would allow him to send the British Library one of the smaller papyri found in the figurines. These fragments could be displayed proudly next to Codex Sinaiticus in the manuscripts room. He would consult on this.

Sammy picked up the phone and called Grace. "I have now spoken with St. James and he really is crushed by the news. I am wondering if we can save face on both sides of the Channel, by allowing the British Library to have one of the small pieces of the Lazarus papyri? What do you think?"

Grace was fine with the idea, "A peace offering! This might pave the way for improved relations between the British Library and the Israeli Museums. May I suggest that the portion you send him is the little scroll that even Art has not looked at yet, the one with the story about the risen Jesus having breakfast at the sea with his disciples and Peter being restored to his role among the disciples. That is such a memorable story, only a few verses and one small piece of papyri, but enormously appreciated in countries of a Christian heritage."

"I knew you would have a good idea about this one, and I am going to push the trustees to get that accomplished—after we sort out the rest of this mess."

"Yes, Sammy, you are a good man," said Grace quietly, "and Wednesday was a good day for two countries."

# 44

## Mending Spirits

THE PRESS CONFERENCE HAD indeed gone well, and Art could only imagine what the headlines would be in next morning's papers. Grace and Sammy had returned to the IAA. Harry, Grayson, and Art enjoyed lunch before splitting up for the day. Plans had already been made for an evening out on the town. Now, alone for the afternoon, and very tired, Art wandered the streets of Jerusalem being trailed by the equally weary Officer Shimon. The shopkeepers in the Cardo were raking in the tourists' money despite the problems of late. Kahlil's shop was open for the first time in many days, and several people were browsing. Art saw Hannah selling a priestly stole on which she herself had stitched some Christian emblems. That's ecumenism, thought Art. "Mind if I pass through into the back."

"By all means," she said. "Our home is your home. Father will enjoying seeing you. But remember, he just got home Tuesday night."

The little apartment in the back of the shop was indeed diminutive. There were two small bedrooms—really more like cubicles—a modest-sized living area, a bathroom, and a kitchen. This was home for Kahlil and Hannah. The living room was piled high with books in at least four different languages. Kahlil might be poor in property but he was rich in soul. Seeing Art come in, Kahlil tried to get up to give him the traditional greeting, but Art said, "Please, stay where you are. We want your wounds to heal, not reopen! How's your head—inside and out!"

Kahlil laughed, "Ah yes, the bump is gone, but so is my memory still! I do dream of a shadowy figure—a familiar man—but not you, my friend, so don't look so worried! But, tell me, how did the big press conference go? Was your rhetoric sharp and compelling? What do you think will come of this?"

"The conference was a lot of fun, actually. I must admit it's a bit of a power trip talking to the press like that. Now that we have thrown down the gauntlet there could be a fairly rapid series of events. Sammy will have his hands full dealing with the British Library. He knows the director, Oliver St. James. I hope they can work together. If Patrick Stone can be found, I think we are heading for a blockbuster trial. Harry definitely wants to be involved. I wonder if Stone knows how much trouble he's caused. Someday, I hope he realizes the mess he created."

"*Insha'Allah*," said Kahlil, invoking God's will. "My friend, once we get past the trial what is next for you? You lacked funds for this season anyway. It will likely be too late to start another dig this summer, and Hannah has no longer been able to keep from me that you received a huge sum of money which you then turned over to the police. Are you still a suspect?"

"You're right, of course, about the summer season of digging, but I plan to spend the rest of the summer studying the scroll, determining in what ways the text we have differs from the Gospel of John and in what ways the Greek text is just a translation of the original or paraphrase at least. This will keep me out of any more trouble! I am still a suspect, suspected of being a collaborator with Stone, I suppose. But enough of my exploits. You came home from the hospital when—Tuesday night? That's impressive! What does the doctor say?"

"Apparently, I was becoming too difficult to keep! The doctor—he gave up—sent me home. He says rest and more rest, but that is all I have been doing lately. I yearn to do something meaningful before I start getting into mischief!"

"Do you think I could persuade you and Hannah to come with me to Le Jazz Hot tonight? Do you even like jazz? Sammy, Grace, and Harry are coming. I've already reserved a table for supper and the early show. We promise to have you home before ten."

"Sounds like a joy to me, let me ask my boss—Hannah!" Kahlil's booming voice reverberated through the shop. She came running.

"Slow down dear; can I persuade you to go to dinner and hear some music tonight. I promise to behave—no whirling dervish dances or the like."

Hannah was obviously tempted. "Well, the doctor did say that the healing of your soul was as important as the healing of your body, so perhaps this will be good thing. We will be home early?"

"Definitely," promised Art. Hannah went back to dealing with customers, and Art offered, "Can I get you some cold juice out of the refrigerator?"

"Hah, you know my pleasures," laughed Kahlil. The two friends sat sipping cherry juice and Art explained that tonight the great James Carter, an American saxophonist, would be playing at the club doing an all John Coltrane tribute.

"Coltrane is my favorite. He was the most amazing and spiritual saxophone player. He's also from my hometown in North Carolina. In honor of your coming home I have brought you some music—John Coltrane's *Ballads*. Can I play it while we talk?"

"By all means," said Kahlil. "The player is over there on the bookshelf."

Art slipped the cassette into the slot, pressed the play button, and immediately the soothing tones of "Say it (Over and Over Again)" came through the speakers. Art turned the volume to a level where the music could be appreciated with the conversation. Art had remembered that Kahlil only had an antiquated cassette recorder so he had bought the cassette after looking a long time for the right one on Ben Yehuda Sttreet.

"So, will your business pick up again?"

"I suppose so," said Kahlil. "It will take some time. When you are closed too long your competition gains the upper hand. But just in the last few hours several old friends—Israelis, Palestinians, tourists—have come in and made a point of buying something. They heard about my adventure, and Hannah says we have already had a full day's worth of sales. Imagine that!"

"As one of my friends likes to say, 'God is good, all the time.'"

"Yes, if only *people* were as well, it would be a happier world."

"Kahlil, I realize this is a difficult subject, and you must forgive me for asking, but in my prayers I'm concerned for Hannah. Is she alright?

She clings to you. She needs a few more friends. Is Sarah her only other friend?"

"Sarah is a wonderful girl, but very busy at the Porch. Believe me, many times I have encouraged her to have a life of her own, but it actually hurts her feelings when I say anything. She feels like I am hinting I don't want her around any more, which is the opposite of the truth. It's just I want her to be happy, even when I am long gone."

"She is the ultimate faithful daughter. I'll keep praying for her." After about another thirty minutes of cordial chat, Art rose to go, saying, "I have one errand to run before we go out tonight. Harry has a nice rental car that is bigger than my car, so he and I will come by and collect you after a while. It will be fun, but please if you get weary, you will tell us, and we can come home early."

Kahlil assured, "If the music is this soothing and pleasant, I may just fall asleep at the club!"

Art left quietly, smiling at Hannah as he went by. He walked out into the market to find a shop that sold Turkish Delight, a confection rather like gum drops only in inch-square cubes. "The rosewater flavored kind please," said Art who knew that Camelia especially loved this sweet treat. Art was thinking maybe this might smooth over some of the bumpy spots between Grace and her mother. Dinner Tuesday night had been a bit strained. But tonight was a night to celebrate—the successful press conference and Grace's birthday!

When he arrived at Grace's apartment he saw the red Mazda parked in its usual spot. He could also hear chatter coming from the open kitchen window on the second floor. Grace and her mother were in animated discussion about something, hopefully not her love life again.

Art hid the candy and a card behind his back, and rang the doorbell. "Who is it?" called Grace through the speaker.

"Oh, nobody special," teased Art. The buzzer went off. Art entered, climbed the stairs, and met Grace waiting at the door. Upon entering, Camelia came out of the kitchen. She liked Art, though of course she thought, "If only he was a good Jewish boy and not a goy."

Art began cheerfully, "Miss Camelia, thank you again for dinner last night. But I must tell you, your daughter did a splendid job at the press conference today—and on her birthday no less! Anyway, I have brought a little something for you two to share." He produced the box of

Turkish Delight. Camelia immediately melted and Grace smiled a wry grin and wagged her finger at Art and said "You!" He then produced a card from behind his back. He had practiced a little speech: "You know what W. C. Fields once said about birthdays?"

"No, but I have a feeling I am about to find out," smiled Grace.

"Be careful, too many of those things can kill you!" Grace burst out laughing, and Camelia stifled a giggle as well.

"Now I first have to show you, Camelia, the card that Grace got me for my last birthday. Yes, I saved it!" The front cover had a picture of an ancient papyrus with a broken jar next to it. Inside, the card read, "Good news, we found your birth certificate!"

"Here, Grace, this card's for you," said Art.

The outside of the card pictured a beautiful sunset on the Sea of Galilee. There was a small boat sailing on the sea that seemed to be gliding off into the west. Grace opened the card and read, "Others age with grace, but you are grace personified. Happy Birthday. Every Blessing, Art."

Grace looked up, and in a rare vulnerable moment gave her mother and Art both a hug. Art felt led to say, "Now listen you two, eat the Turkish Delight and maybe it will help you be sweeter to each other." They both nodded as they stuffed their mouths with the first pieces of the rosewater-flavored treat.

Art then asked, "Miss Camelia are you sure you won't come join us at the jazz club, we won't be late?"

"No," said Camelia, "I never much liked jazz, unless it was of a klezmer sort. You folks go on and have a good time."

"Time to hit the road, birthday girl. We have some celebratin' to do! We are going to the jazz club with some special guests! I'll let you be surprised later." Art waved goodbye to Camelia who was hanging out the window, and Grace waved as well.

"You are such a smoothie," said Grace. "How did you know things had been bumpy at home?"

"Men's intuition," said Art in a sassy voice. They road off to pick up Harry and the El Saids for a night on the town. Sammy would join them if work allowed. Healing and mending come in many forms. As Shakespeare once said, "Music soothes the savage breast." Even Officer Shimon, who had trailed them to the club, relaxed and enjoyed the music.

# 45

## Big Breaks

SAMMY COHEN WAS A man on fire working late into the night. That same day, St. James rose to the occasion, pushing the paperwork and cutting through the red tape all day. Hopefully, by Friday the Swiss bank assets of Stone—wherever he was—would be frozen. At eight o'clock, Sammy got a surprising phone call from Levi Shimon. Stone's real passport had been used to leave Monaco that very afternoon. At nine o'clock, Sammy got a shocking phone call from Avi Hoffner. Patrick Stone himself had tried to call Ray Simpson. He had already learned that Stone had been in the south of France.

Despite the late hour, Cohen couldn't resist. He personally visited Ray Simpson, still sulking behind bars. Sammy and Officer Shimon relayed the news that it was only time now before Stone would be brought back to Jerusalem. If Ray was willing to cooperate there could be a lighter sentence for him, perhaps even parole. Simpson seemed amenable for the first time to talk deal.

Art was sitting at home in front of his computer. He realized that if he was going to really make an impact with his press conference next week he must marshal his evidence as judiciously as possible. Too many in the academic world had closed their minds to the concept of miracles a long time ago. It was an odd phenomenon though. Academics pretended to be broad-minded or open to new ideas, but in fact most people, including Art, were committed to their own presuppositions and interpretations.

Art learned long ago that fundamentalism was not a theological position; it was a mindset. There could be fundamentalist liberals who shut out the concept of miracles on an *a priori* basis. He had studied the arguments: "Such things don't happen now, and so they have never happened"; or, worse still, "Since I have never experienced a miracle, miracles can't happen." Of course, at the other extreme are fundamentalist conservatives who rarely entertain the notion that anything natural can happen without a miracle. Thus, they emphasize a literal seven-day creation over any sort of natural evolution.

Anachronism, the reading back into the Bible modern interpretations, is just as much a sin of fundamentalist liberals as of fundamentalist conservatives. How then was Art going to present the truth about Lazarus's resurrection in a winsome way without turning off most of his audience? How could he inform the people without sounding like he was preaching to them in a condescending way? In fact, if he was perceived as preaching, he could be in hot water with the Israeli law that forbade proselytizing of Jews and other non-Christians. He wanted to do something that glorified God and edified human beings, even unbelievers. He did not want to be obnoxious for Jesus.

Art took a few minutes just to pray through this situation. He began to see a way forward. He would talk first about the rise of the concept of resurrection in early Judaism, and how widely the idea was believed by Pharisees and other early Jews. He would stress the Jewishness of the idea. Yes, this was the right approach in Jerusalem. Jerusalem was going to hear a lot of interesting things in the next few weeks.

Returning to the kitchen, Art fetched two glasses of sherry—a nightcap.

He handed one to Harry and they sat reminiscing about the great concert Wednesday night. Harry admitted he was feeling better about his relationship with Sammy Cohen. The phone rang at ten-thirty—it was Sammy.

"I know it's late Art—if you were planning on sleeping, this news won't help!" he began laughing. "Patrick Stone tried to contact Raymond tonight. Your friend Grayson handled the call just fine. But there's more. We've been looking in England—that's the last time his real passport was used—but now we have word he has been somewhere in Monaco and the south of France as well. We are closing in."

"Wow, Monaco!" exclaimed Art. "I must admit the guy has good taste! Thanks for the news. What's next?"

"The long, slow process of searching the area, hoping he doesn't fly off again, and getting extradition papers for France and Monaco."

"Sounds complicated. It's late. You must be exhausted. I'll check with you tomorrow." Both men signed off.

Art turned to Harry, "The snowball is rolling faster down the hill, and it's surely going to melt soon!"

"Yes," said Art, "but the question is, am I going to be entangled in this prosecution or extricated from it, since I had nothing to do with this theft and sale of the stone?"

"Patience," said Harry, "things have a way of working out."

"Unfortunately, it's not one of my virtues," sighed Art.

# 46

## Stone at Home

PATRICK STONE AROSE FRIDAY, packed his bags, paid his tab, and revved his engine for a trip back to Monaco. This time, the Chateau gates opened for its new owner. He arrived in time for afternoon tea on the terrace. Anjolie brought him fresh shrimp salad in an avocado shell, a glass of local white wine, and the recent editions of the papers—it was time to catch up on the news.

Stone tended to read the papers back to front, doing the crossword and the comics first, leafing through the sports and the business news, and finally looking at the dreary and depressing headlines. He came to Thursday's headlines. At that moment, he choked and spent the next minute trying to stop coughing while he wiped his eyes.

On page one of every major newspaper to be found in Monaco there was a story about the Lazarus stone and the other related artifacts.

*The Times of London*: "Stone Stolen: Museum Hoodwinked"

*The NY Times*: "Lazarus Stone Raises Legal Issues"

*The International Herald Tribune*: "Lazarus Stone Real, but Not the Deal"

Reading the articles closely now he noticed that his name was nowhere mentioned, thankfully, but the story did say that the British Library was cooperating with the Jerusalem authorities. Reading on, he discovered a quotation from the Jerusalem press conference—"prosecute to the full extent of the law." Stone murmured to himself, "I'm a US citizen. The long arm of the Jerusalem law can't stretch this far. Besides, they don't even know I'm here. I haven't used my real passport since London, or any credit cards. How can they find me?" He was wrong about that, for he had forgotten to use his fake passport at the Monaco border so preoccupied was he with he thoughts about the house.

All the same, he decided he would go ahead and transfer the rest of his millions into his Credit Lyonnais account, because he remembered that St. James had his Swiss bank account number. Going back into the house to the library where he had set up his laptop he hopped on the internet, went to the bank website, punched in his access code and account number and the following message came up ACCESS DENIED: ACCOUNT FROZEN. A wave of panic hit Stone and his thoughts began to race in various directions.

Thus far he had paid $2.5 million for the house, $100,000 plus on the car, and who knows how much on hotel tabs, food, clothes and the realtor's fees. He had been informed that the upkeep on the house and the staff cost $10,000 a month. There were in addition the usual expenses like gas, food, heating, and cooling, not to mention the enormous insurance premiums.

When Stone calmed down he figured he still had plenty of money left from the $10 million he had transferred into Credit Lyonnais. He knew the Swiss Bank would never give out the number of the account into which the money had been shifted. They were famous, or infamous, for stonewalling such requests. Nevertheless, he decided he had best retain an attorney, so on the advice of his butler he called a local firm, chatted for a while with one of the barristers, promised to send in a retainer fee, and felt altogether better. Let the world fuss and fume, he was safe here in his fortress, his Chateau Puissant, his powerful home.

Authorities on both sides of the French border with Monaco were busy Friday after being alerted to the possibility of an alleged international criminal in their midst. Extradition papers were being drawn up. The Duchy especially had no desire to harbor a rich thief in a nation full of rich people worried about neighbors who steal stuff. Should Dr. Stone use his real passport again, they would be ready.

A weekend of intense detective work determined that one Dr. Patrick Stone had purchased Chateau Puissant in Monaco just three days earlier. A very unhappy Francois Boule was obliged on Sunday to open his files and reveal details about his client. Stone lived alone. Boule described a quiet man happy just to sit in a library. He knew Jacques, the butler, quite well. Quiet phone calls were made to the estate. The coast was clear; all was ready.

Sunday evening at eight o'clock, Stone was taking a bubble bath in a huge porcelain claw-foot tub. He had nearly dozed off and never heard the police enter the room. Stone opened his eyes to see a gun pointing at his face!

Stone screamed.

"Dr. Stone, please step out of the tub, here is your robe." Stone was in such shock that he actually did what he was told like a robot. He was taken to his bedroom, told to dress and then handcuffed with his arms behind his back.

The staff, having been roused by Jacques, was lined up at the main door. Anjolie cried—she rather liked the little man. Stone was marched out, put in the back of the police van, and driven off. All the paperwork being in order, Stone was turned over to the Israeli authorities, who had a jet waiting at the airport. Tel Aviv was a short flight away, where yet another police van was waiting. So too were the press—and the presses were held long enough to roll with the story and photos of Stone's capture. But would he implicate Art West, or blame him entirely? Thus far he remained silent, as a stone.

# 47

## Jacta Alea Est

SAMMY COHEN BOUGHT EVERY paper he could find at Steinmatsky's on Ben Yehuda and took them to work early Monday morning. Grace had already arrived.

The *Jerusalem Post* reported, "Stone Caught with His Pants Down."

*Ha'Aretz* in modern Hebrew read, "Stone Wiped Clean."

The *International Herald Tribune* led with, "Stone Turned Over to Jewish Authorities."

"I reckon this begins to redeem our honor," he said to Grace.

"Not until the trial sorts things out," she replied cautiously.

"You sure do know how to take the fun out of things," he said grumpily. "I am on my way to the jail to interview our Dr. Stone. It should be a most enlightening morning."

By mid-morning, Sammy was on the phone with the local authorities. Judge Joshua Dershowitz had set a pre-trial hearing for Thursday, and it was clear that the Israeli court system was clearing its dockets to make room for an expeditious trial. There would be no delaying motions slowing down this juggernaut. Patrick Stone, of course, was entitled to expert legal counsel, and it would take time for him to choose a lawyer and prepare for trial. Stone had been savvy enough and had enough wits about him to demand a trial by jury, since he was an American citizen.

Sammy had spoken with the firm of Levi, Levi, and Strauss and they had informed him that they were the team selected to prosecute

.Stone. The senior partner, Mr. Benjamin Levi, told Sammy that the best way to head off extradition to Britain was to make clear to Judge Dershowitz that the crimes Stone had committed occurred right here in Jerusalem, with the exception of selling the inscribed stone to the British Library. Sammy quite agreed. He also informed Benjamin that Harry Scholer, an American lawyer and expert in antiquities, was in town and familiar with the case. Mr. Levi agreed to invite Harry to work with him and come to the pretrial hearing. Sammy was feeling good about his mended relationship with Harry. He called Art and invited them both to the IAA office.

Sammy's secretary ushered them both in as soon as they arrived. Sammy handed the papers to Harry and Art, who remarked, "Well, they got their man. It sounds as if it was humiliating though—the butler must have known Stone was still in the tub! How did he get caught?"

"I interviewed Stone this morning. He had two passports—one real, and one not. Thursday Interpol tracked down the information that he had just purchased a house in Monaco, complete with street address! Trust me, Stone is genuinely in shock at having been caught. He's either very naive or very stupid!"

After rehashing all the news stories and Sammy's interview, Harry exclaimed, "*Jacta alea est!*" Art smiled, and remembered his years taking Latin in senior high school. Julius Caesar, crossing the Rubicon, cries out, "Let the dice fly!" Indeed many in Jerusalem would be riveted to the trial for the next few weeks. For this very reason Art had decided to have his press conference on the Lazarus findings just before the trial began, otherwise it would receive little notice at all in the aftermath of the trial.

Lunchtime was approaching. Harry and Sammy agreed to continue their conversation over local Mediterranean delicacies. Art decided to join Grace, busy working on manuscripts for the day. He caught her in the midst of examining the smaller papyri fragments from the Lazarus tomb.

"I've decided to do the press conference before the trial, giving my lecture on the religious implications of the Lazarus scroll this week. It's just too much competition to wait until later. I've notified the press I will do this day after tomorrow, and Hebrew University is amenable. Will you come and introduce me?" said Art.

"Of course. This is a wise move in my judgment, as Jerusalem is going to be talking about this trial and its outcome for a long time. Hey, I've discovered lots of surprising details about these little manuscripts. Care to spend the afternoon here?"

"Absolutely, but let me ring up Hannah. I want to know if they've seen the papers and how Kahlil reacted." Art called the shop. Hannah was excited. Her words tumbled over themselves.

"You will never guess what happened this morning. When I showed the picture on the front page of the Palestinian paper to my father, he cried out, 'There he is! I remember him now! He is the man who shot me!'"

Hannah rushed on. "But I said to father, 'We have shown you this picture before! Why now do you remember?' All he said was, 'I don't know, my daughter, but Allah's will be done!'"

Art turned to Grace. "I have some surprising details for you too," he laughed and related his conversation with Hannah.

For the rest of Monday afternoon, Grace and Art enjoyed pouring over the Aramaic of the Lazarus documents. Grace brought out the fragment of John 21 with the story of the breakfast by the sea.

"Notice that this fragment is in the same hand as the main manuscript, but the fragment that tells the tale of the demise of the Beloved Disciple, right at the end of John 21, may be in another hand. The last few verses, 23 to 25, certainly are in another hand. Note the part that reads,

> But Jesus did not say that he would not die; he only said,
> "If I want him to remain alive until I return, what is that to you?"

"Plus, the following verses about the Beloved Disciple writing these things down and there not being enough books to contain Jesus' stories are clearly by the later hand. The comment about thinking the Beloved Disciple would not die before the second coming makes good sense, assuming the Beloved Disciple was Lazarus and had been raised from the dead. You can see the disciples thinking, Jesus had already raised him from the dead, surely he would not die again. It must have been something of a shock when he did die again."

"I agree," said Art, "and I have been pondering another mystery. We have no fragments of the so-called prologue that begins John's Gospel. When was it added? Apparently it was added by the final editor of the Gospel sometime later, and perhaps in a very different venue. The logos hymn is profound and reflects on the idea that the divine Son of God existed before all time, helped in making all of creation, and then took on flesh himself and became Jesus. It is the kind of philosophical reflection one might expect in the Diaspora, when there was concern to witness to Gentiles who knew Plato and Aristotle but did not know the Old Testament. And here's another interesting and tantalizing clue. You remember the story about Jesus speaking to the Greeks, probably Greek-speaking Jews? In this Aramaic manuscript it makes clear that Jesus is speaking to Jews from the Diaspora present in Jerusalem for the festival who speak Greek, but in the Gospel of John it is ambiguous, it could actually refer to Greeks, or Gentiles in general."

"Fascinating," said Grace. "Do you think then that Lazarus knew he was coming close to the end, and that while he had written down individual stories all along during his life—stories say like the woman caught in adultery—that when he sought to compose his memoirs, he had way too much material for one piece of papyrus, and so many of the stories got left out—he had to pick and choose? This is what John 21:25 suggests—frustration due to the limitations of working with a papyrus. If the writer of that verse had been dealing with a codex, a book to which leaves could be added, then we might not have that verse added by the editor."

"No, and now we clearly know that the Beloved Disciple, Eliezer, had other tales to tell, but they wouldn't fit in this papyrus. We are just fortunate to have what we have. This is going to revolutionize Gospel studies, and historical Jesus studies.

"Suppose for a minute, Grace, that the earliest image of Jesus we have is the image in the Fourth Gospel. I have argued that this is perfectly possible since this Gospel bears a clear resemblance to other early Jewish wisdom literature like the Wisdom of Solomon and Sirach. The so-called high Christology of this Gospel is not the residue of a long evolution of thinking about Jesus that started with the idea he was a man and finished with the idea he was divine as well as human. Suppose again this Gospel is the earliest portrait of Jesus. Then what? It certainly shoots the Jesus Seminar ideas about Jesus all to pieces."

"Yes," said Grace, "and most contemporary Jewish ideas about Jesus receive a pretty good challenge as well. I am going to go back and read through Wisdom of Solomon, Sirach, and this Gospel again and see what I can come up with. I'll let you know whether I think it is possible this is the earliest Gospel tale."

"But Grace, on the basis of the textual evidence we now know beyond reasonable doubt that this is the earliest Gospel material. One can say that it involves the perspective of a unique person and therefore a unique perspective, but one can't question the timing, I don't think. This means too that the divine and human Jesus portrayed for instance in Paul's letters, say in Philippians 2:5-11, is not a creation of Paul, who in any case was writing in the fifties, not after the eyewitnesses had all died off."

"Well," said Grace, "it's a theory. I'll think about it. I just have a hard time getting my mind wrapped around the idea of monotheistic early Jews thinking of Jesus, a real human being, as God, or divine. I mean Jesus was a real human being, not like the Jewish notion of two powers in heaven, God and Metatron. As Acts 17 says, 'We will talk about these things . . . another time.'"

The small article that appeared on the first page of *Ha' Aretz* on Tuesday morning announced that Professor West would be lecturing at 10 a.m. on Wednesday morning on the theological and historical implications of the Lazarus tomb artifacts. It caught the attention of many, including the TV crews already arriving for the trial. But by far the most important person who noticed this article lived on the north side of Jerusalem, cut out the article tacked it to his bulletin board, and wrote over it THIS MUST BE STOPPED NOW.

# 48

## The Siegal Has Landed

S IMON SIEGAL WAS MINDING his own business sitting in his favorite café in Harvard Square, drinking an iced latté, and checking the headlines on his laptop. A photo of an American citizen, a Yale professor, arrested and extradited to Jerusalem on charges of theft, forgery, and attempted murder certainly caught his attention. Here was a legal situation that made anyone sit up and take notice.

Standing 5' 9" tall with curly hair, some said he looked like Billy Crystal. Simon Siegal had a propensity to talk at 900 miles an hour with a thick New England accent. His detractors called him "Simon Siegal, the legal beagle" but he wouldn't have generated such responses if he hadn't become a very high profile lawyer who loved to throw himself into high profile cases. He wasn't an ambulance chaser but the analogy with piranha in a feeding frenzy described pretty aptly how he normally behaved in courtroom. Simon loved both the challenge and the spotlight.

Siegal was born and raised in Portland, Maine, and did his schooling through college in that northernmost New England state. He went to Harvard Law School on a full-ride scholarship. After some years of being part of a law firm in Boston, Simon was asked to join the American Civil Liberties Union, an offer he could hardly refuse as it gave him the opportunity to be involved in some of the most interesting cases imaginable.

He had successfully defended all of the following sorts of people: 1) African-Americans fired from jobs apparently because of their race; 2) a Klan member denied the right to attend a major university because of his politics and racial opinions; 3) a prominent rap star on trial for using obscene gestures and even more obscene lyrics at concerts.

On the downside, he was still smarting over a recent loss. His client, a major tobacco company, was now required to pay out huge sums in a class action suit by cancer victims. He would like to be "The King of Torts," as John Grisham put it, but his path took him in another direction. While he had won more detractors than admirers in most of those trials, he had also gained a reputation of being able to defend the indefensible. What was perhaps most interesting about Siegal on this morning is that for a period of three years right after law school Siegal had gone to Israel and had been first a law clerk and then a lawyer in the Israeli court system before beginning his Boston job.

Today, Siegal had no official plans—he was on vacation hoping to visit family and friends in the New England area. He made a spontaneous decision to use his influence to contact the Israeli authorities and offer his legal services to one Patrick Stone. This case was too juicy to ignore. His mind was already working on how he would defend Stone in the Israeli system. For now, however, he started a list: return to his apartment, contact his buddies at ACLU, pack, and catch the last flight to Tel Aviv—yes, Monday, June 14 had now become a major calendar event.

Monday night's trans-Atlantic flight proved bouncy—but he arrived in Tel Aviv about 3 p.m. Tuesday. On the flight, Siegal tracked the story over the Internet and knew that the pre-trial hearing was scheduled for Thursday morning. He would need to act fast. While waiting for his baggage at Tel Aviv airport, Siegel called the authorities.

"Jerusalem police, how may I direct your call?"

"Yes, this is Mr. Simon Siegal of the United States. Dr. Patrick Stone's new lawyer. I have just arrived from Boston. I need to speak to my client immediately!" said Siegal with all the power he could muster. Siegal realized his chances were slim of getting Stone himself, but he also knew he would get someone's attention just by mentioning the name. Surprisingly, Patrick Stone himself was put on the line!

"Hello, is this really Simon Siegal?"

"Yes, and Simon says he is here to represent you!"

Stone's response was instantaneous for he had heard much about Siegal and knew his reputation, "Wow! I convinced the police here that you really were my lawyer, even if you weren't on record yet. I figured it was either the real you or someone at least interesting to talk to. That was quite a bluff on your part! When can you start?"

"I already have," said Simon. "I'll be in Jerusalem in about one hour. Until I arrive, and from now on, say nothing to anyone, got it? Wednesday morning, first thing, I will see the judge. Then I will visit you. So, for now, just sit tight."

"Right!" exclaimed Patrick, his spirits reviving a bit. Perhaps there was hope after all.

"Oh, one more thing, we need cash," reminded Siegal.

"You will have to check all my accounts—Tennessee, Connecticut, Switzerland, Cannes—who knows what's left?" said Stone, once again dejected, "There should be plenty still in the Credit Lyonnais account."

"I'll look into it," said Siegal, "We will need secretaries and detectives to gather information. I would rather not engage a firm here to help me. There are some people here I can call on; I once worked in this legal system and know it fairly well."

Even if he couldn't get Patrick Stone exonerated, he could go for lesser charges, a lighter sentence—the legal limit. Siegal's name would be in the news for some time.

Siegal rented a car, drove to Jerusalem and checked into the Seven Arches Hotel in time for a late dinner. True, it was a touristy spot, but he loved the view of the city from atop the Mount of Olives. Standing on the front steps, he looked across the Kidron Valley at the Dome of the Rock gleaming golden in the sunset. The city looked awash in twilight and shadow. Peaceful enough, now. Tomorrow Siegel would spread his legal wings. Thursday he would land in the courtroom.

# 49

## The Siegal System Versus
## the Legal System

JUDGE JOSHUA DERSHOWITZ HAD been on the bench for many years and had gained a reputation for being tough on crime, while staying within the spirit of the law. Carrying his briefcase and computer bag, Siegal announced himself to the Judge's secretary, "I am Simon Siegal, attorney-at-law, and I need to see Judge Dershowitz urgently as I am representing Patrick Stone."

The secretary spoke into her call box and relayed the message. "Please have a seat and help yourself to a cherry Danish while you are waiting."

"Don't mind if I do," said Siegal. In about fifteen minutes Siegal was summoned. Wiping crumbs from his mouth with a handkerchief, he marched forward into battle.

Simon had met Dershowitz once many years ago when Simon was just a law clerk, and Dershowitz was not yet a judge. Simon had been impressed with the tenacity of the man in the search for something resembling truth and justice. They shared a number of cases at that time. But now both men were much older and more seasoned, and it would be interesting to see how they would interact—the irresistible force meets the immovable object. Something had to give.

Dershowitz looked up from his desk, stood as Siegal came in, and said "*Shalom alechem*," to which Siegal responded, "*Alechem shalom.*"

"I see you haven't forgotten your Jewish manners. Please have a seat Mr. Siegal, make yourself comfortable. You are here about the Patrick Stone matter?"

"Yes, indeed your honor, and I'm impressed that you remember me."

"I do indeed. First, let me tell you that I have spoken with the US ambassador and he understands and accepts the need for justice to be done in this case here in Israel. The US government will not be intervening on Dr. Stone's behalf. He got himself into this hot water, and it appears it will be your job to try and extricate him from his legal quagmire. Do you intend to do this solely on your own?"

"At this point, yes, but I'm keeping other options open. I presume my client cannot be tried here for any crime he allegedly committed in England."

The judge pondered this and said, "Yes, you are right. Currently, he is being charged with forgery, attempted homicide, and theft of an antiquity. That's a legal bundle for now. I'll have my secretary give you a copy of the formal charges. The British authorities will want to try him for fraud. They are currently out of a great deal of money—insurance is pending of course."

"Yes, that is an interesting list of allegations," said Siegal smiling. "The pre-trial hearing is Thursday morning, I believe. I hope you will give me sufficient time to prepare my case."

"No more, no less, than the usual. If you need more time, then I suggest you hire more help or, better yet, work with one of our excellent legal offices."

Siegal realized at this point that Judge Dershowitz would not appreciate an American stealing the limelight. He decided to gracefully bow out of the office.

Siegal had never been in this police building in Jerusalem because it was relatively new. However, when he arrived at the jail itself it looked anything but new. He noted the primitive conditions and the lack of air conditioning. His brain put this item in the credit ledger for the trial. Maybe he could allege poor treatment of Stone in general, or in particular for his US citizenship.

Siegal waited in an interrogation room until Stone was brought in. The guard left them alone and waited outside the door. Siegal began, "First of all we must try to clean you up and make you look good for the papers for the pre-trial hearing tomorrow. Have you any other clothes?"

"Well, some of my belongings are still in my apartment. I left quickly with just two suitcases. Anything decent, well it's all back in Monaco."

"Fine, I will go get you a suit. Just write down your measurements. I will also bring you the necessary toiletries. You must look your best. There will be a lot of press nosing about and taking pictures. I need to ask you a few questions if I may? These questions will help me determine how to pursue the case and you must be candid with me."

"OK," said Stone with a sigh, realizing that nothing he was about to say was great for his case.

"Did you or did you not shoot Kahlil El Said?" asked Siegal.

Patrick began to relive the horror. "Yes, I did. We had had an argument in his shop on Tuesday, June first, and he refused to help me broker the Lazarus stone. I followed him later that night waiting for a good place to talk to him. He sat down on a bench in the park behind the Shrine of the Book. I intended to reason with him—and threaten him if necessary to sell the stone. At the least I wanted him to keep silent about my having the stone. I drew my derringer to scare him. The foolish man grabbed my hand! The gun went off—I didn't even know it was loaded. He fell on me, grazing his head on the hard park bench on the way down. My arm was trapped under him. He is a very large man. I panicked, yanking my arm out from under him. I left the little derringer behind."

"So the prosecution, may in fact have some fingerprints of yours from the derringer, right?"

"I suppose, I didn't mean to hurt him, you know."

"OK, tell me about your derringer?"

"It's a Civil War antique—belonged to my father. It only has one shot and only works at close range. Not very deadly I guess. I didn't mean to hurt him, you know."

"You keep saying that. Third question, did you or did you not steal the Lazarus stone from the tomb?"

"Oh yes. Stupid I realize, but after all those years of being treated like an also-ran compared to people like Arthur West—just looking at that stone—it was incredible. My teaching assistant, Ray Simpson, followed Art West when he was scouting out the tel behind the church in Bethany. He rang me when he was sure Art had found something. I got to the scene and West was already in the tel discovering this, that, and the other. I got angry. Simpson and I decided to entomb him—just to scare him." Stone started laughing inanely.

"You didn't really answer my question, Dr. Stone. But let's talk about Simpson—was he in on this from the beginning?"

"Well, he agreed to follow Art West. That's not kosher either, is it? Anyway, he agreed to help me entomb West. I convinced Ray it was a prank—to get him back for whatever. We figured he'd get out quickly enough—I planned to come back and check on him."

"And you did go back, right?"

"Yes, around 11:30. I went alone. West was already gone—I guess the cemetery ghosts really scared him away! The opening wasn't even closed up tight—sloppy work on West's part. I think he got help from the church caretaker. I saw him earlier. Anyway, I photographed the inscription. I chiseled out the stone."

"Finally. For the record, who made the copy of the stone and sent it to West?"

"Like I said, I took good pictures. And Ray is good at making copies. He knew I got that stone from the tomb, however. I didn't even have to tell him. He's not stupid. But he made the copy. I had him bring it to a courier and ship it to Art West to arrive Wednesday morning."

"I have already made sure that any charges related to acts in the U.K. have been excluded. So, are there any other shady things done here in Israel I need to know about?"

"Well, there's the papyri!"

"What, there's more?"

"Oh yeah, I found a small jar in an empty niche. It was full of manuscript fragments. You won't believe what I did with those." Stone started giggling again.

Siegal groaned as Patrick explained how he hid the manuscripts in the figurines before fleeing to the UK with the inscription.

"What have I gotten myself into?" thought Siegal. How could this mild-mannered professor, who never did anything wrong before, get himself into so much trouble?

"Very good," said Siegal, although he was really thinking, very bad, indeed. "Let's get ready to rumble. I'm going shopping for you and will be back later in the day. I'm hoping they will let me interview Raymond today. Do you have any friends or family that can come and support you?"

"No, there's no one. Thanks so much, I could use a friend right now," said Stone politely, hardly looking like a criminal of any sort.

But Siegal had already requested to be let out. He was in motion. So was this case—and that was all that mattered to him.

# 50

## Pressing Things Too Far

T HE PRESS CONFERENCE WAS to be at nine o'clock Wednesday morn- ing in order to provide time for filing stories. Art decided to wear his best suit, a navy blue silk suit, and his yellow tie with the navy stripes. Grace would be introducing him on the platform; Harry was not able to attend because of legal work in preparation for the trial. When Art got to the University, Grayson was there anxious to speak with him. "Dr. Art, I would be happy to go take some pictures at the tomb of Lazarus in those extra niches, are you interested?"

"Sure," said Art, "go right ahead. We'll talk about it later."

"Awesome," said Grayson with a big grin as he sat down on the front row.

"I'm eager to get to Bethany again," said Art, "but first things first."

Grace came up to him and gave him a big hug. "I just wanted to tell you, you are somebody special. My mother adores you and as you put it, the Turkish Delight helped produce a Lazarus effect in our relationship. It's never been better. We must celebrate later."

Grace mounted the stage and got up behind the podium. The room was not quite filled but people were still coming in. The news media that had come from abroad were all on hand, and the banks of lights on both sides of the auditorium were blinding. Art saw many of his friends from the Institute of Holy Land studies and Sammy Cohen was there as well. "This will be fun," Art said to himself.

Grace tapped the microphone and said, "It gives me very great pleasure to present to you, Dr. Arthur West, who will explain the significance of the recent finds in Bethany. He will then take questions. Without further ado, I give you the discoverer of the Lazarus stone."

There was good applause throughout the room. Art had not considered how the Lazarus effect might change his career, but it would. He had been too busy focusing on helping others. He was pleased with the phone call from the Discovery Channel folks last night saying he had been renewed for another season starting in the fall. Guess what his first few shows would be about? Art took his clicker and began the lecture.

"Ossuaries, or bone boxes, were a popular means of burial during the period 20 BC to 70 AD. The practice involved reburial of bones after the flesh had been allowed to desiccate for a year's time, which is about how long it took in Jerusalem for the flesh to disappear. Jews did not practice embalming like Egyptians, they would simply wrap a body in a winding sheet, having cleaned and anointed the body, and wrap spices in the winding sheet to retard the odor of the body during the period of mourning and visitation of the tomb. This is the practice we read about in the Gospels with regard to Jesus. He was destined for an ossuary, but the process got interrupted. You might say he experienced the Lazarus effect." Art proceeded to show various slides of ossuaries, bones, tombs, and niches, including the ossuary of Caiaphas.

"In my judgment it is no accident that in fact the rise of the Pharisaic movement with their strong beliefs about the bodily resurrection coincides with the practice of osslegium or reburial in an ossuary. The ossuary is a burial ritual that reflects a strong belief in the afterlife, in particular that bodily resurrection would happen, and so the bones needed to be kept together. Many of you will remember that old spiritual based on Ezekiel 37—"Dem bones, dem bones, dem dry bones gonna rise up one day." Art sang these words in a deep baritone voice. You could tell he was loosening up and letting it rip.

"This brings us to these whole series of remarkable finds at the Church of Mary and Martha, which are still ongoing.

"Here is the inscription in one of the other niches that flanks where Lazarus was buried, indicating that Martha was buried in this tomb as well.

"Obviously, in terms of inscriptional evidence the most striking is this inscription over the Lazarus niche reading, 'Twice dead under Pilate, twice raised in Yeshua (i.e. Jesus), in sure hope of resurrection.' This attests that Lazarus had already been raised from the dead once by Jesus and then had died again. It also attests that he had been reborn and raised by Jesus during his lifetime and still looked forward to a future bodily resurrection.

"I must stress that resurrection, almost without exception, in early Judaism refers to something that happens to a human body, or at least involves a human body either raised or transformed. It is not a terminology applied to visions, dreams, hallucinations, dying and going to heaven or the like. It has a very specific meaning—the raising up of the body or into a body. Usually in Pharisaic Judaism the focus of this was on what would happen to the righteous. I need not remind you that just down this ridge a little further near the Seven Arches Hotel there are plenty of orthodox Jews buried on the top of the Mount of Olives so that at the resurrection they can be first up to greet Messiah when he comes. Orthodox Jews and orthodox Christians share this belief in future bodily resurrection. It is not merely a historic or ancient belief. Once Jesus died and rose again, the belief among his followers became that those who were in Christ would die and rise again and be conformed to his image.

"I could talk for hours about the scroll that was discovered in the ossuary of Lazarus, but here I must just sum up my conclusions:

"First this scroll was written by the Beloved Disciple also known as Eliezer and we know him as Lazarus.

"Second, it contains the better part of the Gospel of John in Aramaic, not in Greek in a beautiful Herodian period Aramaic script.

"Third, the scroll does not call Lazarus the beloved disciple directly, rather where John's Gospel has those words, this scroll has the name Eliezer, the ancient version of Lazarus.

"Fourth, this scroll was found in the ossuary which had an inscription reading Eliezer, son of Simon. Simon then is the father of Lazarus, which makes good sense in view of the fact that Mark's Gospel says of the events that the anointing of Jesus took place in the house of Simon the leper.

"Fifth, this may explain why Lazarus, Martha, and Mary were apparently all single. A member of their family was a leper, and indeed Lazarus himself may have died of leprosy.

"Sixth, this scroll pre-dates any written Greek Gospel that we have or know of, and makes evident that the belief that Jesus was both divine and human was held very early on after Jesus' death. I would attribute the triggering of this belief to the fact that Jesus appeared to his disciples in the flesh after his death.

"Seventh, this conclusion that a high Christological view of Jesus as both divine and human was a belief that arose soon after Easter is confirmed by the Aramaic prayer prayed by the earliest followers of Jesus—*maran atha*—'Come, O Lord,' which we find in 1 Corinthians 16. Early Jewish followers of Jesus prayed this prayer and they did not believe they were praying to a mere rabbi to come back from the dead. The fact that they prayed TO Jesus is critical.

"Eighth, this means they considered him already a part of the Godhead. In other words, Jesus precipitated a rethinking of what monotheism meant. Monotheism was redefined to include Jesus. What we are dealing with in the Lazarus stone is an affirmation of miracle. What we are dealing with in the Aramaic document found in Lazarus's ossuary is a Christological reformulation of early Jewish monotheism.

"Ninth, it is important also to note that the earliest Christians were all Jews and they all believed they were already living in the end times and that therefore eschatological events were coming to pass back then, all involving Jesus and his community of followers. In short they did not focus on offering up prophecies about the late twentieth or early twenty-first century and would not have been encouraging us to look for correspondences between Biblical prophecies and our own day, but rather between OT prophecies and Jesus' day and the NT era. This in my judgment . . ."

Art was interrupted in mid-sentence by two noises that sounded like thunder inside the auditorium. He paused, looked down at his blue suit and saw it turning red beneath his right shoulder. Dizzy, he began falling; he saw Grace rising and running to catch him; his mind for some reason, turned to the verse in Judges 5:27. He began mumbling the poetry in Hebrew: "At her feet he sank, he fell; there he lay. At her feet he sank, he fell; where he sank, there he fell—dead." Then blackness and silence engulfed him.

# 51

## Pre-trial Jitters

L ATE WEDNESDAY MORNING, THE phone rang in Benjamin Levi's office. The Judge's secretary was on the line.

"Judge Dershowitz has asked me to inform you that Simon Siegal has been retained as counsel for the defense. Apparently, he has worked in Israel before. The Judge also wants to remind you that the trial must deal strictly with the evidence and the crimes committed in Israel. One more thing, I just got word of a shooting of Dr. West over at Hebrew University, know anything about it?"

"No," said Benjamin, "I'll ask Harry Scholer."

Harry had been sitting in the outer room chitchatting with the secretary.

She was asking him, "What are your plans for the rest of the day? Have you time for lunch with Mr. Levi?"

"In my country I would ask for a rain check—but if I did that here I could starve this summer!" They both laughed.

As Levi was hanging up, his secretary announced that Harry Scholer was in the outer room. Levi greeted him with a quick question.

"What do you know of an American lawyer named Simon Siegal? Seems he flew here in a hurry Monday night and has agreed to represent Dr. Stone."

Harry's eyes went wide. "You're kidding? Simon Siegal! High profile lawyer, very talkative, usually wins his cases. Last I knew he was working for the ACLU. I wonder how much experience he has with Israeli law? Can we check on that?"

"I'll put a paralegal on that right away—we need to know as much about Siegel as we do about Stone. And then there's Ray Simpson. Have you thought of how we can use Simpson to our advantage?"

Harry was more encouraging on that point. "Yes, we can use him to establish motive, as well as relate the facts of what happened at the tomb in the morning. Art is not planning to press charges concerning his brief 'entombment' with Lazarus. I guess he feels it was a learning experience. I've already talked to Simpson and his lawyer. As part of a plea bargain for a lesser sentence he will testify against Stone."

"As legal counsel to the IAA, we recommend a suspended sentence, a major fine, and two years of parole where he does community service, here in Israel. Then he can leave the country," said Levi.

"Raymond's no master mind, that's for sure! At least in the US, there's the whole issue of power relationships. There are legal precedents in regard to the relationship between professors and students where the latter can be exonerated of all kinds of things on the basis that they could not say 'No' to their superior."

"Very true," said Levi. "Besides the student is going to get the sympathy vote in a trial. It will be good to have your knowledge of the moral issues. Thank you for being willing to help. Apparently, with Simon Siegal on board, we have our hands full."

"And now Harry, I was trying to figure out how to tell you this but instead of tiptoeing around it I will just say it. I must share some bad news—it looks like one of our star witnesses, Art West has just been shot, are you aware of this?"

Harry sat down stunned. "Where have they taken him, I must go at once."

He flipped open his cell phone and called Grace Levine. The phone rang for what seemed like an eternity, but finally she picked up. "Hello yes," she said curtly.

"Grace, this is Harry, what has happened with Art?"

"He's been shot, the ambulance is taking him just now to Sinai hospital, it doesn't look good. Its madness here at the auditorium with police scrambling everywhere trying to catch the shooter or shooters, it appears there were two shots, I must go. If you've got it in you, you better start praying now."

"Oh no," said Harry, and buried his face in his hands. He flashed back to when his brother had been brutally murdered in Jerusalem only four years ago while he was minding his own business sitting in a café in Tel Aviv and a bomb went off.

"Who could have wanted to kill someone as harmless as Art?" Harry realized he had better get to the hospital fast.

# 52

## Auditing the Auditorium

PANDEMONIUM HAD BROKEN OUT once the shots were fired. Officer Shimon had been on the stage once again, and from his vantage point the shots seemed to have come from behind one of the two banks of lights on either side of the auditorium, or in other words from behind the cameramen. He had called for an immediate lock down of the room on his walkie-talkie, but some people had already fled the room upon first hearing the huge noise of the shots. The acoustics in this auditorium were so alive that the sound had been amplified several fold, sounding more like a bazooka than a handgun or rifle. Shimon had called for back up and the police station had all but emptied to respond to his urgent call.

There were people screaming, and lying down in the aisles, and covering their heads. Grace had acted fast, but had not quite reached Art before he hit his head on the microphone stand as he fell and then the floor. He was bleeding profusely from just below his right shoulder and he was totally unconscious, but breathing. Grace opened her cell phone and dialed 919* at once and summoned the ambulance to the back door of the Golda Meir auditorium. She took her scarf off and tried to staunch the wound that was bleeding profusely. The question rattling around in her head was "Who could have done this to Art?" It couldn't be Stone or Simpson, they were both in custody. The ambulance had better get here fast. Fortunately there was a back route they could take to the back door of the auditorium. She looked up and saw

Grayson Johnson kneeling on the floor in front of the stage praying and praying. "Thank goodness someone is intervening with God just now," she muttered.

The air was hot and heavy and Sedek Hadar was moving fast down the hill into the Kidron Valley on foot. He had chosen deliberately to go the crowded route so he could be lost in the multitudes, walking down the road that goes by the chapel known as Dominus Flevit and then the Garden of Gethsemane. He knew he could catch the #2 bus right at the corner where the road bent just beyond the Garden of Gethsemane. His emotions ran the gamut from fear to exhilaration. He had finally done something to stop the Christian blasphemy of the God who is One. Whatever the legal consequences, if he was caught, he knew he would be praised by those whose opinions mattered most to him—Rabbi Menachem and the sons of Zion. He would go report to them first, and then he would disappear and go visit relatives in an obscure neighborhood in Hebron. He thought about calling Jamison Parkes Law, but he decided against it. He wasn't entirely sure how he would react to this latest exploit of his.

Pinned to the floor on the left side of the auditorium was a young man with a backpack and a gun on the floor next to him. Officer Hoffner had been standing at the back left hand corner of the auditorium and had seen the young man get out of his seat, walk forward toward the cameras, lean against the far wall, and then suddenly whip out a pistol and take dead aim at Art West and fire. Hoffner had gotten there only seconds after the shot knocking over one of the cameramen as he pinned the young man to the floor.

"What is your name?" Hoffner kept saying to the young man, whose arm was pinned behind his back.

The youth would only say, "I want my lawyer, Jamison Parkes Law. I should be allowed to call him now."

Law, thought Hoffner, wasn't he that fundamentalist lawyer from Texas. Could he be behind this shooting? He decided to allow the young man to make his call and then interrupt it.

The boy used speed dial and soon he had Law on the line. "Guess what Mr. Law," said the youth, "I think I scored one for the good guys, I just put a stop to Art West's criticism of your views on prophecy. You said he was a loose cannon who needed to have a rag put in his mouth at our last meeting of the Millennial Dawn Society. I did it."

Jamison was pacing the floor of his flat. "What have you done?" he screamed over the phone line.

"I shot the dude, and put an end to his big mouth," bragged the young man.

"You did what?" Law screamed.

" I thought you would be pleased," said the youth glumly.

At this juncture Hoffner interrupted and took the phone. "Mr. Law it sounds as though your follower has been more than a little over zealous. You will need to come down to the station and make a statement ASAP. We are carting the young man off to jail right now."

"What did you say your name was young man?"

"James is the last name. My first name is Yeshua, son of messianic Jewish parents, but most people call me Jesse— Jesse James."

"Well," said Hoffner, "this is the last round up for you cowboy."

Mohammed could hardly believe his luck—finally most of the officers were leaving the station. For days he had staked out the police station trying to figure a way into it, in a desperate ploy to see if he could kidnap a celebrity prisoner and then negotiate a hostage exchange for one of the Hamas leaders he particularly admired. He knew it was a desperate gambit, but Hosni, the great Hamas leader was only two days away from being taken to a maximum security prison for the rest of his life. Lurking on the opposite street corner from the police station, he reviewed the plans he had made over a week before. He knew the station was old and did not even have air conditioning vents. Apparently no one had installed security systems on the back of the building, not expecting people to be brazen enough to try and break into the building.

Once the vast majority of police cars had peeled out of the station, Mohammed went around the back, put on his ski-mask, picked the lock, disabled the ancient bell alarm, turned out all the lights and went down the basement corridor where the cells were. Mohammed had read the papers closely enough to know there was an important American or two in custody. He wanted the one that would put up the least resistance. Looking into the cell on the left-hand side of the corridor he saw a disheveled older man. He had found his mark. Shining his light right in his face he said in the bad English he had practiced for weeks, "You no speak, I shoot you now for sure."

Stone raised his hands and stood up quivering, while Mohammed rather easily jimmied the lock on the cell. Pushing the older man down the dark corridor and holding his pistol firmly in the small of the man's back, Mohammed and his prisoner rapidly exited the building.

The next thing Stone knew, he was first in broad daylight, then he was blindfolded, thrown into the back of a car, and then for good measure knocked over the head with the butt of a gun. The last thing he remembered hearing before all went blank was the screeching of tires as the small getaway car headed somewhere fast.

# 53

## Miracle at Sinai?

THE AMBULANCE HAD COME with some dispatch and Art's vital signs were holding steady when they were monitored by the EMT in the ambulance. "Coming in, get ready, we've got a bleeder and surgery is going to be needed immediately," said one of them to the emergency room staff.

"OK," was the only reply on the other end of the line.

"Oh yes, and you had better call Dr. Mordecai and get him prepped at once."

"Right."

The ambulance, with full sirens blaring, was racing up the hill towards the hospital, and the gurney in the back on which Art was lying was swaying back and forth with every curve. He was hooked up to a heart monitor, and one of the EMT staff was busy applying direct pressure to the wound hoping to slow down the flow of blood.

"We had better get there quick," said the staffer, "his blood pressure is beginning to drop rapidly."

The entrance to the emergency room at Sinai Hospital was under a portico, and as the ambulance wheeled its way in three nurses were standing waiting for the back doors of the ambulance to open so they could wheel Art right into surgery. Everything was prepped and ready.

Dr. Mordecai was standing just inside the door, and the minute he saw the blood pressure of Art and his pale demeanor he was yelling for units of blood. "Stat," he said. This was a life and death matter, no ordinary surgery. The first task would be to stop the bleeding.

The lights in the operating theater were blazing hot and bright, and the nurses had already ripped West's suit off of him and covered him in a thin blue blanket. Blood was pouring out of the wound, and almost before the gurney had come to a rest and West was transferred to the operating table, Dr. Mordecai was making an incision right next to the wound and immediately clamping off the hemorrhaging artery.

"OK, we have stopped the bleeding," said Mordecai. "Now get the miniature X-ray machine over here quick, and let's see if we can find the bullet."

As they were wheeling the machine over, Mordecai told the nurse to raise West and look for an exit wound, and sure enough there was one. "Well one good thing, we don't have to fish any metal out of him, but do the X-ray anyway."

But the X-ray showed that there was indeed a piece of metal in Art, a bullet.

"So he was shot more than once," said the Doctor, "and from different angles. Job two is to get the other shell out of him." This was a delicate matter as the bullet had entered from the left side and had lodged itself next to the liver and gall bladder without actually entering either one. Delicately Dr. Mordecai used forceps to extract the bullet. "Sponge," he said to the nearest nurse, and she wiped the doctor's forehead as he was beginning to sweat profusely. "Alright, get the units of blood ready to go. Go ahead and feed him a pint or two, as we've got to go in and sow up that ruptured artery."

The surgery on the artery was indeed delicate and it took over two hours to finish the job without disrupting anything else. At one juncture Art's pulse had gotten so low that they were contemplating sticking a needle in him with a stimulant, but it proved to be unnecessary. By late afternoon, the Doctor had done everything he could to save Art West, and he was prepared to tell those waiting outside the ICU that he was critical but stable.

As he walked into the waiting area he saw the familiar long faces of Kahlil and Hannah, and Grace Levine, as well as one other gentlemen the doctor didn't know, Harry Scholer. They all looked grim, as though they had been weeping or praying or both. Dr. Mordecai said "The next 24 hours are critical, but Dr. West has his fitness and luck on his side. One bullet exited through his right back, the other lodged next to his liver coming from a very different angle. Were their two shooters shooting from two different angles?"

Grace did a double take and said: "Well there were two noises but we thought they came from two shots from the one shooter. Are you telling me that two people were trying to terminate Art West?"

"Yes, it certainly looks like the bullets came from two very different angles," said Dr. Mordecai. "In any event you are welcome to wait out the night here, I will have the nurses give you regular reports. We have done all we can for now. It is now in the hands of the God."

Grace said thank you to the doctor for everyone, and then added "I think it best if we say nothing to the media until we know what will transpire with Art, but Harry would you call Officer Hoffner and tell him there was another shooter who may have gotten away?"

"Right away," said Harry, glad to have something constructive to do.

# 54

# The Wisdom of the Rabbi

R ABBI MENACHEM WAS SOME 79 years of age, and while he had always been radical as well as ultra-orthodox in his views, he had never sanctioned murder to silence an opponent who was not himself violently attacking Jews. So it was with considerable consternation that he sat and listened to Sedek Hadar, having already promised to keep this a confidential conversation.

"Rabbi I have, since I have joined the sons of Zion, always followed your teaching, and it was my understanding that the blasphemers had to be stopped. Was that not your teaching?"

"Yes my child, but have you not noticed that I myself have never used more than non-violent protest and legal means to achieve such ends? Do you not remember the day in front of the McDonalds on Ben Yehuda St.? Did you hear anyone tell you to start firing at that upstart of a woman?"

"No rabbi, I did not," Sedek said glumly.

"Very well then, what you have done, though I do not doubt your motives were good, was wrong, wrong in the way you went about this. We cannot sanction violence against those who have not physically attacked us. Hamas, is a different story, as you know."

"Yes, but rabbi, it is hard to tell the difference sometimes. Aren't ideas as dangerous as weapons sometimes?"

"Yes, sometimes they are but the Torah is very clear—'only an eye for an eye' and so on. That command was meant to limit violence to a proportional response not license it. The proper response to West was to refute his ideas of course, not shoot him!" and here the rabbi became animated.

"But what should I do now rabbi? If I turn myself in, it will not go well with me, and I will never be of service to the sons of Zion again. And perhaps I have only wounded him."

The rabbi pondered this. He did not want to betray a confidence, but he also did not want his own name associated with immoral acts of violence. "Let us wait a day or two and decide shall we? Let us wait and see what happens to Professor West who has so disturbed you. But you must promise me this my child."

"Yes rabbi, what is it?"

"You must promise me you will contact me in two days, and then you must abide by what we decide on that occasion. In the meantime, go visit your relatives in Hebron as you said you would do. Put your house in order. Pray and read the Torah, especially the Psalms, and as I said, call me in two days."

Sedek nodded and said, "Shalom," as he left in sadness.

When he had closed the front door, the rabbi murmured to himself, "Man is made for trouble, as the sparks fly up."

# 55

## The Price of Freedom

H E AWOKE WITH A pounding headache and a huge lump on the back of his head. Just touching it made him woozier. He had absolutely no idea where he was, other than he was in a dark room, handcuffed to a bedpost, and the room had no ventilation or air-conditioning. Sweat dripped down his forehead, and in the midst of all his chaotic thoughts another dismal one came to him "They will think I tried to escape! Just marvelous!" said Stone to no one in particular.

Mohammed was sitting in the next room mulling over exactly who he should call about his prisoner. He had had enough sense to buy a new Go phone that would be difficult to trace and had lots of minutes on it. He had bought it in the name of a distant, deceased relative at a now defunct address in Bethlehem. They would never trace it to him. Finally he decided the smart move was to call the American press. It was they who most cared about what happened to Stone. He did not want a ransom, just a straightforward prisoner exchange.

Almost immediately someone picked up the phone at the *Herald Tribune* office in Jerusalem. "Hello, yes," came a female voice across the line in Hebrew.

Mohammed, speaking through a cloth over the phone, said, "Do you speak Arabic?"

"Yes," said the girl.

"Good, then listen very carefully. We have kidnapped Dr. Patrick Stone and have him in a safe house. Unless Hosni, the great Hamas leader is released by the police by nine o'clock tomorrow morning, Dr. Stone will be executed. Am I clear? Do you understand the message?"

"I understand," said the shaky voice at the other end of the line.

"Then you must tell your editor this at once, and tell them to call the police. I will call back in two hours. The police must give you clear directions as to when and where the exchange can be made. No games, no tricks, or Stone is dead—understand?"

"I get it, and now I must go," and she rang off.

Mohammed was counting on the fact that the Israeli police could not afford to look bad in front of the worldwide press, which had shown up for the trial of Stone. If anything went wrong the Israelis would have a lot of explaining to do to Washington, and their own supposedly impregnable security and police force would lose face even with their own people. Mohammed thought he had the Israelis right where he wanted them.

Officer Hoffner was the first man back to the station and when he walked in the front door, Office David was sitting at the desk. He had the disgruntled Jesse James in handcuffs with him.

"All been quiet here?" Hoffner asked David.

"Yes, but it's time to do the afternoon check on the prisoners."

Officer David got up, but suddenly the phone rang.

"I've got to get this, can you go downstairs and check on Simpson and Stone?"

"Certainly," said Officer Hoffner. "I've got to install this young man in one of those cells anyway." Hoffner had gotten about halfway down the stairwell when Officer David began screaming, "Someone on the phone says Stone has been kidnapped! Impossible! Check quick!"

Within two minutes Hoffner was standing in front of the open cell door and just shaking his head. "How in the world do we explain this to Officer Shimon? What do we have here—a revolving door? What else can go wrong today?"

Hoffner led James to the next cell down and opened the door.

"In you go son. With any luck your lawyer friend will be by to see you soon."

Jesse just hung his head, cried, and shuffled into the cell offering no resistance. In his mind he had gone from hero to zero in nothing flat.

# 56

## Marking Time

Harry enjoyed the warm, dry weather of Jerusalem. Cold, wet, and rainy days in Washington did not appeal to him at all. When Grace could stand the pacing of Harry and the El Saids no longer, she sent them all off to Kahlil's shop to give them something to do, promising she would call them the minute she had any word at all. At the antiquities shop, Hannah had prepared a light lunch, including pita bread and baba ghanoush. Lots of fruit and nuts were piled on another plate.

Kahlil was doing much better. His head sported a small bandage, his badge of courage. He was back to his jovial self in the shop. Only now he was humming Coltrane tunes. And business had returned as well, with the huge press of tourists in town buying all sorts of things. The publicity surrounding the Lazarus stone had made stone objects from the biblical period all that much more popular. Kahlil could hardly keep tablets in stock.

Harry enjoyed a pleasant two hours eating, talking and even haggling.

He realized he was spending more and more time with Hannah—and enjoying every minute. But there was business to consider. He slowly and gently began to prepare Kahlil and Hannah for the trial ahead, but his unspoken and greater concern was for Art. Would he survive this, and even if he did, would he ever be his effervescent self again?

~

Jamison Parkes Law now had a real situation on his hands. Jesse James, an American citizen was in jail for shooting Art West, and all because he misunderstood what Law had been urging his disciples to do. Never in his wildest imagination did he think his young followers would see his moral call to arms as a literal call to arms. He too was learning something on this day about dangerous ideas and dangerous forms of rhetoric. "Damage control," he kept saying to himself, "damage control." As he road in his Volvo down to the police station he reflected on what he was going to say to the police. Of course he would disavow the violence, but what else should he say? Should he tell them he would be the legal representative for James? He knew he must resist the temptation to simply abandon James, or else the rest of his following might abandon him. They had all liked James immensely, he was just too impetuous, too much of a "shoot first and ask questions later" kind of person, and now he had proved it quite literally. He was only 19 years of age. What was to be done? Law decided he would provide counsel for James, and he would advise him to say nothing, while waiting to see what would happen with West. More than one person was now marking time, as West struggled for survival.

# 57

## Over Jordan, but not Overjoyed

THE PRIME MINISTER HIMSELF had called in his top hostage negotiator, Avner Galal, to deal with the Stone-Hosni mess. However
much the Prime Minister had enjoyed using the rhetoric that he did
not negotiate with terrorists, this time the consequences of not doing
so were too severe. Naturally once the exchange was made they would
track the terrorists down and run them to ground.

Galal was a no-nonsense kind of man. He had served with Yadin
in the '67 war, and he knew all the ins and outs of negotiation and
exchange, or at least he thought he did. But he had never heard of a hostage exchange being made on the Allenby Bridge itself. This was a first.
Galal had been given the full use of the para-military boys who worked
with the Mossad, the secret police, but he had chosen just four of their
finest to accompany him with Hosni to the bridge. Officer Shimon had
come with him as well to identify Stone.

Did this location mean that the terrorist that had Stone was a
Jordanian? It seemed unlikely since Jordan had been in the process of
normalizing things with Israel to some degree, and their authorities denied knowing anything about this. He tried to envision in his mind the
exchange on the bridge and all the possibilities, but there were too many
contingencies to consider. What especially worried him was the request
to have Hosni placed in full body armor for the exchange. He guessed
they wanted to eliminate the eliminating of Hosni by long-range rifle

fire after the exchange. He was already sweating, his camouflage uniform turning darker shades of green and brown by the minute.

Stone could hardly believe it when he had stepped out of the car in the middle of the night and, while still blindfolded, was ordered to start gradually walking through the shallow waters of the Jordan to the other side, a gun planted firmly in his back. How in the world had he gotten to a place where he could cross over Jordan into another country without notice? His head was still killing him, but at least the kidnapper had given him some pita bread and hummus before they left the safe house and got in the car. He surmised that they wanted to keep the "merchandise" in tact until the exchange or ransom was paid. He had no idea what the arrangements were.

Mohammed, like many older Palestinians, carried a Jordanian passport because, of course, until the war, all of the eastern part of Israel right up to eastern Jerusalem belonged to Jordan. He had called his friend Ishmael who lived in Jordan and worked in the duty free shops and asked him not only to meet him at the bridge, but to tell the guards that one of their own was escaping from Israel and its secret police. Well—it was mostly true. They would be sympathetic.

Thus, when Mohammed, with Stone in tow, had gotten up the east bank of the Jordan and came up on the back side of the shops at the checkpoint just beyond Allenby bridge, Mohammed walked directly with Stone to the guard's booth where he told Ishmael to meet him. In the bright light of the booth he could see they were playing cards. Nothing could be easier.

"Salam Alaykum," he said in a quiet voice so as not to startle them. Ishmael flashed a big smile and returned the greeting, hopping up and giving Mohammed a big hug.

"It has been too many years . . . Let me introduce you to my friend—this is one of Jordan's finest—Hussein."

Hussein stood up and noticed the disheveled old man and came to attention—"And who in the world is this?"

"Do not worry," said Mohammed, "he will not be with us long. But you must notify your superiors as he will shortly be exchanged for the great Hosni."

"Hosni, the one known as the jackal? Hosni the one who killed a whole busload of people outside of Jerusalem last year? That Hosni?" queried the guard.

"Yes that one," said Mohammed.

"Who then is this, that is worthy of such an exchange?" asked Ishmael.

"I present to you Dr. Patrick Stone—the great antiquities thief!"

Stunned, both Jordanians looked hard at the short, balding, older man in rumpled clothes and could hardly believe their eyes. This was the man they had seen on the Jordanian news?

Hussein was on the phone at once, calling and waking up his superior, General Atta.

He would want to be in on this matter. Atta had quickly phoned King Abdullah to alert him to what was happening, and the King had given Atta specific instructions on how to handle this matter. After the recent bombings at hotels in Amman, Abdullah was not interested in cozying up with terrorist of any kind. So it appeared that everyone was going to be in for a surprise when the sun came up on Allenby Bridge in the morning.

# 58

# Foreign Exchange

Dawn came quickly over the Jordan River, and there was not a breath of wind on this hot morning. There was, however, a weather report that the first hamsin—the dreaded heat and dust storm—might come through later in the day. General Atta had arrived an hour before dawn in his full dress uniform, with three other Jordanian soldiers armed to the teeth. Nothing was going to be left to chance.

The light began to creep over the Golan onto the bridge itself, which Mohammed could now see clearly for the first time from the checkpoint booth. Atta had already briefed Mohammed as to what he wanted to do.

"I expect to receive a phone call from Lt. Galal shortly, and after that we will work out the details." His voice was authoritative and cold. Unlike his Jordanian friend at the guard booth, the General was not even cordial to Mohammed, much less did the general treat him like a hero. This made Mohammed nervous. Had he made a mistake?

The cell phone of the General began to ring, playing a Arabic dance tune. Grabbing his jacket, which held the phone, the General flipped open the phone and said "Salam Alaykum."

"And shalom to you as well," said Avner. "We have an agreement then as to how this is to transpire—yes? No soldiers crossing the bridge, no funny business. Just Stone walking our way and 'the Jackal' walking in your direction across the bridge?" The arrangements had already been made through channels; the decisions were simply conveyed to

Avner and General Atta. There would be no delicate negotiations, no haggling, no baksheesh—just a one-for-one swap, done by the book. The exchange was to take place at precisely 8 a.m.

"Indeed," said the General, "simple and clean. We are understood then," and he hung up his phone.

Meanwhile Stone was at the point of collapse. It had all been too much for him, the aging overweight, academic. It was like he was caught in the middle of the plot of a B movie. At the moment he was sitting in the toilet shaking, trying to go to the bathroom one more time; he was so nervous. No one had tortured him, but still the situation seemed ominous to him. Certainly no one was offering him food or water, nor did anyone speak to him. The guard stood right outside his stall waiting for him to emerge.

Suddenly a wave of nausea came over Stone and he stood up, turned around and started vomiting into the toilet. The guard could here this, and became concerned. The exchange was only five minutes away.

"General Atta! This man is sick. What should we do?"

It was clear that Stone was in no condition to travel, and might only barely be able to walk across the bridge. Atta immediately called Avner.

"We have a problem," he said. "Stone is busying throwing up in the guard's toilet and is extremely weak. Give me an extra thirty minutes to clean him up. There will be no tricks. We don't want any part of this antiquities thief!"

Avner listened for a moment and thought—"is this some kind of ruse? Surely not since the General seems thoroughly disgusted with the 'marked man.'"

"OK, but lets get this over with quick, I hear the sirocco or dust storm is coming."

Looking out of the guard booth and up at the sky Atta noticed that it had gone from blue to a sort of light tan color. This did not bode well.

"You are right," said the General, "I will call you back as soon as we are ready."

The guard had to help Stone out of the toilet he was so shaky. They gave him some cool water, and an aspirin for his headache.

"Here, take this—you will feel better."

Stifling the desire to wretch again, Stone drank down the water and swallowed the pill without difficulty. He was quickly escorted to the bridge. The time was 8:15.

The General phoned Avner once more—"We are as ready as we can be. Stone may need help from you once he gets to your half of the bridge."

"Right, we anticipated that, and Officer Shimon, whom you can now see standing at the other end of the bridge if you look through a rifle scope, will be waiting, in case he is needed. He is not armed. I repeat he is not armed. One more thing: part of the deal was that 'the jackal' be in full body armor. It's bound to be stiflingly hot in this weather, but we are doing exactly what was asked."

The Jordan River is in fact not very wide at all at the Allenby bridge crossing. It is more like a creek than a river, especially in June, and so the walk for the prisoners would not be a long one. The sun, which had risen earlier, had now given way to an annoying haze. Atta looked up again, and listened intently. He began to hear the distant roar, sounding at first like continuously rolling thunder. He frantically phoned Avner—"Right now, quickly get your man on the bridge, the hamsin is coming."

Stone was shoved out on the bridge at precisely 8:17, and Hosni was as well on the other side. The two men began walking, the latter with a better stride than the former. From the middle of the road Mohammed watched this. It seemed more like a death march than a flight to freedom. Yet he was excited thinking about the prospect of meeting his hero—"The Jackal."

Shuffling his way along, then stumbling once, Stone was about halfway across the bridge when the hamsin hit full force—at first with only twenty-mile-an-hour winds. The jackal had made it almost entirely to the Jordanian side before the strong, biting, sand-filled wind hit, but not Stone. Stone fell flat on his face on the concrete with a thud.

Atta and one of his guards ran to Hosni and grabbed him and dragged him the rest of the way across the bridge. There was no danger of any gunfire from the Israelis since they could not see a thing at the far end of the bridge. At the same time, Shimon, running as fast as he could into the wind and shielding his eyes by putting on his shooting goggles started yelling—"I am coming Dr. Stone, I am coming."

There was no response, except a low moan, which might have been the wind or it might have been Stone. Reaching the spot where Stone fell, Shimon picked the man up in his arms and turned toward Israel. At least the wind was with him. Shimon was a large man—6'6" and with strong arms. In his earlier years he had been on the Israeli Olympic team as a weight lifter. Carrying Stone was not a huge task, if only the wind would not blow him down.

Shimon could not see a thing as he tried to traverse the last 100 yards of the bridge. Avner was standing facing the wind shouting, "Here, here, come in this direction. Over here."

Meanwhile "The Jackal" was in the custody of General Atta and his men.

Flashing a smile, which revealed at least two teeth missing, Hosni said to the General, "Allah akbar."

The General replied, "Allah is indeed great but you are nothing but trouble. We will be escorting you to a Jordanian prison. And as for your hero-worshipping friend Mohammed, we have plans for him as well. He will be confined to the Palestinian refugee camp outside Amman."

Mohammed could hardly believe what he was hearing. "How can this be? You also are Muslims!"

General Atta replied curtly—"Most Muslims do not believe in terrorism and kidnapping as a solution to our problems. You shame the faith that you name!" And with that both Hosni, now stripped of the battle regalia, and Mohammed were handcuffed and thrust into the back of an armored vehicle, never to be seen again in Israel.

Meanwhile, Shimon, his arms getting heavy, had finally reached the end of the bridge and could just see Lt. Galal. "I have made it, praise be heaven," said Shimon as he gave out of gas, and set Stone gently down. Stone, breathing heavily, was nonetheless conscious.

"Where am I?" he asked feebly.

"Welcome back to the Promised Land Dr. Stone. We will take you back to the comfort of your cell and some military food now." Stone just grunted and gently set himself down in the back of the jeep. His resistance was so low he had no fight left in him. They could do as they like with him—he didn't care any more.

# 59

# Bail Denied

SIMON SIEGAL COULD HARDLY believe his luck. His client, who had a shaky case at best, had now become an object of no little sympathy from the press, which had plastered pictures of him back on the front page of the *Herald Tribune* and the *Jerusalem Post*. The Tribune especially had run a full-length article with their secretary and correspondent being interviewed about the phone call from Mohammed and what ensued thereafter. Their photographer had managed to get a shot of Stone when he was returned to the police station looking distraught, distressed, and disheveled—in fact, totally pathetic. Siegal was sure that the sympathy vote generated by this story would help the case.

Friday morning's pre-trial hearing was gaveled into session and the line up for the trial was set. On one side of the docket was Simon Siegal, and on the other was Benjamin Levi, Harry Scholer, and various legal aides. Stone had been allowed to rest in his cell, rather than appear before the judge at this juncture. Judge Dershowitz was noted for acting with dispatch as a no-nonsense judge. The charges were officially read into the court records. "Counselor Siegal, how does your client plead?"

"Not guilty on all counts," said Siegal emphatically, "and we request release of my client with an appropriate bail."

Dershowitz looked at Siegal and said, "Nice try, counselor, but since this man has already fled the country once and been dragged out of the country a second time, and has access to considerable funds once he is out of jail, I am denying bail. He will be remanded to the congenial custody of the police in the Jerusalem police facility, and if he needs medical attention we will send it his way from Sinai hospital. Any other motions Mr. Siegal?"

"Yes, your honor. We request that cameras and reporters be kept out of the courtroom since this is such a high-profile case."

"I am inclined to agree with you on that, counselor. Mr. Levi, have you any objections to a closed trial?"

"No, your honor," said Benjamin Levi, "but we would like permission to speak to the press each day once the day's proceedings are done."

"You may do so, and I will also have the court reporter hand out a summary of the proceedings each day as well. Is that satisfactory to both parties?"

"Yes, your honor," came the collective reply.

Then Mr. Siegal interjected, "I have one more matter to bring up, your honor."

"Proceed," ordered the judge.

"I have a motion to dismiss the gun as evidence since my client's fingerprints were never found on it."

The judge looked at the affidavit, and then asked, "What does the prosecution say to this motion?"

At this juncture Harry leapt into action. "Your honor, this is a typical tactic of Mr. Siegal, who likes to exclude one piece of evidence after another until he makes them all disappear. The prosecution is prepared to present clear evidence that the gun found on the scene belonged to Patrick Stone's father, Leroy, who lived in Johnson City, Tennessee, and that though Dr. Stone's prints were not on the gun, his DNA was found from the hair fibers on the coat Said wore the night of the shooting, a coat which has the powder residue from the gun on it."

"That's enough for me for now," said the judge. "Motion to suppress the weapon is denied. Anything else?"

"Yes your honor," said Harry, "As you no doubt know one of our main witnesses, Art West is clinging to life at Sinai hospital, and we are having some trouble getting one of our witnesses here in time, Dr. William Arnold. There may be a need for a motion for a long recess and continuance at some point."

"I understand, and must allow it if it comes to that. We want this to be a fair trial for both sides," said the judge. "That's all for today gentleman." The gavel sounded the end of the proceedings.

As they were leaving the courtroom Benjamin said to Harry, "Nice work, I am glad you know Siegal's tactics. I am quite certain he has more rabbits up his sleeve."

"Indeed," said Harry, " but last I checked, June is rabbit hunting season." Both men smiled as they walked down the courthouse steps. Harry was trying to portray a positive demeanor but he was inwardly more than a little troubled. Stone would now have the sympathy vote on his side—he could be called a victim of Hamas terrorism, something an Israeli jury would have feelings about. And how was Art? How could they win the trial without Art? Suddenly Harry was jolted out of his revere by the insistent ringing of his cell phone.

"Grace here," said the voice at the other end. "Art's vital signs are stable and his blood pressure is back to normal, but he is not conscious yet, by the design of the doctor, who wants his body to repair for a while before waking him. Nonetheless, the news we have is good."

"I am so relieved to hear this, be sure to call Kahlil and let him know as well."

"I will," said Grace, and rang off. Surely, thought Harry, things must begin to get better soon.

# 60

## Grayson Goes Grave Diggin'

GRAYSON JOHNSON WAS ENJOYING his Thursday off as much as he could, considering that he had not been allowed to see Dr. West at the hospital and had been told by Dr. Levine that perhaps he had best go do some of the tasks Dr. West would want him to be doing just now. He thought this was a good way to keep himself occupied and so he resolved to go back to the tomb in Bethany.

Grayson rather missed Avi Hoffner's company. After recording last Thursday's phone call, Avi was busy with other detective work. But as a reward for his cooperation in these matters he had been given an IAA pass to crawl around in the Lazarus tomb. When Hoffner informed him of this on Tuesday, Grayson nearly leapt out of his Nike sneakers. "Awesome! I am for sure honored and you can count on me to comb every square inch of that tomb. I'll take my digital camera. I've got Thursday off!" Art had already given him a few basic guidelines of what he could and could not do at a dig site, but he felt confident that Grayson would do just fine.

Grayson set out with his backpack and a determined look in his eye. When he arrived at the tomb, he noticed it was cordoned off. On instructions from Art, he went in the church and showed Mustafa his badge, a note from Art West, and another from Officer Hoffner. Mustafa, a man used to interesting characters, said, "That is fine. Please be careful. Do not break anything or take anything."

Taking out his heavy-duty flashlight, Grayson shimmied through the hole in the back of the tomb, turned on the flashlight and began combing the walls first. There was really nothing but carved out rock to see.

But his next object for attention was the niche on the right which had thus far not been examined closely. Crawling into the empty space and lighting the roof of the enclosure, Grayson found an inscription similar to the one Art had found in the other niche. This inscription, however, was not in Aramaic; it was in Greek. Grayson, budding scholar that he was, took two years of Greek at Fruitland Bible Institute. Slowly, he made out the poetic words one by one:

> *Here lay Mary, the one who anointed Jesus*
> *Now Mary resides where the departed martyrs dwell*

Carefully taking three pictures, Grayson crawled out of the niche and pondered the allusion in the inscription. Grayson knew his Bible well, especially his New Testament. As a fan of the "Left Behind" series he had studied the book of Revelation many times. He recognized the reference to Revelation 6, which speaks of the departed saints being under the altar in heaven.

"OK," said Grayson, "but are we being told that Mary and her ossuary were like, raptured to heaven? Even Mr. LaHaye said nothing about caskets being beamed up. So probably that's a bogus idea." He decided to look over the rest of the tomb once more and think about the inscription while he did. There turned out to be nothing more that was new in the tomb.

Crawling out of the tomb, he checked his pictures and found that the inscription showed up clearly. He went back to talk to Mustafa.

"Sir, is there any record of Mary and Martha's bones being moved under the altar of this church a long time ago."

"The church you see is a rather modern church with a modern altar. But it is built on the foundations of the ancient church of Mary and Martha. I have always wondered why the church was not also named for Lazarus. Sometimes churches were named for those buried under the altar in that place. I tell you what I will do. The crypt in this church is off limits to tourists due to its dangers. But I shall take a trip down there and see what can be found. I am sure the priest will approve."

Grayson smiled and said, "OK, gotta run, but would you call me if anything comes to light. Here is my phone number at the house. Later Dude."

At least one good thing had turned up today. Grayson made a mental note to spend an hour or so once he was home, just praying for Dr. West's health. He decided to pray as though he were the voice of Dr. West beseeching God, using Psalm 18:

> I call to the Lord, who is worthy of praise, and I am saved from my enemies. The cords of death entangled me; the torrents of destruction overwhelmed me. The cords of the grave coiled around me; the snares of death confronted me. In my distress I called to the Lord; I cried to my God for help. From his temple he heard my voice; my cry came before him, into his ears . . . He reached down from on high and took hold of me; he drew me out of deep waters. He rescued me from my powerful enemy, from my foes who were too strong for me . . . He brought me out into a spacious place; he rescued me because he delighted in me.

Dr. West was in the hands of God, reasoned Grayson, the best place he could be. On that thought he was able to lie down and get his first good night's rest in three days.

# 61

## Life Lines and Death Watches

THE DOCTOR HAD COME into Art's room and told the nurse not to give Art any more "magic sleeping potion." It was time for him to be allowed to wake up. Grace had been sitting patiently in the room they had wheeled Art into waiting to hear from the doctor again. Dr. Mordecai smiled and said, "Your Dr. West is a fighter, I think he is out of danger now."

"That's both a relief and a laugh," said Grace, "Art West the fighting pacifist. I always knew he was a bundle of outrageous extremes. But seriously, how long realistically before he might be allowed to go home so we can stop this death watch?"

"If when he awakes, all is well, I would say another 3–4 days, but we will have to wait and see. He should be awake in an hour or so." The Doctor smiled again and left.

Grace bided her time by reading the latest issue of Harry Scholer's magazine, *Biblical Artifacts*. She had been particularly intrigued by the article arguing for a reassessment of the Jehoash Tablet and its authenticity. At about ten in the morning Art began to stir in his bed, and calling for water.

Grace slipped some ice chips in his mouth, and he said, "Thanks nurse," having not yet opened his eyes. Grace turned on her best New England accent and replied, "Why you are most welcome! This is Nurse Levine from Brookline, Mass."

Art opened his eyes with a start and said, "Grace, its you," and began to weep. "What am I doing here?" Grace began to tear up as well and said, "Well there was this little matter of two different assassins trying to gun you down while you were lecturing on resurrection. I guess they wanted to see if you could embody your theology literally."

Art smiled and said, "It hurts too much to laugh, but that was a good one. Hey, did you hear the one about President Bush and Moses?"

"No," said Grace, "but I can hardly wait to do so." This was good; Art was trying to be his old self.

"Well it seems the President was walking down the corridor in an airport with his secret service guys when he saw this man who looked remarkably like Moses, and he went up to him and asked, 'Are you Moses?' But the man never stopped and just kept walking. The President was miffed and so he sent one of his secret service men after the guy and told him to ask the man if he was Moses. The secret service quickly caught up with the man and said, 'Excuse me sir, are you Moses, you sure look like Moses. Why didn't you respond to the President when he spoke to you?' Moses replied, "Yes I am Moses, but the last time I spoke with a bush, I got in big trouble."

Grace just burst out laughing. Art said, "Please don't make me laugh, the stitches you know, the stitches on both sides!" Grace got out her cell phone and dialed up Harry. "Harry," she said, "we've got a live one here, the death watch is over. Art just cracked a joke." She handed the phone to Art. "Hi friend," said Art, "How are you and the trial getting along?"

"Just fine Art, only we are going to need your testimony, so I am thinking maybe we will send a videographer over your way tomorrow morning if you are feeling up to it."

"Sure" said Art, "I've got nothing better to do."

"Except get well from two bullet wounds," hollered Grace from the other side of Art's bed.

"Harry, please call Kahlil and tell him I am back in the land of the living will you?"

"Sure thing," said Harry "Things are beginning to look up. Back to trial preparation."

"Once a lawyer, always a lawyer," said Art turning to Grace and adding, "Did I tell you the one about the man who was on his death bed and had his wife call his two lawyers, telling her to get them over to his house quick, as he wanted to die like Jesus, between two thieves?"

Grace said, "Enough, enough, I am beginning to think the anesthesia has so altered your brain waves that you've been turned into a candidate for Christian Comedy Central. Give it and yourself a rest, and I'll be back after a visit to the IAA office."

"Right," said Art and as she was leaving he said, "But did I tell you the one about King David being the first to ride a motorcycle? The Bible says, 'His triumph was heard throughout the land.'"

"Gevalt, " said Grace and smiled, "Someone put him back to sleep . . . please!"

# 62

## Clash of the Titans

THE COURTROOM WAS GLEAMING with sunlight pouring in through the windows on this hot June day. The lights hardly needed to be on. But the searching white-hot spotlight of truth would be bringing the real heat and light in this room. The courtroom had filled up an hour before time for the trial, and the press in great hordes was camping outside the building waiting for any and every bit of news possible. The headline in the *Jerusalem Post* this morning read, CLASH OF THE TITANS. Two famous Jewish lawyers were about to have a go at it in public over the most famous theft in the Holy Land in recent memory.

When the combatants entered the room Benjamin Levi was wearing a dark blue, pin-stripe suit, as was Harry Scholer, the difference being that Levi went for the reserved dark tie whereas Harry wore his natty red bow tie. Various legal aides trundled into court behind them like participants in a Roman triumph.

Simon Siegal made a striking entrance wearing a hunter green suit.

Patrick Stone looked better than he had in many days, wearing a brown tweed jacket and looking every inch the Yale professor he was, but with enough of a limp to remind those in the courtroom of his recent travails. Apparently someone really had looked after him and coached him on how to behave.

Certain documents had already been made available to all the parties concerned and entered into the court records. They included

Stone's passports, hotel receipts, a copy of the agreement made between Stone and the British Library, copies of Stone's bank statements, and the purchase agreement for Chateau Puissant. The IAA had dropped the charges concerning the manuscripts found in the figurines. And, Art West by conversation with Harry had told him to drop all charges pertaining to his short entombment in Bethany. That left charges of theft, forgery, and attempted murder.

Jury selection had begun the Monday after the pre-trial hearing. The jury pool had already been skimmed by the two principle attorneys, with each rejecting four jurors for cause. A lot of pre-trial publicity had made jury selection difficult.

Judge Dershowitz then addressed Siegal and Levi, "Gentlemen, you may make your opening statements to the jury, Mr. Levi first."

"Ladies and gentleman of the jury, this is no ordinary trial. Because the nature of this crime strikes at the heart of both the Jewish and Christian heritage here in Eretz Israel, and endangers our ability to continue to have and pass on that legacy, we are dealing with far more than theft and assault. We are dealing with an attempt to get rich by stripping a people of its heritage and identity. This is the crime of all looters and forgers who seek to profit by illicit means.

"The Lazarus stone is no ordinary artifact. The British Library paid the enormous sum of 20 million pounds sterling to obtain it. The theft of this object would be equivalent to the theft of the chariot of King Tut or the Rosetta stone. And what makes this crime all the more heinous is that it has been perpetrated not by a petty thief or ordinary tomb raider, but by a well-known professor from a prestigious university in the United States.

"Unlike the ordinary thief who cannot read ancient languages, this thief," Levi continued, pointing to Patrick Stone, "this thief knew precisely what he had found and precisely what its value was likely to be. So desperate was he to have this object that he was prepared to attempt murder with his own gun to silence the one man, an antiquities dealer here in Jerusalem, a good and honest man, who knew he had possession of this stone. Stopping at nothing Stone connived to get the Lazarus stone out of the country and sell it to the British Library before anyone could stop him. On top of this he tried to blacken the name of another man, Professor West, and throw the scent off his own trail by having the British Library transfer over a million dollars into West's

Jerusalem bank account, fingering him as the one really guilty of stealing the Lazarus stone.

"Here is a driven, self-centered, greedy man who wanted to cash in on someone else's inheritance. Unlike the case of Jacob and Esau, this man," again pointing at Stone, "didn't bargain for another man's inheritance, he stole it outright. Outrageous! It is our contention that Patrick Stone should feel the full brunt of Israeli justice, not least so that it will be a deterrent for all that might seek to follow in his footsteps. By early Jewish law, he himself should be stoned at least for the attempted murder of Mr. El Said! We need to make an example out of Dr. Patrick Stone, and we intend to leave no evidentiary stone unturned until justice is done!"

There was a round of applause in the courtroom, which Dershowitz gaveled into submission. Simon Siegal arose looking confident.

"It is a sad day when anyone loses something precious, all the more so if it has great historical significance. But this artifact is not lost. Indeed it is being held for eventual display to the public at one of the world's leading museums—the British Library, home to other Jewish artifacts. One could argue that Professor Stone has done the world a favor, by personally bringing the inscription to London. With our outdated laws pertaining to relics, the inscription might never leave Israel. Indeed, it would probably languish in some laboratory examined by scholars alone—much like other scrolls that have not been released to the public. And you know, ladies and gentleman, far more people visit London, where it is safer. Our terrorist environment frightens tourists away!" There. Siegal had already managed to remind the audience of terrorists in general, and now he could build on that. He could not resist adding, "Our terrorist environment even led to the kidnapping of Dr. Stone by a member of Hamas, right out from under our noses. I am sure you have all read about the brutal treatment of Dr. Stone, who is still healing from his injuries at terrorists' hand.

"Furthermore, this Lazarus stone is of much greater importance to the Christian world, than it is to us. For us, it is an interesting curiosity that raises a few questions. For devout Christians the inscription confirms the Gospel accounts that Jesus actually was a faith healer! That Jesus raised the dead! For Christians, the words on the stone provide a witness that Jesus and resurrection go together, that Jesus and messiahship go together!

"Ask any of the IAA members here who have seen this stone whether it has that significance for them as Jews. I think not. So let us not exaggerate the nature of this theft. There is a reason why Dr. Stone went to a Christian nation to sell this object.

"But wait, what if Dr. Stone did not steal this object at all? Suppose he obtained it from his over-zealous teaching assistant, Raymond Simpson, whose fingerprints were all over the forged copy of the stone and its mail wrapper? The testimony will show that Simpson was in the tomb and made the copy of the inscription. Can any one of you here say that if this object were brought to you, you would not be tempted to keep it? Can any of you say that once you had the valuable object and had sought to have it brokered to the proper people right here in Jerusalem, but were turned down by a leading antiquities dealer, that you would not be very angry with that dealer? Even admitting that Kahlil El Said was harmed in the process, the evidence will show that no assault was intended, that Kahlil El Said's wounds were accidental only.

"Though you see here a well-known, international scholar, it was not always so. In fact, Patrick Stone comes from humble origins—from Johnson City, Tennessee. His grandparents sold illegal whiskey, or 'moonshine' as it is called, to put food on the table. Patrick's father, Leroy, rose to be mayor of that small town; he was a heavy drinker, who beat his son Patrick, telling him he was no good and would never amount to much. The lashing out of his father in word and in deed drove Patrick to spend his life trying hard to prove that he was somebody, somebody important. His father belittled his academic accomplishments, calling his son an educated fool.

"Do you know ladies and gentleman what that does to a person's psyche when a parent abuses, neglects, and belittles? I think you do know the lasting effects of such abuse. Now picture in your mind Patrick Stone. Though he was a grown man who had accomplished much in academia, it was never enough, never validated him to the one person he most wanted approval from—his father. There is often a great gap between who a person is, and how they see themselves. This was clearly the case with Patrick Stone. Good enough was never good enough.

"On that fateful day when the Lazarus stone came into Patrick's possession, he was like a child in a toy store, only now the child within him saw a way to finally prove to at least the scholars at one of the world's greatest museums that he was somebody, somebody important.

He managed to turn the stone over to the world's most famous museum, which promised to keep his identity a secret—imagine the humility in that act! In his heart, he knew he had broken away from the need to please—he had done the right thing!

"It is a sad and tragic story, the tale of Patrick Stone, who in a moment of weakness made a tragic error in judgment despite a previously spotless record of integrity. Which one of us has not had such a moment of weakness? Who are we to cast the first stone, as Mr. Levi has suggested we should? I submit to you, ladies and gentlemen of the jury, that Patrick Stone deserves a better fate. I trust that when you judge the evidence in light of the man, you will judge with mercy and fairness."

By the time Siegal had finished his amazing opening salvo, some members of the jury were in tears. Harry whispered to Benjamin, "Like I said, we really have our work cut out for us in this case."

The gavel brought everyone back to reality. "We will recess until after lunch," said Dershowitz firmly.

# 63

# The Case for the Prosecution

THE LUNCH RECESS HAD been uneventful, and Harry had not eaten much, so revved up was he after Levi had told him he would be first up to bat to do the inquisition on Ray Simpson.

Scholer had tirelessly prepared himself, and so he stood up before the court, cleared his throat, and said, "The prosecution calls Raymond Simpson."

Dressed simply but neatly in khaki slacks and a plaid sport shirt, not a suit, as the prosecution did not wish to portray him as a professional of any kind, Ray took the stand. After he was sworn in, Scholer began to grill him.

"Mr. Simpson what, is your relationship with Patrick Stone?"

"I am his teaching assistant at Yale, and his doctoral student."

"And what was it that brought you to Israel?"

"Dr. Stone asked me to come and help him with his research, and I was excited to do so. It will look good on my resume."

"Very good, and how would you describe the work Dr. Stone asked you to do this past month while in Israel?"

"Nothing at all like what he asked me to do when I was at Yale."

"What do you mean? Describe what he asked you to do."

"Well, for one thing, instead of doing research or digging, he had me trailing Dr. Arthur West. He even had me trail him to a bank and get his checking account number by devious means. He was obsessed with finding out what Dr. West was doing in Bethany."

"Objection," said Siegal. "Some of this calls for speculation about the state of mind of Dr. Stone."

"Sustained," said Dershowitz. "The last sentence will be stricken from the record."

Scholer continued, "Tell us more about what he had you do besides follow Dr. West."

"Well, here's a short list. First, he asked me to help trap West in the tomb behind the Church of Mary and Martha. It took both of us to move that stone quickly before Dr. West could get out. Second, later that same day, Dr. Stone brought me pictures of an inscription. He asked me to make a quick copy. Third, he asked me to wrap up the copy, take it to a courier, and make sure the copy would arrive on Dr. West's doorstep the following morning. Finally, on Tuesday afternoon he left me a number of figurines and a note that I later threw away. The note said to store the figurines in my locker at the Bethlehem bus station."

"Did you know where the inscription came from?"

"I read the text—I knew it was from the Bethany Church. I'm sorry about all that."

"And the figurines—did you know what was in them. Didn't you find the request rather strange?"

"I swear I didn't know what was in the figurines. And I couldn't figure out why he would want them hidden in *my* locker of all places. If they weren't valuable, why not leave them at his apartment?"

"Thank you, Mr. Simpson. We enter into the records exhibits A, B, and C—the copy of the stone inscription including the paper wrapping, the four figurines, and the key to the locker. However, for security sake, the manuscripts have been removed."

Dershowitz once again took control.

"Do you wish to cross-examine this witness, Mr. Siegal?"

"Certainly your honor, I have but a few questions for him."

"Mr. Simpson, how old are you?"

"Twenty-seven, sir."

"And would you consider yourself a responsible adult?"

"More like an educated fool!"

"And did Professor Stone actually order you to do anything?"

"No, it would be more correct to say he strongly urged me to help."

'Very good, and so he did not threaten you in any way, right?"

"Well, indirectly, I suppose, in the sense that he told me if I helped him that he would write me a glowing recommendation for a job at Johns Hopkins. Believe me, when Dr. Stone says 'jump,' I just reply 'how high.'"

"Yes, of course, he is your superior. Would it be true to say, Mr. Simpson, that you have been offered a more lenient sentence for your cooperation with the prosecution."

"Yes, that's so. I'll be doing community service for some time."

"One more thing, were you present with Dr. Stone either when he was alleged to be in the antiquities shop or later when he is alleged to have assaulted Mr. El Said?"

"No sir, I was home with my roommate, Grayson Johnson, drinking Maccabee beer, and eating Cheetos." Laughter broke out in the courtroom.

"Exactly so, and so you have no personal knowledge at all of Dr. Stone committing any act of violence on those occasions—correct?"

"I wasn't in either place."

"Lastly, did Dr. Stone tell you where he was going and what he was doing when he fled the country?"

"No sir, his note simply said he was going home, and that he would see me back at school. He even left me money and the use of his flat."

"Very generous of him, wouldn't you say?"

Before Raymond could answer the question, Siegal turned and said, "No further questions."

"Redirect, your honor!" cried Levi.

"Mr. Simpson, if Dr. Stone was such a great mentor, why then did you feel compelled to attempt to flee the country?"

"Because I knew that Dr. Stone and I had done something wrong, and I was afraid he would leave me holding the bag." This led to some murmuring in the courtroom, but Simpson was allowed to step down.

As Raymond was dismissed, Levi called his next witness, Kahlil El Said.

"Mr. El Said, what is your profession?"

"I am an antiquities dealer in the old city."

"And is it not correct to say you are one of the leading experts amongst the dealers in ancient stone objects?"

"Yes. I am proud of my reputation as an honest antiquities dealer."

"So then it is in no way surprising that Dr. Stone came and showed *you* what we now call the Lazarus stone, seeking to sell it to you or have you broker it to another."

"No, it is not surprising."

"What was the demeanor of Dr. Stone when he came into the shop?"

"He was pacing the floor. When I turned him down, he called me an imbecile! Then he rudely referred to my shop as a 'small business in a God-forsaken part of town!' He was most insulting. I was shocked that one claiming to be an academic would say such demeaning things."

"Not surprising by American standards. Sorry, your honor for the sarcasm. Now, Mr. El Said, are you quite certain that it was Dr. Stone, the man sitting over there, who came to your shop."

"Absolutely sure."

"Mr. El Said, I see that you have a bandage on your head. Can you tell the court how you came to injure yourself?"

"I was shot. When I fell I hit my head on an iron bench in the park behind the Shrine of the Book. I spent a week in the hospital."

"Do you have any idea who shot you, could you see his face in the dark?"

"Yes, that man!" Kahlil pointed to Patrick Stone.

"Did you have a conversation with Patrick Stone before he shot you?"

"He said, 'How could you deny me like that? Surely I can convince you to broker the inscription for me!'"

"You took that to refer to the conversation earlier in the day?"

"Yes, I did."

"Then what happened?"

"He pulled out a small gun and began to wave it at me. I grabbed his hand. Apparently, the gun went off. That is all I remember."

"But you are sure it was Dr. Patrick Stone that shot you."

"Without a doubt."

"Thank you, Mr. El Said, nothing further. I hope your full health returns."

Again Dershowitz pronounced, "Mr. Siegal, do you have any questions at this point?"

Siegal arose and approached El Said.

"At any time before he pulled the gun, did you feel threatened?"

"Not really, he had already shown his true colors in my shop."

"Why did you grab the gun?"

"It was foolish, perhaps, but I just wanted that gun to go away!"

"Do you feel that your actions caused the gun to go off—that my client never intended to hurt you, merely to scare you?"

"I agree, that is possible."

"Is it not the case that you were in a coma for a long time after the shooting?"

"Yes, for several days, and then I had amnesia, but my memory is clear now."

"Is it not possible that some other angry client assailed you and you thought it was Stone because his anger was fresh in your mind? Isn't it possible in light of your concussion that you have muddled things up in your mind?"

"I don't believe so, and besides the man spoke English with an American not an Israeli or Palestinian accent. I have not had other Americans angry with me of late."

"No more questions, your honor."

Judge Dershowitz was impressed by Siegal's probing questions. He definitely steered the onus of the crime away from his client. "Call your next witness, Mr. Levi."

Levi's voice rang out, "The court calls Detective Hoffner to the stand.

"Detective, can you tell us in what capacity you have been involved in these matters."

"In various ways. I examined both the weapon and the coat. I was also involved in the recovery of the manuscripts in the figurines, and monitoring the whereabouts of Dr. Stone."

"Let me enter into record, exhibits D, E, and F—the gun, the coat, and the tape recoding. Very good. Tell us first what you found when you examined the gun. Where was this found?"

"It was found on the park bench beside the body of Mr. El Said when we arrived at the crime scene."

"I see, tell us about this weapon," Levi held up Exhibit D, the gun.

"It is a nineteenth-century derringer, one shot only. I tracked it to a gun shop in Johnson City, Tennessee. The owner of the shop claimed that such a gun was owned by Dr. Stone's father, Leroy. We now have an affidavit showing that the gun used to shoot El Said matches the description of the gun owned by Dr. Stone and his father. We also have documents from Dr. Shelby Hande of the United States explaining the historical significance of this antique weapon."

"Yes, we have those reports. And were there any fingerprints found on the weapon?"

"Yes, but not those of the defendant. Rather they were the prints of Dr. Arthur West who arrived at the scene apparently after the shooting."

"I see. But if there are no prints of the gun, how do we know Dr. Stone is the perpetrator and not Dr. West?"

"It involves two bits of evidence. First, Dr. Stone's DNA was found in hairs on El Said's coat that he wore that night. This can hardly be explained if he was not there, and the gun was right next to the body. Secondly, as I said before, we have a sworn deposition from Johnson City, Tennessee that such a gun belonged at one time to Dr. Stone's father, Leroy. The natural inference must be that he is the shooter."

"And not Dr. West?"

"No sir, he was immediately tested for gun powder residue and blood splatters. He was clean."

"Nothing further your honor," said Benjamin Levi.

The Judge's gaze shifted, "Mr. Siegal?"

Siegal strode forward and looked Hoffner in the eye.

"Detective Hoffner, how long have you been on the force? And what is your area of expertise?"

"Eight years now specializing in forensic science including guns and ballistics."

"Very good. Have you ever dealt with a handgun quite like this before?"

"No sir."

"And you do not know that Leroy gave his son such a weapon, do you?"

"No sir, but it is a logical inference."

"Yes, well many things are logical if you are arguing in a circle. Would you consider yourself an expert in the forensic matter of examining DNA evidence based on hair fibers?"

"Well . . . not technically, but our lab boys do know about these things."

"Detective Hoffner, can you please tell us about the phone call you monitored in the house of Raymond Simpson here in Jerusalem earlier this month?"

"Yes sir. Simpson was already in custody, but Stone did not know that, and so he spoke with Simpson's roommate Grayson Johnson."

"What was said?"

"It is all on tape. Exhibit F I believe. Stone was wanting to ask Johnson to tell Simpson to return the figurines!"

"And these figurines, Exhibit B, contain priceless manuscripts, is that correct?

"The very same sir."

"Let me be clear about this, he turned to the jury, Mr. Stone wished for Raymond Simpson to *return* the figurines! To the Three Arches shop?"

"He specifically said not to return them to the shop. He wanted to give Raymond specific directions on how to return those figurines. He didn't mention they contained manuscripts."

"So Dr. Stone planned to return the manuscripts to their rightful owner."

Benjamin Levi jumped up, "Objection your owner, calls for speculation."

"Sustained. Be careful, Mr. Siegal," said the Judge firmly.

"Detective, was this a *legal* wire tap?"

"Yes sir, by the book."

"Very good, nothing further."

Harry and Benjamin looked at each other—the testimony about the figurines certainly painted Stone in a more pleasing light. Levi arose, and said,

"I have one last witness, and I will be brief your honor."

"When is a loquacious man like you ever brief? Carry on," smiled the judge.

"I call Mustafa el Din, caretaker of the Church of Mary and Martha."

Mustafa came to the dock wearing his clerical robe.

"Mustafa, I have but one question for you. Have you ever seen the defendant wandering around the inside or outside of the Church of Mary and Martha?"

"Yes, on Tuesday, June 1, I saw two men roaming around the church in the morning. One was the man sitting there, Dr. Stone. The other man was younger, and I did not see his face clearly. I was busy in the church the rest of the day and saw no one else."

"Did you see them wandering around the back of the church?'

"I saw them wandering in that direction in the morning, yes."

"That's all I have for this witness."

The judge looked at Siegal, "Your turn."

"Mr. el Din, is it your testimony that on June first my client was wandering around your church? Did you actually see him behind your church?"

"No, I saw two men heading in that direction, and then I went back in the church. One of the men was Dr. Stone for sure."

"But at the time you didn't know who they were, nor did it seem important to you to see what they were up to since you went back in the church? Is that not right?"

"I was very busy on that day. There was no reason to be alarmed."

"Ah, they posed no threat?" said Siegal who turned, held up his hands, and went to his seat before objections could even be raised.

Dershowitz gaveled the first day's proceedings to an end. It had been a draining experience for all. Harry turned to Levi and said, "So far so good. All evidence points to his guilt."

But as Siegal turned to leave he whispered to Stone, "So far so good. You never came across as a true criminal. You are a good man who never meant to hurt anyone, and with your latest escapade you are a victim of terrorism as well." Things were looking up for Patrick Stone.

# 64

## Turning Points

THE VIDEOGRAPHER HAD COME right on time—with both Simon Siegal and Harry Scholer in tow—to film Art West's testimony and responses. At that moment Art was sitting up in his bed drinking Haifa orange juice and trying not to look like death warmed over. He had shaved for the first time, and with the help of the nurse he had showered and combed his hair. "You can't make a silk purse out of a sow's ear," said Art to himself. Art had talked to Grace at some length about what he would say at the trial, talking through with her his strong feeling of wanting the court to have mercy on Stone. Grace had reminded him that that must be left in the judge's and jury's hands.

"OK," said Art, "I am as ready as I can be. Roll the tape . . ."

Jamison Parkes Law had called the guard to let him out of Jesse James's cell. The word was out that West was out of danger, and so the most James could be charged with was assault with a deadly weapon. But, Art West had told Harry the night before by phone that he did not plan to press charges against his assailants. The office of the prosecuting attorney was mulling over whether to charge James anyway. Law turned and said to James, "Remember, the less said the better. We will wait to see what the prosecuting attorney intends to do."

"Right," said Jesse, "but you know I don't feel bad about what went down. The man was a menace."

"I told you to zip it!" said Law, "the authorities are monitoring this place." And he walked out in disgust. "I think I know how Jesus must have felt about Judas, on some occasions," he muttered to himself.

Rabbi Menachem's phone in his study was ringing off the hook. Finally he managed to get to his chair and pick it up. He moved slowly these days. The last few weeks had really taxed his patience and wisdom. It turned out to be a police officer in Migdal. "Is this Rabbi Menachem?"

"Yes," said the Rabbi, "What may I do for you?"

"I have here a note from someone named Sedek Hadar, do you recognize that name?"

"Yes," said the Rabbi, "he was supposed to have called me yesterday, but he failed to do so."

"Well rabbi, that would have been impossible as Sedek yesterday morning, after charging a group of Palestinians who were throwing stones at the Jewish settlement where he lived in Hebron, was shot dead by one of the members of Hamas who had been goading the children into throwing stones."

A tear began to form in the rabbi's right eye.

"Rabbi, this note is to you from Hadar, and so I thought I should read it: 'Rabbi, I am sorry to have failed you in various ways, but perhaps in the end I can redeem the honor of my name, which means 'Righteous' as you know very well, and show myself worth of being a son of Zion by standing up against those who seek to destroy our Jewish settlements here in Hebron. Tomorrow morning I plan to go out and stand against the rock throwers and the guns, and tell them to leave us alone. If you receive this note, you will know I have died in a noble cause, as I have left it in my pocket to be found by the police. May God be with you and your righteous teachings.'"

"Thank you officer," said the Rabbi, and hung up with tears now streaming down his face. Quoting Sirach he said to himself "'Blessed are those who die in the Lord . . .' There is now no reason to tell anyone about Sedek's mistakes. He has paid the ultimate penalty already, and is past the point of no return. I shall arrange for an honorable funeral for him now."

For some reason a line from a poem the rabbi had learned as a child came to mind "Life and death upon one tether . . . and running beautiful together."

# 65

## The Case for the Defense

T HE SECOND MORNING OF the trial began with Simon Siegal striding
into the courtroom in a bright blue jacket. Someone had failed to
turn on the air conditioner early enough, and everyone was sweating at
ten o'clock in the morning.

The first witness that Siegal called was Dr. Shelby Hande of
Memphis, Tennessee. Harry and Levi had no idea why Siegal thought it
was so important to bring this gentleman all the way from the US. They
looked forward to this piece of testimony.

Dr. Hande looked rather like Colonel Sanders given his gray hair,
goatee, and mustache. He was dressed in a tweed jacket and dark pants
held up by red suspenders. He cut quite a figure; the word colorful was
more than appropriate.

"Dr. Hande, thank you for coming all the way to Jerusalem."

"Least I could do considering you were paying. I plan to enjoy a
little sightseeing afterwards. I didn't realize you were Civil War buffs."

There was a little ironic laughter in the room, since what the term
"Civil War" meant to most Israelis was the struggle between Palestinians
and Israelis, and to others it was an oxymoron—there had never been
a war that was civil.

"Mr. Hande, here we have exhibit C, the derringer alleged to have
been used in the shooting of Kahlil El Said." He handed the weapon to
Shelby who looked it over carefully.

"Do you recognize this type of gun?"

"Yes, indeed I do. It's a nineteenth-century, single-bore, one-shot derringer, carried on one's person as a last line of defense."

"Defense, you say?"

"You hard a hearin'? Yes sir, defense, both during and after the American Civil War. A derringer like this one is hardly an offensive weapon. It produced no velocity to the bullet and if you were more than five feet from the intended target little damage would be done. As I said, it's a last line of defense weapon, to be used only at close range. They're more of a souvenir or a curiosity item, kept as a family heirloom."

"Now, Dr. Hande, in your judgment would an intelligent person, a knowledgeable person from Tennessee like yourself know that this was no assault weapon?"

"Objection. Calls for speculation about what Dr. Stone knows," called out Harry Scholer.

"Rephrase the question," ordered the judge.

"OK. Dr. Hande, in your judgment if someone knew anything about this antique derringer, would they set out with this weapon to assault someone?"

"No sir, that's ludicrous on the face of things. If I wanted to kill someone, I'd use a Colt 45!" The jury now had visions of the Wild West.

"But perhaps someone might bring it for protection or as a threat perhaps?"

"Yes, that's far more plausible."

"Thank you very much, Dr. Hande."

"Cross-examine?" asked Dershowitz.

Harry rose up. "Dr. Hande, I have long been an admirer of your volumes on the Civil War, and I have no dispute with what you say about this gun, but let me ask you, Was this weapon ever known to be used to kill anyone, any record of anyone killed by being shot by this gun?"

"Yes, but only in very close quarters. More often it might be used to finish someone off."

"But as you yourself have said, this weapon carried only one bullet. You might well feel malicious and angry enough to shoot someone with this weapon without worrying too much that you were likely to kill them, isn't that true?"

"Derringers like this were used in duels if it was to be real close quarters. This was a regular thing. Sometimes there would be sword fights—with some wounds. Then derringers would finish the duel, again to redeem one's honor."

"Very good, is honor a major consideration for people raised in Tennessee?"

"Nowadays, no," said Shelby. "Folks have lost their sense of honor and shame mostly, in America, even in the South, but for men of my age or thereabouts, raised in the old South, then yes, it could be an honor thing."

"One more thing. If you had a precious antiquity from the Civil War that you wanted to sell, say Robert E. Lee's sword, or the saddle worn by Traveler his horse, if you went to a Civil War memorabilia dealer and he refused to even talk price with you, would that make you angry, would you feel shamed by that exchange?"

"Yes I would, and so would many other Southern gentlemen."

"So speaking again only for yourself, might this lead you to try and do something to redeem your honor in regard to the one who shamed you?"

"Yes sir, that is entirely possible."

"Thank you, nothing further."

The Judge's voice rang out in the heat of the morning, "Mr. Siegal, call your next witness."

"I would like to call Dr. Arthur West to the stand but since that is clearly impossible being that he is in the hospital, I have gone to him and asked my questions, as has Mr. Scholer. I am happy to report he is on the mend."

Siegal popped the video tape into the large TV/VCR unit which was hooked up in tandem with a second unit so all of the principles including the judge and the jury could watch this crucial testimony. Siegal began the questioning

"Dr. West, I must be direct with you, though I am mindful of not overtaxing you today."

"Go right ahead."

"Were you scheduled to have a meeting with Kahlil El Said at nine o' clock in the park behind the Shrine of the Book on the night he was shot?"

"Yes, I was."

"And did you make that meeting?'

"Well in a manner of speaking. When I got there Kahlil was already shot and on the ground. I heard the shot as I was walking up the hill near the Shrine."

"Would it be correct to say that your fingerprints were the only one's found on that derringer?"

"Yes, that is correct."

Harry Scholer got carried away at that point. Sticking his face in the camera he said: "Your honor, testimony has already been heard clearing Dr. West of the shooting."

Siegal continued: "And would it be correct to say that you were the person who discovered the Lazarus stone, and also had a close relationship with Kahlil El Said."

"Yes, I have known Kahlil El Said for many years."

"And lastly would it also be correct to say that you were short on money for this season's dig, and so selling a precious piece of antiquity might have funded you quite well?"

"As to the first part of the question, you are right. I was short on funds. As for the second part, my integrity has been upheld in this matter, and I am not on trial here. I would never sell something found more recently than 1978 in this land. Never. This ought to be clear from the fact that I turned over to the police all the money that mysteriously appeared in my bank account a few days ago. It's against the law to sell such antiquities."

"But it is strange that you are the only one who has a self-admitted link to the crime scenes and to Kahlil, whom Dr. Stone had not met before, and it is only you who have prints on the gun. And last but not least, you were found in possession of the forged copy of the stone. Is that not so?" By now Simon was becoming more insistent and strident in his tone.

"All of these things are true, and yet I have committed no crime. All of the evidence so far presented accurately explains all of these situations."

"Thank you, Professor West, enlightening but not convincing since you are the only one who has admitted to all the right connections in this case."

Harry Scholer then appeared in front of the camera.

"Dr. West," he began, "can you tell the court where you went the very morning you discovered the Lazarus stone in the tomb?"

"After a quick shower and change of clothes at home, I went straight to the IAA with my digital pictures, which are even dated as to time. They show that I reached the IAA office within an hour of taking that picture."

"Very good, and tell me would it have been logistically possible, since no one before you even knew there was a Lazarus stone, to have taken that picture, then chiseled the stone out of its place and hidden it, then showered, gone straight to the IAA and shown them the picture, then returned to the tomb and acted surprised it was gone? Would such a course of actions made any sense at all?"

"In my judgment no," said Art, "and anyway, the date and time on the picture shows I did not have time to chisel out the stone and hide it before going to the IAA. That's a delicate operation which takes at least an hour in itself, as limestone is fragile and the stone would have broken if it had not been chiseled out with care."

"So you are saying, just to be completely clear, that there is no way you stole the Lazarus stone and sold it to someone?"

"Correct," said Art, "as should have been apparent since we now know that Patrick Stone had it in his possession and sold it to the British Library since the Museum has told the court so."

"How would you characterize your relationship with Patrick Stone? Have you been friends or close colleagues?"

"No we have not, indeed for whatever reason Dr. Stone has avoided me, and there seems to be some antipathy. We have never hit it off, and he has never been in my house either in the States or here."

"So anyone who knows you, would know that a scheme that would involve both you and Patrick Stone in some antiquities crime is highly unlikely?"

"Indeed," said Art, " and the British Library also attested that it was Stone who gave them my account number to wire the money to."

"How in the world did Stone get your account number, if you were not close friends and he had never visited you?"

"I have no idea, but it had to be by some nefarious means."

Harry interjected, "Let the record show that Simpson has already testified he got the number for his mentor when he followed West to the bank one day."

This was the end of the videotape testimony and it was clear that the wounded warrior West had cut a sympathetic figure on tape.

The Judge called out, "Mr. Siegal, have you a further witness?"

"Well no your honor but I'd like to recall, Kahlil El Said."

"I object, your honor," said Levi, "The man has already testified."

"He is here in the court, I believe, so I will allow it," said the Judge.

"Mr. El Said, I am sorry to trouble you further, but I must ask one more time. Had you ever personally met Dr. Stone before that day you claim he was in your shop?"

"No sir."

"And even on that occasion, did you know that he was Dr. Stone?"

"No, it was a brief exchange, but memorable after all."

"So you had never seen Stone before that day in your shop, didn't know he was Stone then, and after that you got a blow on the head and your memory came back slowly—right?"

"If you say so," said Kahlil fuming a bit.

"No more questions."

Harry rose and asked Kahlil, "Hasn't the doctor cleared you to go back to work in the shop on the assumption that you are now of sound mind?"

"Yes, that is correct," said Kahlil feeling a bit better.

Harry nodded his head toward the judge who said, "You may step down, Mr. El Said."

At that point, Levi asked if he could approach the bench. A courier had quietly entered the courtroom during Kahlil's testimony. The judge summoned both Siegal and Levi to the bar. Harry said, "We have a witness in the hall who couldn't get here yesterday."

"Mr. Siegal, I am trusting that since you didn't challenge this name before you will not challenge the name now—William Arnold."

Siegal was not pleased, but tried to maintain a poker face. He said, "Alright, he can come in but I have the right to cross-examine him."

"Indeed you do."

"The prosecution calls William Arnold."

William Arnold came into the court wearing a seersucker blazer and white gauze shirt. His dark features and goatee made him stand out from the crowd.

"Mr. Arnold, can you state your profession?"

"Yes, and it's Dr. Arnold. I am a professor of Aramaic and Biblical Studies at a leading seminary in Kentucky, Asbury Seminary."

"Very good, and to get right to the point, were you in Kahlil's shop the day Patrick Stone came in? If so, please describe what happened."

"Yes I was. It was late afternoon, Tuesday, June 1. I had just finished purchasing some coins. I have here the receipt to prove that I was there on that day. I carefully save receipts from such purchases. It even has a time stamp on it." He handed the receipt to Harry who passed it to the Judge.

Harry smiled, "I'm glad you are very careful with your money, Dr. Arnold. And do you give equal attention to the details about people's names and faces?"

"I do indeed."

"Do you know Dr. Patrick Stone?"

"I have met him at ASOR meetings several times—that's the American Society of Oriental Religion."

"And did you see him in Kahlil's shop on the day in question, fuming, and trying to sell something?"

"Yes, I saw him on that precise day with the package in his hand. I couldn't see the contents from where I was sitting in the back of the shop. He started shouting. Hannah El Said, I believe, was hiding behind a desk."

"Nothing further."

Siegal leapt up. "Dr Arnold, you say you know Patrick Stone, and yet how can you be sure? Are you a personal friend of his?"

"No, I am not, but I have certainly met him before and spoken briefly with him. Here is an ASOR program from three years ago. There was a listing of the panelists for a discussion—Patrick Stone and William Arnold were listed side by side."

"This proves nothing. For all we know Dr. Stone did not show up for this panel discussion."

"Ah, but he did," smiled Dr. Arnold. "In the very next issue of ASOR we have the dialogue that he, I, and the other scholar had on that occasion." He handed the journal to Siegel who was obliged to enter it into evidence.

"You have no idea, however, what was in the package?"

"No, I never saw it. When Mr. El Said returned, embarrassed, he dismissed the incident."

"You are a much younger man that Patrick Stone, still making your reputation—yes?"

"Yes."

"And so it would be to your advantage to claim you had a relationship with the famous Patrick Stone of Yale—yes?"

"Not any more," said Arnold and smiled.

Siegal made a face and said, "Nothing further your honor."

"Mr. Siegal, have you any more witnesses?"

"Since we believe we have shown reasonable doubt about Dr. Stone's guilt in these matters, the defense rests, now your honor," said Siegal.

"Very good, we will hear closing statements on Monday at 10 a.m. Court is dismissed."

On the steps of the courthouse the press stuck microphones first in the face of Siegal and then in the faces of Levi and Scholer, asking for comments. On this day both parties said, "The transcripts which will be available in about a half hour, speak for themselves, we are confident of victory in this matter."

# 66

# Closing Arguments

HARRY SPENT MOST OF the weekend working on and practicing his closing speech to the jury. Art had finally come home and was lying on the couch listening periodically but had a habit of dozing off. He was physically and emotionally drained. He had told the truth in the videotape, but why did he feel so sorry for Stone? He prayed a prayer that mercy tempered with justice, rather than the reverse, would prevail.

On the other end of town, Simon Siegal spent the weekend having long talks with Patrick Stone. Saturday afternoon was no exception.

"I think a guilty verdict will possibly come your way. The prosecution is probably so smug at this point, that I doubt they would be open to a plea bargain. Sentencing will be important. I think I've built a good sympathy case for you."

"Sympathy, you say. How much damage did Arnold do me?"

"Probably a good deal. I was doing damage control to stop the 'ugly American' characterization."

"What would jail time look like?" said Stone.

"Well, on the theft charge, they could sentence you to twenty years. But I think we've shown that you had no intention of hurting Kahlil—even though you left the scene of the crime. What we will have to do is plead for the minimum time and early parole."

Stone thought for a while and said, "I'm sixty-eight years old. I've kept all of this from my mother. She's senile, you know. She'll probably never miss me."

Siegal was not used to losing, but on this occasion he had a sick feeling in his stomach. He decided that he had better come up with a tour-de-force closing statement to evoke maximum mercy from the court.

Judge Dershowitz spent his weekend mulling over his options for sentencing. He was not a man lacking in sympathy for the weaknesses of human beings, especially the desire to secure oneself in old age. He knew the jury would likely go for a guilty verdict—but they may opt for lesser charges. There were mitigating circumstances to consider. He had felt a nudge in the direction of justice tempered with mercy. The Lazarus stone would be returned. He believed that Stone had not planned to hurt El Said. He was surprised to learn that Stone planned to give back the small manuscripts. Stone was not the usual criminal—but a man suddenly out of control after a fairly controlled life.

Monday morning came too early for all the participants in the trial. Most of them loaded up on caffeine. The new Starbucks coffee shop near the courthouse had been doing a big business since the trial began. Siegal went to the jail to escort Patrick into court. Art arose earlier than usual for morning devotions but decided he needed to not go through the emotional trauma of the end of the trial and so he would stay at home. His spirit was troubled. Sammy Cohen and Grace Levine decided to come together. They had not missed one minute of the proceedings. The matter with Ray Simpson had been resolved. He was ready to begin community service, but today he was allowed to attend the final session.

It was difficult even to climb the steps to get into the Maccabee Courthouse on this morning. Harry and Benjamin barged their way through the crowd. Siegal and Stone, of course, were escorted by the police.

Judge Dershowitz gaveled the session into order, and invited Siegal to deliver his closing arguments. On this day Siegel wore a dark business suit, and his mood was serious. No flippant remarks today. He wanted to look penitent and invoke the sympathies of the jury today.

"In Ecclesiastes we read, 'There is no righteous man on earth who solely does what is right and never sins.' Paul in Romans says the same thing, 'All have sinned and fallen short of God's glory.' I have not put my client on the stand because he is not a young man, and burdened with the weight of his current problems. Patrick Stone would be the first to admit he has his failings. He made some mistakes in regard to the Lazarus stone. The evidence seems to suggest he stole it, but remember that he did not keep the stone; he delivered it safely into the hands of the British Library. Mr. El Said suffered a severe blow to the head, which may have affected his memory, but the gun seems to suggest that my client did indeed shoot El Said. I absolutely believe my client when he tells me that his shooting of Kahlil El Said was entirely an accident, brought on by Mr. El Said himself when he grabbed the gun. And the gun—a derringer—we have heard testimony that this gun is hardly offensive. At most, Stone meant to instill some fear in the man. There is certainly reasonable doubt in regard to the charge of attempted murder!

"Dr. Stone's life has not been an easy one. His upbringing was hard; his lack of recognition even by family is galling, and it appears he was envious of Dr. Arthur West and his accomplishments. I asked you before jury, as I do again now, have you never been tempted to cheat when someone or fate offered you the chance of a lifetime? I think you know very well we have all had such temptations.

"The difference is, Dr. Stone followed through. Nothing pre-meditated. Hasty plans. A lot of luck. He found himself with money, a way to take care of his dear mother, and make his retirement years comfortable.

"Remember, Dr. Stone has not one crime to his record in sixty-eight years. He has been a well-respected academic. Should all of that go for naught because of one colossal blunder? Is there no such thing as a second chance for a man who has only crossed the boundaries of the law once?

"It is my hope that you feel some pity, some mercy in your heart for this man. Garnish his ill-gotten gains, return the stone to the Israeli museum, but if you impose a harsh sentence now, he will never see the light of day again. He is sixty-eight years old and hardly in the peak of health. If he goes to jail for any length of time at all, he will never have a chance to bounce back, to redeem himself, to try again to be a good man. Furthermore, he has been a recent victim of a terrorist's kidnapping—a harrowing experience to be sure.

"Ladies and gentleman of the jury. Let that stone," Siegal said as he pointed to the picture of the Lazarus stone set on an easel, "be returned. But let that Stone," pointing to Patrick, "be returned to his home, not the jailer."

There was a hush in the courtroom. The speech had been eloquent and moving, and there were plenty of tears, especially among the older persons in the room. To watch the ruination of a once proud and note-worthy human being was hard even for the most hard-hearted.

Harry Scholer arose, sipped a little water out of a glass, and walked around to face the jury. He looked each one in the eye before he said a word. "Friends," he said, "this is a sad day. No one should be gloating over the ruination of a man's life. But the saddest part of it all is that Dr. Patrick Stone has no one but himself to blame. He cannot blame his parents; he cannot blame his culture. He had coped well and not violated the law his whole life. He earned a PhD and though not the most notable of scholars, he was a professor at a prestigious university.

"Stone made a tragic series of decisions recently. Who knows why it happened now? Perhaps he ceased to fear or even believe in God? Perhaps he became tired of being an academic with no real prospects of further achievement. Perhaps he was just tired of living a mundane, lonely life. But consider for a moment a contrast.

"When Arthur West was at the scene of Kahlil El Said's shoot-ing, and had actually touched the gun that shot Kahlil, he called both the ambulance and the police. He did not think of himself first; he did not run and hide. In fact, he went to the hospital and gave blood for Kahlil.

"When Arthur West first discovered the Lazarus stone, he took pictures and reported his findings to the IAA. Even when the forged copy of the stone was found in his house he did not run away. He faced the police inquiry with dignity. When Art West had a huge amount of money unexpectedly turn up in his bank account he turned it over to the police!

"What a contrast with the man who stole the stone, ran from a crime scene, left his teaching assistant in the lurch, swindled the British Library, and snuck off to a life of luxury in Monaco! Which of these sets of actions are the actions of an honest and good man? I am sure you know the answer to that question.

"We have presented clear and compelling evidence of the guilt of Dr. Stone, both in regard to the theft and forgery, and in regard to the shooting. In regard to the theft, Dr. Stone was seen in the area of the tomb at the church; he was seen in Kahlil's shop with the stone and positively identified by William Arnold, and we have the affidavits of Dr. Oliver St. James of the British Library who handled the so-called sale of the stone for millions of dollars. All of this has been entered into evidence.

"In regard to the forgery, it is clear that Patrick Stone ordered Raymond Simpson to make the copy and have it delivered to Arthur West.

"In regard to the shooting, it was his family heirloom, a derringer, that shot Kahlil El Said, and his hair fiber was found on the jacket Kahlil wore that day. His memory may be fuzzy about the details, but Mr. El Said has stated that Patrick Stone did indeed shoot him.

"The testimonial evidence against Dr. Stone is both clear and compelling. And I would remind you again of this fact—the IAA has been working very hard in recent years to stop looting and forging. The Lazarus stone is a major archaeological find. Don't send the wrong signals to looters that they can get off with a slap on the wrist when they try and steal our history for the sake of money and personal gain. Don't let it happen. As the Bible says, 'Whatsoever a man soweth, that he shall also reap.' Thank you."

Harry sat down feeling he had risen to the occasion and at least had left the right message ringing in the jurors' ears. The judge dismissed the jury with the charge, "Come back with a unanimous verdict on these various counts as soon as you reasonably can."

The jury left the courtroom, as did everyone else. As usual, all the counselors spoke to the media saying they were confident justice would be done. Everybody put their cell phones on ring, and went out to eat.

# 67

# And the Winner Is . . .

THE JURY WAS OUT only five hours. At four o'clock, the foreman of the jury called the judge and said, "We are ready to deliver the verdicts." Legal aides stationed at the courthouse started calling all the principles. The verdict was in.

The courtroom was packed and the jury came in all looking somber. The judge sat down in his seat, used his gavel, and said, "Members of the jury, have you reached a verdict in this case?"

The foreman stood up and handed the judge a folded piece of paper. Slowly Judge Dershowitz surveyed the verdicts. He turned to the foreman. "On the count of stealing the Lazarus stone, how do you find?"

"We find the defendant guilty, your honor."

"On the count of forgery, how do you find?"

"We find the defendant guilty, your honor"

Then the judge took a deep breath, "In regard to the attempted murder of Kahlil El Said, how do you find?"

"We find the defendant NOT guilty of attempted murder, but guilty of aggravated assault."

Stone buried his head in his hands and wept, his shoulders and torso shaking.

"Thank you jury, you are dismissed from further duties."

Then, surprisingly, Judge Dershowitz said, "Since it is within my powers to pass sentence NOW, I intend to do so. This was obviously a serious set of crimes committed by Dr. Stone, and he should not receive preferential treatment because of his academic contributions to society. I have determined that the following sentence meets the requirements of justice tempered with mercy.

"First, Dr. Stone must serve ten years in prison; however, he will be eligible for parole after five years.

"Secondly, all ill-gotten gains must be returned to the British Library through the garnishing of his two bank accounts, and the sale of his house and car in Monaco. If there is a windfall of extra money upon the sale of the house, the extra money must be set aside for the building of the Lazarus stone and papyri museum, next door to the Shrine of the book.

"Thirdly, in consultation with the IAA we have worked out an agreement with the British Library whereby one piece of the small papyri will go into the collection in the British Library, in exchange for the return of the Lazarus stone.

"Fourthly, the El Said family is free to sue Dr. Stone at any point if they so choose.

"Finally, Mr. Simon, I am afraid you will have to accept that your work was pro bono." At this, the gavel smashed down for the last time.

Harry stood up and yelled, "Hallelujah!" He hugged Benjamin Levi and his son, and Grace, and anyone else he could hug. Simon Siegal shook Dr. Patrick Stone's hand and watched as he was led away. They would discuss appeals but he could not see any reason to argue for a lesser sentence.

Art for his part was glad to hear by phone from Harry that Stone had not gotten life in prison. Of course, now he would lose his academic post as well, but there was nothing to be done about that. Now he could go back to concentrating on his work again. Suddenly the phone rang. It was Hannah.

"Are you feeling well enough to go out tonight for a while? Want to catch the 9 o'clock show at the Le Jazz Hot? You won't believe it, but Diana Krall is in town."

"Wow," said Art, "You bet. I've been wanting to hear her. I'm going to call Grace and see if she will come."

Hannah replied shyly, "You could also invite that nice Harry Scholer. And I should tell you, my father and I will not be suing poor Dr. Stone. It is time to forgive and forget."

Art figured the fastest way to find Grace was to phone her. He invited her to the show. She hesitated, "I would love to go but I have a favor to ask. Can we bring my mother? She and I have been enjoying each other's company of late. And she was fascinated by my description of the jazz club. Let's bring her!"

"Sure, the more the merrier," agreed Art. The Lazarus Effect, thought Art, things brought back from the dead, even troublesome relationships, even me from two gunshot wounds.

The line to get into Le Jazz Hot was reasonable, and soon the whole crew had arrived and was sharing a meal. An interesting group it was: Hannah and her father, Kahlil; Grace and her mother, Camelia; Art and his friend, Harry Scholer. When they were finishing their baklava and coffee, they wandered down to the little tables in the front of the small club. Not ten minutes later a beautiful blond in a black jump suit appeared. Her guitar player, bassist, and drummer started out without her. She then joined them with a rousing rendition of Coltrane's version of the Broadway tune, "My Favorite Things." Before Art knew what was happening Hannah and Harry were up on the dance floor! Art smiled a huge smile, and simply said, "The Lazarus Effect."

# 68

## The Lazarus Effect

TUESDAY MORNING ABOUT TEN o'clock, Art's phone rang. This time
it was Mustafa. "Brother Art, you must come soon. I have been
working with Grayson Johnson for some days. And now, we have a
surprise for you here at the church."

"How about I come this afternoon, say about one o'clock. Shall I
bring anyone?"

"Yes, you may bring everybody! I hope it will be a joyful time!
You must all come!" With that rather unusual barrage, Mustafa, a man
*normally* of few words, hung up. Now Art was eager just to do what he
had prayed about and then get himself to Bethany.

The headlines in the *Jerusalem Post* this morning said it all: STONE
GUILTY OF STEALING STONE.

They'd be talking about that trial and its sentencing for a long
time. The general sentiment on the street was that Patrick Stone got
off lightly, but no one was complaining too loudly since the inscription
would be coming back to Israel soon enough, and without cost to the
country. There was much to say, and much to share, and the impact of
the Lazarus findings would reverberate for a long time to come.

Art spoke to Grace, and said, "You gotta come with me and
Grayson. I hear there is another surprise at the Church of Mary and
Martha."

"Another one? This I have to see."

"I've got to go over to the police station and retrieve my passport and do one other errand. They are finally giving me the passport back. I guess that means I'm truly in the clear."

"Of course you are," said Grace, "shall we meet for lunch at Solomon's Porch and then go to the church?"

"Sure," said Art, "my appetite is coming back and I could really use some shwarma and rice."

"The shwarma, the better," quipped Grace.

"My bad puns are rubbing off on you, see ya soon."

The police station was remarkably quiet on this day, and Officer Shimon was surprised to see the tall figure walk slowly into the station. "I'm here to retrieve my passport and to see Yeshua James."

"Not a problem," said Hoffner, "I will accompany you."

Art took the walk down stairs to the cells slowly as he didn't want to push himself too hard just yet. He came to the cell where Stone had once been, but now Yeshua was sitting there biding his time.

"Officer will you give me a private minute with this man, he's not armed now? Would you just wait down at the end of the hall, and I will call for you when I'm done? Open the cell and lock me in there for a minute."

Art could see the stunned look on James's face and how uncomfortable he was with this surprising development, but he shrugged his shoulders and said nothing.

Art sat down next to the young man and said, "Jesse, I wanted to come and say personally to you that I forgive you, as does Jesus. You misjudged me, misjudged me badly. I am not the betrayer of the Bible or of Bible prophecy. Genuinely orthodox Christians like myself and Jamison Law can disagree on some things and still be genuine Christians. So I want to say again, I forgive you, but you need to get right with the Lord. You need to seek his face. You need to receive the forgiveness he has to offer not merely acknowledge that it exists. What you did was wrong, very wrong, but I have no intent to prosecute or persecute or lecture you about it."

Jesse finally looked up and looked deeply into Art's eyes.

"Really," said Jesse, his voice quavering.

"Yes," said Art, "really, the heart of the Gospel is forgiveness."

"Dr. West would you pray with me, I feel so lost and alone and scared."

"Sure, lets just pray the prayer Jesus taught us all to pray."

They began the Lord's prayer, but when they got to the line about forgive us as we forgiven others, Jesse broke down and wept unashamedly, holding on to Art's hand, and said "Thank you, thank you, now I can face tomorrow." After a few more minutes Art gave Jesse a hug, and called for Officer Hoffner. He turned as he was leaving and smiled at Jesse one last time.

Lunch was rather subdued, and Grace could see Art was pondering things, so she was quiet. They had truly enjoyed the shwarma and rice at lunch, but it was time to meet Mustafa and Grayson at the church. Art thanked Sarah, and Grace insisted on getting the tab. They decided to go to the church in Grace's snazzy red Mazda. It took only twenty minutes driving along the top of the Mount of Olives to get to the church. Grayson came on the run. Slowly, behind him, came another young man.

"Come and see down in the crypt, come and see!"

"Slow down, Grayson." West's eyes shifted to the young man coming towards him—Raymond Simpson! West's surprised look said it all. The two men shook hands while Grayson explained.

"Yeah, Dr. Art, you know Raymond, my roomie. I told you I saw him everyday in jail—I didn't bail on him like 'you know who' if you get my drift. Anyway, the Gospel is powerful, man. Raymond's really on board now."

"Well, welcome, Raymond. Praise the Lord! With your expertise in antiquities, we could use you around here."

"Well, the authorities are a bit nervous about me being around digs!" Raymond laughed. "But I've been helping Grayson and Mustafa. And with your recommendation, anything is possible."

Mustafa came and handed them all flashlights. Bending over, Mustafa led everyone down into the crypt that lay directly under the high altar in the church. After many steps they reached the bottom.

Mustafa said, "Shine your lights straight ahead." They did so, and could see what looked like a primitive stone altar, but a very unusual one as it was an altar standing on high legs. Underneath the altar could be seen something protruding out each end.

"Come and see," said Mustafa, his voice almost breaking into tears.

Art, Grace, Grayson, and Raymond went over to the altar, and Mustafa said, "Shine your lights underneath."

They did so, and there were two small ossuaries, one with the Aramaic name Miriam, which was Mary, the other with the name for Martha.

"They are here," said Mustafa. "All along they are here beneath the altar of our church. The inscription that Grayson found in tomb said, 'Mary buried like saints in Revelation 6 under altar.'" His English was falling apart because of the excitement, but they caught his meaning.

Art sat down on the damp stone, overcome. He shone his light on the front ledge of the altar and he saw a faint inscription in Greek. It too was from the book of Revelation.

Allow me, said Raymond. "Blessed are those who die in the Lord, henceforth." Tears welled up in his eyes.

Art was also overcome. "It's all here, all these years, waiting to be discovered, and now this crypt will mean the revival of this church. People will come from everywhere to see all of this."

To Grace he said, "L'Chaim, to life.

To Mustafa, "To the One who came to give life and give it abundantly."

To Raymond and Grayson, "To life everlasting."

And to each one of them, "To the Lazarus Effect."

They all responded in unison, "To the Lazarus Effect!"